The UK Ninja Foodi 2-Basket Air Fryer Cookbook

Easy and Affordable Recipes for a Different Way to Eat Every Day. Includes Side Dishes, Desserts, Snacks and More.

Rafael Caviness

The UK Ninja Foodi
2-Basket Air Fryer Cookbook

Table of Contents

Table of Contents 3
Introduction 7
Getting Started with the Ninja Foodi Dual Zone Air Fryer 7

What Is the Ninja Foodi 2-Basket Air Fryer? 7
Main Functions of the Ninja Foodi Dual Zone Air Fryers 8
The Benefit You'll Gain from Your Air Fryer 9

Tips for Cooking Success 9
Maintaining and Cleaning the Appliance 10

Appetizers And Snacks 11

Sweet Apple Fries 11
Enchilada Chicken Dip 11
Honey-mustard Chicken Wings 11
Buffalo Cauliflower 12
Avocado Toast With Lemony Shrimp 12
Basil Feta Crostini 12
Cheesy Green Pitas 12
Greek Street Tacos 13
Crunchy Spicy Chickpeas 13
Parmesan Eggplant Bites 13
Tasty Roasted Black Olives & Tomatoes 13
Parmesan Pizza Nuggets 13
Loaded Potato Skins 14
Sweet Potato Chips 14
Seafood Egg Rolls 14
Hot Shrimp 15
Crab Rangoon 15
Avocado Fries With Quick Salsa Fresca 15

Fried Peaches 16
Roasted Red Pepper Dip 16
Cinnamon Honeyed Pretzel Bites 16
Home-style Buffalo Chicken Wings 17
Crispy Tofu Bites 17
Fried Goat Cheese 17
Hungarian Spiralized Fries 17
Mediterranean Potato Skins 18
Grilled Cheese Sandwich Deluxe 18
Crispy Curried Sweet Potato Fries 18
Potato Chips 18
Cheesy Zucchini Chips 18
Maple Loaded Sweet Potatoes 19
Fried Gyoza 19
Crunchy Tortellini Bites 19
Potato Chips With Sour Cream And Onion Dip 20
Avocado Fries 20

Vegetable Side Dishes Recipes 21

Sage & Thyme Potatoes 21
Green Peas With Mint 21
Almond-crusted Zucchini Fries 21
Fried Okra 21
Brown Rice And Goat Cheese Croquettes 21
Fingerling Potatoes 22
Garlicky Bell Pepper Mix 22
Spicy Bean Stuffed Potatoes 22
Pecorino Dill Muffins 23
Five-spice Roasted Sweet Potatoes 23
Perfect French Fries 23
Buttery Radish Wedges 23
Jerk Rubbed Corn On The Cob 24
Herbed Baby Red Potato Hasselback 24
Roasted Broccoli And Red Bean Salad 24
Southern Okra Chips 24
Mushrooms 25
Moroccan Cauliflower 25

Savory Brussels Sprouts 25
Provence French Fries 25
Roasted Fennel Salad 25
Buttery Stuffed Tomatoes 26
Rich Baked Sweet Potatoes 26
Vegetable Roast 26
Summer Watermelon And Cucumber Salad 26
Corn Au Gratin 27
Tandoori Cauliflower 27
The Ultimate Mac`n´cheese 27
Curried Fruit 27
Grits Casserole 27
Cinnamon Roasted Pumpkin 28
Roasted Bell Peppers With Garlic & Dill 28
Hasselbacks 28
Fried Corn On The Cob 28
Lemony Green Bean Sautée 29

Bread And Breakfast 30

Canadian Bacon & Cheese Sandwich 30
Cajun Breakfast Potatoes 30
Almond Cranberry Granola 30
Sweet Potato-cinnamon Toast 30

Quesadillas 31
Bacon, Broccoli And Swiss Cheese Bread Pudding 31
Apple Fritters 31
Wild Blueberry Lemon Chia Bread 32

The UK Ninja Foodi
2-Basket Air Fryer Cookbook

Hashbrown Potatoes Lyonnaise 32
Eggless Mung Bean Tart 32
Favorite Blueberry Muffins 32
Blueberry French Toast Sticks 33
Thai Turkey Sausage Patties 33
Cinnamon Pear Oat Muffins 33
Cinnamon Biscuit Rolls 33
Mini Everything Bagels 34
Meaty Omelet 34
All-in-one Breakfast Toast 34
Parma Ham & Egg Toast Cups 35
Mascarpone Iced Cinnamon Rolls 35
Crunchy French Toast Sticks 35
Effortless Toffee Zucchini Bread 36
Oat Muffins With Blueberries 36
Bread Boat Eggs 36
Breakfast Chimichangas 36
Zucchini Walnut Bread 37
Pesto Egg & Ham Sandwiches 37

Sugar-dusted Beignets 37
Orange Trail Oatmeal 37
Banana-blackberry Muffins 38
Scones 38
Home-style Pumpkin Crumble 38
Zucchini Hash Browns 39
Cheesy Egg Bites 39
Strawberry Streusel Muffins 39
Coconut & Peanut Rice Cereal 39
Green Egg Quiche 40
Shakshuka Cups 40
Spring Vegetable Omelet 40
Southern Sweet Cornbread 40
Hole In One 41
Veggie & Feta Scramble Bowls 41
Honey Donuts 41
Sweet Potato & Mushroom Hash 41
Chicken Scotch Eggs 42

Beef , pork & Lamb Recipes 43

Paprika Fried Beef 43
Leftover Roast Beef Risotto 43
Albóndigas 43
Canadian-style Rib Eye Steak 43
Aromatic Pork Tenderloin 44
Smokehouse-style Beef Ribs 44
Mini Meatloaves With Pancetta 44
Boneless Ribeyes 44
Honey Mustard Pork Roast 45
Cal-mex Chimichangas 45
Kentucky-style Pork Tenderloin 45
Honey Pork Links 45
Santorini Steak Bowls 45
Extra Crispy Country-style Pork Riblets 46
Beef & Barley Stuffed Bell Peppers 46
Pork Cutlets With Aloha Salsa 46
Stress-free Beef Patties 47
Provençal Grilled Rib-eye 47
Mustard-crusted Rib-eye 47
Better-than-chinese-take-out Sesame Beef 47
Apple Cornbread Stuffed Pork Loin With Apple Gravy 48
Pork Cutlets With Almond-lemon Crust 48
Delicious Juicy Pork Meatballs 49
Barbecue-style London Broil 49
Balsamic Short Ribs 49
Sage Pork With Potatoes 50
Spicy Hoisin Bbq Pork Chops 50
Mushroom & Quinoa-stuffed Pork Loins 50
Red Curry Flank Steak 50
Pork Loin 51
Country-style Pork Ribs(1) 51
Mongolian Beef 51
Greek Pork Chops 52

Sloppy Joes 52
Garlic And Oregano Lamb Chops 52
Grilled Pork & Bell Pepper Salad 52
Skirt Steak Fajitas 53
Bacon, Blue Cheese And Pear Stuffed Pork Chops 53
Pork & Beef Egg Rolls 54
Lamb Chops In Currant Sauce 54
Broccoli & Mushroom Beef 54
Chicken Fried Steak 54
Chipotle Pork Meatballs 55
City "chicken" 55
Tasty Filet Mignon 55
Natchitoches Meat Pies 55
Barbecue Country-style Pork Ribs 56
Italian Sausage & Peppers 56
Traditional Italian Beef Meatballs 57
Taco Pie With Meatballs 57
Berbere Beef Steaks 57
Citrus Pork Lettuce Wraps 57
Italian Meatballs 58
Calzones South Of The Border 58
Basil Cheese & Ham Stromboli 58
Crispy Pork Medallions With Radicchio
And Endive Salad 59
Crispy Pork Pork Escalopes 59
Beef And Spinach Braciole 59
Balsamic London Broil 60
Meat Loaves 60
Stuffed Pork Chops 60
Cajun Pork Loin Chops 6
Oktoberfest Bratwursts 6
Meatloaf With Tangy Tomato Glaze 6
Thyme Steak Finger Strips 6

Fish And Seafood Recipes 63

Dijon Shrimp Cakes 63
Cheesy Tuna Tower 63
Rich Salmon Burgers With Broccoli Slaw 63
Southern Shrimp With Cocktail Sauce 63
Bacon-wrapped Scallops 64
The Best Oysters Rockefeller 64
Fried Oysters 64
Potato-wrapped Salmon Fillets 64
Baltimore Crab Cakes 65
Crab Cakes On A Budget 65
British Fish & Chips 65
Basil Crab Cakes With Fresh Salad 66
Firecracker Popcorn Shrimp 66
King Prawns Al Ajillo 66
Malaysian Shrimp With Sambal Mayo 66
Hot Calamari Rings 67
Holiday Shrimp Scampi 67
Fish Tacos With Jalapeño-lime Sauce 67
Mediterranean Salmon Cakes 68
Maple Balsamic Glazed Salmon 68
Mojo Sea Bass 68
Popcorn Crawfish 68
Almond Topped Trout 69
Crabmeat-stuffed Flounder 69
Holliday Lobster Salad 69
Herby Prawn & Zucchini Bake 69
Spiced Shrimp Empanadas 70
Easy Scallops With Lemon Butter 70
Yummy Salmon Burgers With Salsa Rosa 70
Coconut-shrimp Po' Boys 71

Flounder Fillets 71
Stuffed Shrimp Wrapped In Bacon 71
Fish Tacos With Hot Coleslaw 72
Catalan-style Crab Samfaina 72
Shrimp "scampi" 72
Beer-breaded Halibut Fish Tacos 72
Southeast Asian-style Tuna Steaks 73
Basil Mushroom & Shrimp Spaghetti 73
Summer Sea Scallops 73
Salmon Patties With Lemon-dill Sauce 74
Garlic-lemon Steamer Clams 74
French Grouper Nicoise 74
Curried Sweet-and-spicy Scallops 74
Almond-crusted Fish 74
Catalan Sardines With Romesco Sauce 75
Tilapia Teriyaki 75
Caribbean Jerk Cod Fillets 75
Italian Tuna Roast 75
Halibut Quesadillas 76
Autenthic Greek Fish Pitas 76
Shrimp, Chorizo And Fingerling Potatoes 76
Crab Stuffed Salmon Roast 76
Shrimp-jalapeño Poppers In Prosciutto 77
Salty German-style Shrimp Pancakes 77
Shrimp Po'boy With Remoulade Sauce 77
Catfish Nuggets 78
Lime Flaming Halibut 78
Fish Goujons With Tartar Sauce 78
Crunchy And Buttery Cod With Ritz® Cracker Crust 78
Salmon 79

Poultry Recipes 80

Parmesan Crusted Chicken Cordon Bleu 80
Fiesta Chicken Plate 80
Spicy Black Bean Turkey Burgers With Cumin-avocado
Spread 80
Party Buffalo Chicken Drumettes 81
Southwest Gluten-free Turkey Meatloaf 81
Chicken Nuggets 82
Quick Chicken For Filling 82
Pesto Chicken Cheeseburgers 82
Crispy Chicken Parmesan 82
Christmas Chicken & Roasted Grape Salad 83
Coconut Chicken With Apricot-ginger Sauce 83
Chicken Adobo 83
Classic Chicken Cobb Salad 83
Yummy Maple-mustard Chicken Kabobs 84
Japanese-style Turkey Meatballs 84
Chicken Parmigiana 84
Herb-marinated Chicken 84
Honey Lemon Thyme Glazed Cornish Hen 85
Buffalo Egg Rolls 85
Jerk Chicken Drumsticks 85
Chicken Cordon Bleu Patties 86
Chicken & Rice Sautée 86

Teriyaki Chicken Bites 86
Basic Chicken Breasts(2) 86
Turkey Scotch Eggs 87
Sage & Paprika Turkey Cutlets 87
Peachy Chicken Chunks With Cherries 87
Chicken Chimichangas 87
Chicago-style Turkey Meatballs 88
Asian Meatball Tacos 88
Southern-fried Chicken Livers 88
Farmer's Fried Chicken 89
Goat Cheese Stuffed Turkey Roulade 89
Chicken Pigs In Blankets 89
Irresistible Cheesy Chicken Sticks 90
Cheesy Chicken-avocado Paninis 90
Granny Pesto Chicken Caprese 90
Chicken Pasta Pie 90
Asian Sweet Chili Chicken 91
Buttered Chicken Thighs 91
Pulled Turkey Quesadillas 91
Masala Chicken With Charred Vegetables 91
Chicken Breasts Wrapped In Bacon 92
Greek Chicken Wings 92
Greek Gyros With Chicken & Rice 92

Country Chicken Hoagies 92
Coconut Curry Chicken With Coconut Rice 93
Spiced Chicken Breasts 93

Sesame Orange Chicken 93
Pickle Brined Fried Chicken 94

Vegetarians Recipes 95

Vegetable Hand Pies 95
Pineapple & Veggie Souvlaki 95
Sweet Corn Bread 95
Pinto Bean Casserole 95
Harissa Veggie Fries 96
Party Giant Nachos 96
Veggie Burgers 96
Fennel Tofu Bites 96
Corn And Pepper Jack Chile Rellenos
With Roasted Tomato Sauce 97
Gorgeous Jalapeño Poppers 97
Spinach And Cheese Calzone 98
Fried Potatoes With Bell Peppers 98
Quinoa & Black Bean Stuffed Peppers 98
Hellenic Zucchini Bites 98
Vegan French Toast 99
Mexican Twice Air-fried Sweet Potatoes 99
Breaded Avocado Tacos 99

Curried Cauliflower 100
Roasted Vegetable, Brown Rice And Black Bean Burrito 100
Tomato & Squash Stuffed Mushrooms 100
Meatless Kimchi Bowls 100
Roasted Vegetable Stromboli 101
Rainbow Quinoa Patties 101
Vegetarian Paella 101
Colorful Vegetable Medley 102
Cheesy Eggplant Rounds 102
Stuffed Portobellos 102
Creamy Broccoli & Mushroom Casserole 102
Fake Shepherd's Pie 103
Tacos 103
Mushroom-rice Stuffed Bell Peppers 103
Charred Cauliflower Tacos 103
Tandoori Paneer Naan Pizza 104
Fried Rice With Curried Tofu 104
Grilled Cheese Sandwich 104

Desserts And Sweets 105

Cherry Hand Pies 105
Easy Bread Pudding 105
Almond-roasted Pears 105
Nutty Banana Bread 105
Giant Buttery Chocolate Chip Cookie 106
Baked Apple 106
Banana Bread Cake 106
Bananas Foster Bread Pudding 107
Magic Giant Chocolate Cookies 107
Mixed Berry Pie 107
Baked Stuffed Pears 108
Fried Oreos 108
Coconut Macaroons 108
Chocolate Soufflés 108
Mango-chocolate Custard 109
Fruit Turnovers 109
Cherry Cheesecake Rolls 109
Fried Snickers Bars 109
Giant Oatmeal–peanut Butter Cookie 110
Caramel Apple Crumble 110

Sea-salted Caramel Cookie Cups 110
Peanut Butter-banana Roll-ups 111
One-bowl Chocolate Buttermilk Cake 111
Strawberry Donuts 111
Lemon Pound Cake Bites 111
Home-style Pumpkin Pie Pudding 112
Annie's Chocolate Chunk Hazelnut Cookies 112
Holiday Peppermint Cake 112
Peanut Butter Cup Doughnut Holes 112
Fall Pumpkin Cake 113
Party S'mores 113
Honey-roasted Mixed Nuts 113
Tortilla Fried Pies 114
Famous Chocolate Lava Cake 114
Pecan-oat Filled Apples 114
Mixed Berry Hand Pies 114
Chocolate Bars 115
Baked Caramelized Peaches 115
Custard 115
Brownies With White Chocolate 115

RECIPE INDEX 116

Introduction

Do you really want to reduce your kitchen time? Do you want to prepare two different meals at one time? Then grab the Ninja Foodi 2-Basket Air Fryer and air fry all your favorite meals in its two cooking chambers. This smart air fryer is specially designed with the amazing dual-zone technology that will help you cook two different meals at a time or a single meal in large portions using smart finish or match cooking technology. That's right! Ninja Kitchen has made it possible. The Ninja Foodi 2-Basket Air Fryer has a total of 8-qt capacity, which is divided into two 4-qt cooking zones-Zone 1 and Zone 2. The number of the zone is given on the crisper plate so you could easily detect them. Each zone has a portion in the display, and it shows their respective settings. You can use the respective keys to set the time and temperature for each zone.

With The UK Ninja Foodi 2-Basket Air Fryer Cookbook, dive into the recipes, and let's get the kitchen worked!

Start your Ninja Foodi 2-Basket Air Fryer journey today!

Getting Started with the Ninja Foodi Dual Zone Air Fryer

What Is the Ninja Foodi 2-Basket Air Fryer?

The Ninja Foodi 2- Basket Air Fryer is the next revolutionary appliance coming from the awesome folks working at Ninja Kitchen! No matter how unbelievable the concept might sound, Ninja Kitchen has put on countless hours of engineering into crafting this meticulously designed appliance that takes the Air Frying game to a whole different level.

At its heart, the Ninja Foodi 2- Basket Air Fryer is a simple and exceedingly effective Air Fryer that gives you all the basic functions that you would expect from an Air Fryer. With this appliance, you can Air Frye, Bake, Broil, Dehydrate, Air Crisp, and more! You know, the usual Air Fryer stuffs.

However, what makes this unique is the super cool "Dual Zone" technology that completely flips the game in the Air Frying market.

If you are looking to cut down your cooking to half, or you want to make two different meals at the same time. The same appliance, then the Ninja Foodi Dual Zone/ 2- Basket Air Fryer is exactly what you need!

Simply put, the Dual Zone technology allows the appliance to be put on either single cook mode or multi cook mode.

Single cook mode works as usual; you cook using just a single basket. However, with the Dual Cook mode, you can seamlessly set the different timer, mode, and temperature for both of the zones individually and cook the meals you require.

Alternatively, you may give the same settings to both of the zones and cook the same meal in a doubled portion without spending any more time than you would need when making just a single portion.

While handling two Air Fryer baskets might sound a little bit complicated at first, the way how Ninja Kitchen has engineered this appliance has made it extremely accessible and easy to handle.

VThe Ninja Foodi Dual Zone Air Fryer is one of the innovative product designs manufactured. If you are looking for a perfect air fryer for your family, then the Ninja Foodi Dual Zone Air Fryer is one of the best options available for you. Some of the important features and benefits of the Ninja Foodi Dual Zone Air Fryer are mentioned as follows.

1. 8-Quart Capacity XL

The enormous 8-quart capacity, which can be divided into two sections, provides ample area for cooking both large and small amounts of food. This oven can cook 2 pounds of fries and 2 pounds of wings and drumettes.

2. Multifunctional Air Fryer

The Ninja Foodi Dual Zone Air Fryer comes with 6 preset functions. These easily customizable functions include max crisp, air fry, roast, bake, reheat and dehydrate. You never need to buy separate appliances for a single cooking function.

3. Safer Than Deep Fryer

Traditional deep frying method involves a large container full of sizzling oil. This can increase the safety risk of splashing hot oil over the skin. While the Ninja Foodi Dual Zone Air Fryer is close from all the sides when getting hot, there is no risk of splashing, spilling or accidental burn during the cooking process.

4. Smart Finish

This culinary marvel can intelligently sync the cook timings of both cooking zones, allowing you to prepare multiple items at the same time while maintaining the same finish time. So, here's how it's done! When you put various foods in the baskets, each one takes a different amount of time to cook. When you use the smart cooking feature and start the operation, the basket with the longer cooking time will run first, while the other basket will remain on hold until the other chamber reaches the same cooking duration. Both sides finish cooking at the same time in this manner.

5. Match Cook

This air fryer's total 8 quartz capacity is divided into two 4-quart air fryer baskets, allowing you to cook various foods and the same dish in both baskets at the same time. You can utilize the same cooking mode for both baskets and utilize the XL capacity with the match cook technology.

6. Reduce the Risk of Acrylamide Formation

Deep frying is one of the high heat cooking methods in which harmful acrylamide is formed. It is one of the causes of developing some cancer like ovarian, endometrial, oesophageal and breast cancer. On the other side, this air fryer cooks your food into very little oil and fat by circulating hot air around the food. This process lowers the risk of acrylamide formation.

7. Use Less Oil and Fats

The cooking basket of the oven comes with ceramic non-stick coatings and allows you to prepare your favorite food using up to 75 to 80 % less fat and oils than the traditional deep frying method.

8. Wide Temperature Range

The Ninja Foodi Dual Zone Air Fryer offers a range of 105 °F to 400 °F temperature. The lower temperature range is suitable for dehydrating your favorite fruits, vegetable, and meat slices, and the higher temperature range allows you to cook thick cuts of meat.

9. Easy to Clean

The interior of this air fryer is made up of a non-stick coating so that you can clean it easily. The cooking tray comes in metallic and dishwasher safe, but you can easily clean it by hand if you want to.

Main Functions of the Ninja Foodi Dual Zone Air Fryers

The Ninja Foodi Dual Zone Air Fryer has six cooking functions: max crisp, air fry, roast, reheat, dehydrate and bake. This appliance has a large capacity. You can prepare food for your big family. If you want to bake a cake with the Ninja Foodi Dual Zone Air Fryer, you can select "bake" cooking mode.

1. Max Crisp

This cooking function is perfect for frozen foods such as chicken nuggets and French fries etc. Using this function, you will get crispy and tender food. With less time, you will get crispy and tender food.

2. Air Fry

This cooking function will allow you to cook food with less oil and fat than other cooking methods. Using this function, you will get crunchy and crispy food from the outside and juicy and tender food from the inside. You can prepare chicken, beef, lamb, pork, and seafood using this cooking option.

3. Roast

Now, you didn't need an oven to roast food. The Ninja Foodi Dual Zone Air Fryer has useful cooking function, "roast". With this function, you can roast chicken, lamb, seafood, and vegetable dishes. It is one of the dry cooking methods that give you a nice brown texture to the food and increase the flavor of your foods.

4. Reheat

The reheat function can quickly warm your food without changing its texture and flavor if you have leftover food. Now, you didn't need to place food onto the stovetop for reheating.

5. Dehydrate

This cooking function is used to dehydrate fruits, meat, and vegetables. Using this cooking method, you can preserve food for a long time. It takes hours to dehydrate the food but gives you a delicious and crispy texture.

6. Bake

This cooking method allows you to bake cakes, muffins, cupcakes, and any other dessert on any occasion or regular day. You didn't need an oven to bake the food. The Ninja Foodi Dual Zone Air Fryer has a baking option for baking your food with delicious texture.

The Benefit You'll Gain from Your Air Fryer

Consider the following reasons why an air fryer might be right for you:

1. Healthy Cooking

Everyone loves the taste of deep-fried foods, but many people must avoid these for health reasons. If you're looking to lower cholesterol or lose weight, your doctor may thank you for using an air fryer. Air fryers use around 75 percent less oil than deep fryers, providing a healthy alternative without sacrificing flavor.

2. Speed of Cooking

The air fryer's small convection oven preheats and cooks more quickly than a conventional oven. You'll have tasty meals in haste, with less wait!

3. Green Cooking

Have you "gone green?" Cooking with an air fryer can help. Most air fryers are energy efficient, and shorter cook times translate to less overall power usage.

4. Simple and Easy

Air fryers utilize simple controls, typically two knobs for cook time and temperature, or an easy to read digital display. You simply toss the food in oil (if desired), place it in the basket, and the air fryer does the rest.

5. Clean Up is a Breeze

The baskets and pans of most air fryers are dishwasher safe for easy cleanup. Also, the enclosed nature of the air fryer prevents the splatters and spills associated with deep frying and pan frying.

6. Safe

Lacking the large oil vats of traditional deep fryers, air fryers eliminate the risk of serious burns from spilled oil. Also, air fryers are designed so that the exterior does not become dangerously hot to the touch.

Tips for Cooking Success

Remember these nifty tips whenever you are cooking with your new air fryer.

- Pressing the Start/Pause button while using the Smart Finish will pause the cooking process on both zones. Press the same button to resume cooking.

- If at any time you need to pause the cooking process in one of the baskets, first select the zone, then the Start/Pause button.

- To stop or end the cooking process, select the zone, then set the time to zero using the arrow down button. The display should show End after a few seconds, and the cooking process in this zone will stop.

- You can adjust the temperature and time in each zone at any time during the cooking process. Select the zone, then adjust the setting using the arrow buttons.
- Place a single layer of food and avoid stacking whenever possible.
- To get the best results, toss or shake the food at least twice within the cooking cycle, especially for foods that overlap, like French fries. This will produce a more even cooking throughout.
- When cooking fresh vegetables, add at least one tablespoon of cooking oil. More oil can be added to create a crispier texture.
- Use the crisper plates when you want your food to become crunchy. Note that the crisper plates will slightly elevate your food to allow hot air to permeate the bottom and result in a crispier texture.
- Follow the correct breading technique for wet battered food. Coat the food with flour first, then with egg, and finally with bread crumbs. Press the crumbs into the food to avoid it from flying around when air frying.

- It is best to regularly check the progress to avoid overcooking. Refer to the cooking chart for different foods in the quick start guide included in the package.
- A food-safe temperature must be reached to avoid any foodborne illness. Use a thermometer to check for doneness, especially when cooking raw meat. Instant-read thermometers are your best choice for this.
- Once cooking time is up or when the desired browning is achieved, promptly remove the food from the unit.
- Do not use metal cutleries or tools that can damage the non-stick coating. Dump the food directly on a plate or use silicon-tipped tongs.
- Small bits of food may be blown away while cooking. You can avoid this by securing pieces of food with toothpicks.
- To cook recipes intended for traditional ovens, simply reduce the temperature by 25 degrees Fahrenheit and regularly check for doneness.
- Do not let food touch the heating elements.
- Never overload the baskets. Not only will this result in uneven cooking, but it may also cause the appliance to malfunction as well.

Maintaining and Cleaning the Appliance

- The Ninja 2-basket air fryer is not intended to be used outdoor.
- It is very important to check the voltage indication are corresponding to the main voltage from the switch.
- Do not immerse the appliance in water.
- Keep the cord away from the hot area.
- Do not touch the outer surface of the air fryer hen using for cooking purposes.
- Put the appliance on a horizontal and flat surface.
- Unplug the appliance after use.
- Cleaning
- First, unplug the power cord of the air fryer.
-
- Make sure the appliance is cooled before cleaning.
- The air fryer should be cleaning after every use.
- To clean the outer surface, use a damp towel.
- Clean the inside of the air fryer with a nonabrasive sponge.
- The accessories of the air fryer are dishwasher safe, but to extend the life of the drawers, it's recommended to wash them manually.

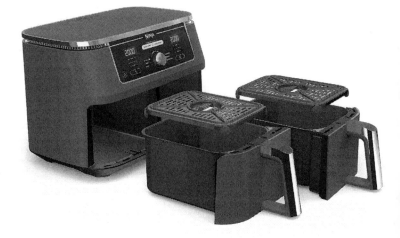

Appetizers And Snacks

Sweet Apple Fries

Servings: 3
Cooking Time: 8 Minutes
Ingredients:

- 2 Medium-size sweet apple(s), such as Gala or Fuji
- 1 Large egg white(s)
- 2 tablespoons Water
- 1½ cups Finely ground gingersnap crumbs (gluten-free, if a concern)
- Vegetable oil spray

Directions:

1. Preheat the air fryer to 375°F (190°C).
2. Peel and core an apple, then cut it into 12 slices Repeat with more apples as necessary.
3. Whisk the egg white(s) and water in a medium bowl until foamy. Add the apple slices and toss well to coat.
4. Spread the gingersnap crumbs across a dinner plate. Using clean hands, pick up an apple slice, let any excess egg white mixture slip back into the rest, and dredge the slice in the crumbs, coating it lightly but evenly on all sides. Set it aside and continue coating the remaining apple slices.
5. Lightly coat the slices on all sides with vegetable oil spray, then set them curved side down in the basket in one layer. Air-fry undisturbed for 6 minutes, or until browned and crisp. You may need to air-fry the slices for 2 minutes longer if the temperature is at 360°F (180°C).
6. Use kitchen tongs to transfer the slices to a wire rack. Cool for 2 to 3 minutes before serving.

Enchilada Chicken Dip

Servings:6
Cooking Time: 20 Minutes
Ingredients:

- 1 cup chopped cooked chicken breasts
- 1 can diced green chiles, including juice
- 8 oz cream cheese, softened
- ¼ cup mayonnaise
- ¼ cup sour cream
- 2 tbsp chopped onion
- 1 jalapeño pepper, minced
- 1 cup shredded mozzarella
- ¼ cup diced tomatoes
- 1 tsp chili powder

Directions:

1. Preheat air fryer to 400°F. Beat the cream cheese, mayonnaise, and sour cream in a bowl until smooth. Stir in the cooked chicken, onion, green chiles, jalapeño, and ½ cup of mozzarella cheese. Spoon the mixture into a baking dish. Sprinkle the remaining cheese on top, and place the dish in the fryer. Bake for 10 minutes. Garnish the dip with diced tomatoes and chili powder. Serve.

Honey-mustard Chicken Wings

Servings: 2
Cooking Time: 14 Minutes
Ingredients:

- 2 pounds chicken wings
- salt and freshly ground black pepper
- 2 tablespoons butter
- ¼ cup honey
- ¼ cup spicy brown mustard
- pinch ground cayenne pepper
- 2 teaspoons Worcestershire sauce

Directions:

1. Prepare the chicken wings by cutting off the wing tips and discarding (or freezing for chicken stock). Divide the drumettes from the wingettes by cutting through the joint. Place the chicken wing pieces in a large bowl.
2. Preheat the air fryer to 400°F (205°C).
3. Season the wings with salt and freshly ground black pepper and air-fry the wings in two batches for 10 minutes per batch, shaking the basket half way through the cooking process.
4. While the wings are air-frying, combine the remaining ingredients in a small saucepan over low heat.
5. When both batches are done, toss all the wings with the honey-mustard sauce and toss them all back into the basket for another 4 minutes to heat through and finish cooking. Give the basket a good shake part way through the cooking process to redistribute the wings. Remove the wings from the air fryer and serve.

Buffalo Cauliflower

Servings: 6
Cooking Time: 12 Minutes
Ingredients:
- 1 large head of cauliflower, washed and cut into medium-size florets
- ½ cup all-purpose flour
- ¼ cup melted butter
- 3 tablespoons hot sauce
- ½ teaspoon garlic powder
- ½ cup blue cheese dip or ranch dressing (optional)

Directions:
1. Preheat the air fryer to 350°F（175°C）.
2. Make sure the cauliflower florets are dry, and then coat them in flour.
3. Liberally spray the air fryer basket with an olive oil mist. Place the cauliflower into the basket, making sure not to stack them on top of each other. Depending on the size of your air fryer, you may need to do this in two batches.
4. Cook for 6 minutes, then shake the basket, and cook another 6 minutes.
5. While cooking, mix the melted butter, hot sauce, and garlic powder in a large bowl.
6. Carefully remove the cauliflower from the air fryer. Toss the cauliflower into the butter mixture to coat. Repeat Steps 2–4 for any leftover cauliflower. Serve warm with the dip of your choice.

Avocado Toast With Lemony Shrimp

Servings: 4
Cooking Time: 6 Minutes
Ingredients:
- 6 ounces Raw medium shrimp (30 to 35 per pound), peeled and deveined
- 1½ teaspoons Finely grated lemon zest
- 2 teaspoons Lemon juice
- 1½ teaspoons Minced garlic
- 1½ teaspoons Ground black pepper
- 4 Rye or whole-wheat bread slices (gluten-free, if a concern)
- 2 Ripe Hass avocado(s), halved, pitted, peeled and roughly chopped
- For garnishing Coarse sea salt or kosher salt

Directions:
1. Preheat the air fryer to 400°F（205°C）.
2. Toss the shrimp, lemon zest, lemon juice, garlic, and pepper in a bowl until the shrimp are evenly coated.
3. When the machine is at temperature, use kitchen tongs to place the shrimp in a single layer in the basket. Air-fry undisturbed for 4 minutes, or until the shrimp are pink and barely firm. Use kitchen tongs to transfer the shrimp to a cutting board.

4. Working in batches, set as many slices of bread as will fit in the basket in one layer. Air-fry undisturbed for 2 minutes, just until warmed through and crisp. The bread will not brown much.
5. Arrange the bread slices on a clean, dry work surface. Divide the avocado bits among them and gently smash the avocado into a coarse paste with the tines of a flatware fork. Top the toasts with the shrimp and sprinkle with salt as a garnish.

Basil Feta Crostini

Servings: 4
Cooking Time: 10 Minutes
Ingredients:
- 1 baguette, sliced
- ¼ cup olive oil
- 2 garlic cloves, minced
- 4 oz feta cheese
- 2 tbsp basil, minced

Directions:
1. Preheat air fryer to 380°F（195°C）. Combine together the olive oil and garlic in a bowl. Brush it over one side of each slice of bread. Put the bread in a single layer in the frying basket and Bake for 5 minutes. In a small bowl, mix together the feta cheese and basil. Remove the toast from the air fryer, then spread a thin layer of the goat cheese mixture over the top of each piece. Serve.

Cheesy Green Pitas

Servings: 4
Cooking Time: 15 Minutes
Ingredients:
- ½ cup canned artichoke hearts, sliced
- 2 whole-wheat pitas
- 2 tbsp olive oil, divided
- 2 garlic cloves, minced
- ¼ tsp salt
- ¼ cup green olives
- ¼ cup grated Pecorino
- ¼ cup crumbled feta
- 2 tbsp chopped chervil

Directions:
1. Preheat air fryer to 380°F（195°C）. Lightly brush each pita with some olive oil, then top with garlic and salt. Divide the artichoke hearts, green olives, and cheeses evenly between the two pitas, and put both into the air fryer. Bake for 10 minutes. Remove the pitas and cut them into 4 pieces each before serving. Top with chervil. Enjoy!
2. Roast the shrimp for 4 minutes, then open the air fryer and place the ramekin with oil and garlic in the basket beside the shrimp packet. Cook for 2 more minutes. Place the shrimp on a serving plate or platter with the ramekin of garlic olive oil on the side for dipping.

Greek Street Tacos

Servings: 8
Cooking Time: 3 Minutes
Ingredients:
- 8 small flour tortillas (4-inch diameter)
- 8 tablespoons hummus
- 4 tablespoons crumbled feta cheese
- 4 tablespoons chopped kalamata or other olives (optional)
- olive oil for misting

Directions:
1. Place 1 tablespoon of hummus or tapenade in the center of each tortilla. Top with 1 teaspoon of feta crumbles and 1 teaspoon of chopped olives, if using.
2. Using your finger or a small spoon, moisten the edges of the tortilla all around with water.
3. Fold tortilla over to make a half-moon shape. Press center gently. Then press the edges firmly to seal in the filling.
4. Mist both sides with olive oil.
5. Place in air fryer basket very close but try not to overlap.
6. Cook at 390°F (200°C) for 3minutes, just until lightly browned and crispy.

Crunchy Spicy Chickpeas

Servings: 6
Cooking Time: 12 Minutes
Ingredients:
- 2½ cups Canned chickpeas, drained and rinsed
- 2½ tablespoons Vegetable or canola oil
- up to 1 tablespoon Cajun or jerk dried seasoning blend (see here for a Cajun blend, here for a jerk blend)
- up to ¾ teaspoon Table salt (optional)

Directions:
1. Preheat the air fryer to 400°F (205°C).
2. Toss the chickpeas, oil, seasoning blend, and salt (if using) in a large bowl until the chickpeas are evenly coated.
3. When the machine is at temperature, pour the chickpeas into the basket. Air-fry for 12 minutes, removing the basket at the 4- and 8-minute marks to toss and rearrange the chickpeas, until very aromatic and perhaps sizzling but not burned.
4. Pour the chickpeas into a large serving bowl. Cool for a couple of minutes, gently stirring once, before you dive in.

Parmesan Eggplant Bites

Servings:4
Cooking Time: 35 Minutes
Ingredients:
- 2 eggs
- 2 tbsp heavy cream
- ½ cup bread crumbs
- ½ tsp Italian seasoning
- ½ cup grated Parmesan
- ½ tsp salt
- 1 eggplant, cut into sticks
- ½ cup tomato sauce, warm

Directions:
1. Preheat air fryer to 400°F (205°C). In a bowl, mix the eggs and heavy cream. In another bowl, combine bread crumbs, Parmesan cheese, Italian seasoning and salt. Dip eggplant fries in egg mixture and dredge them in crumb mixture.
2. Place the fries in the greased frying basket and Air Fry for 12 minutes, shaking once. Transfer to a large serving plate and serve with warmed tomato sauce.

Tasty Roasted Black Olives & Tomatoes

Servings: 6
Cooking Time: 25 Minutes
Ingredients:
- 2 cups grape tomatoes
- 4 garlic cloves, chopped
- ½ red onion, chopped
- 1 cup black olives
- 1 cup green olives
- 1 tbsp thyme, minced
- 1 tbsp oregano, minced
- 2 tbsp olive oil
- ½ tsp salt

Directions:
1. Preheat air fryer to 380°F (195°C). Add all ingredients to a bowl and toss well to coat. Pour the mixture into the frying basket and Roast for 10 minutes. Stir the mixture, then Roast for an additional 10 minutes. Serve and enjoy!

Parmesan Pizza Nuggets

Servings: 8
Cooking Time: 6 Minutes
Ingredients:
- ¾ cup warm filtered water
- 1 package fast-rising yeast
- ½ teaspoon salt
- 2 cups all-purpose flour
- ¼ cup finely grated Parmesan cheese
- 1 teaspoon Italian seasoning
- 2 tablespoon extra-virgin olive oil
- 1 teaspoon kosher salt

Directions:
1. Preheat the air fryer to 370°F (185°C).

2. In a large microwave-safe bowl, add the water. Heat for 40 seconds in the microwave. Remove and mix in the yeast and salt. Let sit 5 minutes.

3. Meanwhile, in a medium bowl, mix the flour with the Parmesan cheese and Italian seasoning. Set aside.

4. Using a stand mixer with a dough hook attachment, add the yeast liquid and then mix in the flour mixture ⅓ cup at a time until all the flour mixture is added and a dough is formed.

5. Remove the bowl from the stand, and then let the dough rise for 1 hour in a warm space, covered with a kitchen towel.

6. After the dough has doubled in size, remove it from the bowl and punch it down a few times on a lightly floured flat surface.

7. Divide the dough into 4 balls, and then roll each ball out into a long, skinny, sticklike shape.

8. Using a sharp knife, cut each dough stick into 6 pieces. Repeat for the remaining dough balls until you have about 24 nuggets formed.

9. Lightly brush the top of each bite with the egg whites and cover with a pinch of sea salt.

10. Spray the air fryer basket with olive oil spray and place the pizza nuggets on top. Cook for 6 minutes, or until lightly browned. Remove and keep warm.

11. Repeat until all the nuggets are cooked.

12. Serve warm.

Loaded Potato Skins

Servings: 8
Cooking Time: 8 Minutes
Ingredients:
- 12 round baby potatoes
- 3 ounces cream cheese
- 4 slices cooked bacon, crumbled or chopped
- 2 green onions, finely chopped
- ½ cup grated cheddar cheese, divided
- ¼ cup sour cream
- 1 tablespoon milk
- 2 teaspoons hot sauce

Directions:
1. Preheat the air fryer to 320°F（160°C）.

2. Poke holes into the baby potatoes with a fork. Place the potatoes onto a microwave-safe plate and microwave on high for 4 to 5 minutes, or until soft to squeeze. Let the potatoes cool until they're safe to handle, about 5 minutes.

3. Meanwhile, in a medium bowl, mix together the cream cheese, bacon, green onions, and ¼ cup of the cheddar cheese; set aside.

4. Slice the baby potatoes in half. Using a spoon, scoop out the pulp, leaving enough pulp on the inside to retain the shape of the potato half. Place the potato pulp into the cream cheese mixture and mash together with a fork. Using a spoon, refill the potato halves with filling.

5. Place the potato halves into the air fryer basket and top with the remaining ¼ cup of cheddar cheese.

6. Cook the loaded baked potato bites in batches for 8 minutes.

7. Meanwhile, make the sour cream sauce. In a small bowl, whisk together the sour cream, milk, and hot sauce. Add more hot sauce if desired.

8. When the potatoes have all finished cooking, place them onto a serving platter and serve with sour cream sauce drizzled over the top or as a dip.

Sweet Potato Chips

Servings: 4
Cooking Time: 10 Minutes
Ingredients:
- 2 medium sweet potatoes, washed
- 2 cups filtered water
- 1 tablespoon avocado oil
- 2 teaspoons brown sugar
- ½ teaspoon salt

Directions:
1. Using a mandolin, slice the potatoes into ⅛-inch pieces.

2. Add the water to a large bowl. Place the potatoes in the bowl, and soak for at least 30 minutes.

3. Preheat the air fryer to 350°F（175°C）.

4. Drain the water and pat the chips dry with a paper towel or kitchen cloth. Toss the chips with the avocado oil, brown sugar, and salt. Liberally spray the air fryer basket with olive oil mist.

5. Set the chips inside the air fryer, separating them so they're not on top of each other. Cook for 5 minutes, shake the basket, and cook another 5 minutes, or until browned.

6. Remove and let cool a few minutes prior to serving. Repeat until all the chips are cooked.

Seafood Egg Rolls

Servings: 6
Cooking Time: 35 Minutes
Ingredients:
- 2 tbsp olive oil
- 1 shallot, chopped
- 2 garlic cloves, minced
- ½ cup shredded carrots
- 1 lb cooked shrimp, chopped
- 1 cup corn kernels
- 1/3 cup chopped cashews
- 1 tbsp soy sauce
- 2 tsp fish sauce
- 12 egg roll wrappers

Directions:

1.   Preheat the air fryer to 400°F（205°C）. Combine the olive oil, shallot, garlic, and carrots in a 6-inch. Put the pan in the frying basket and Air Fry for 3-5 minutes, stirring once. Remove the pan and put the veggies in a bowl. Add shrimp, corn, cashews, soy sauce, and fish sauce to the veggies and combine. Lay the egg roll wrappers on the clean work surface and brush the edges with water. Divide the filling equally and fill them, then brush the edges with water again. Roll up, folding in the side, enclosing the filling inside. Place 4 egg rolls in the basket and spray with cooking oil. Air Fry for 10-12 minutes, rotating once halfway through cooking until golden and crispy. Repeat with remaining rolls. Serve hot.

Hot Shrimp

Servings: 4
Cooking Time: 15 Minutes
Ingredients:
- 1 lb shrimp, cleaned and deveined
- 4 tbsp olive oil
- ½ lime, juiced
- 3 garlic cloves, minced
- ½ tsp salt
- ¼ tsp chili powder

Directions:
1.   Preheat air fryer to 380°F（195°C）. Toss the shrimp with 2 tbsp of olive oil, lime juice, 1/3 of garlic, salt, and red chili powder in a bowl. Mix the remaining olive oil and garlic in a small ramekin. Pour the shrimp into the center of a piece of aluminum foil, then fold the sides up and crimp the edges so that it forms an aluminum foil bowl that is open on top. Put the resulting packet into the frying basket.

Crab Rangoon

Servings: 18
Cooking Time: 6 Minutes
Ingredients:
- 4½ tablespoons (a little more than ¼ pound) Crabmeat, preferably backfin or claw, picked over for shells and cartilage
- 1½ ounces (3 tablespoons) Regular or low-fat cream cheese (not fat-free), softened to room temperature
- 1½ tablespoons Minced scallion
- 1½ teaspoons Minced garlic
- 1½ teaspoons Worcestershire sauce
- 18 Wonton wrappers (thawed, if necessary)
- Vegetable oil spray

Directions:
.   Preheat the air fryer to 400°F（205°C）.
.   Gently stir the crab, cream cheese, scallion, garlic, and Worcestershire sauce in a medium bowl until well combined.

3.   Set a bowl of water on a clean, dry work surface or next to a large cutting board. Set one wonton wrapper on the surface, then put a teaspoonful of the crab mixture in the center of the wrapper. Dip your clean finger in the water and run it around the edge of the wrapper. Bring all four sides up to the center and over the filling, and pinch them together in the middle to seal without covering all of the filling. The traditional look is for the corners of the filled wonton to become four open "flower petals" radiating out from the filled center. Set the filled wonton aside and continue making more as needed. (If you want a video tutorial on filling these, see ours at our YouTube channel, Cooking with Bruce and Mark.)
4.   Generously coat the filled wontons with vegetable oil spray. Set them sealed side up in the basket with a little room among them. Air-fry undisturbed for 6 minutes, or until golden brown and crisp.
5.   Use a nonstick-safe spatula to gently transfer the wontons to a wire rack. Cool for 5 minutes before serving warm.

Avocado Fries With Quick Salsa Fresca

Servings: 4
Cooking Time: 6 Minutes
Ingredients:
- ½ cup flour*
- 2 teaspoons salt
- 2 eggs, lightly beaten
- 1 cup panko breadcrumbs*
- ⅛ teaspoon cayenne pepper
- ¼ teaspoon smoked paprika (optional)
- 2 large avocados, just ripe
- vegetable oil, in a spray bottle
- Quick Salsa Fresca
- 1 cup cherry tomatoes
- 1 tablespoon-sized chunk of shallot or red onion
- 2 teaspoons fresh lime juice
- 1 teaspoon chopped fresh cilantro or parsley
- salt and freshly ground black pepper

Directions:
1.   Set up a dredging station with three shallow dishes. Place the flour and salt in the first shallow dish. Place the eggs into the second dish. Combine the breadcrumbs, cayenne pepper and paprika (if using) in the third dish.
2.   Preheat the air fryer to 400°F（205°C）.
3.   Cut the avocado in half around the pit and separate the two sides. Slice the avocados into long strips while still in their skin. Run a spoon around the slices, separating them from the avocado skin. Try to keep the slices whole, but don't worry if they break – you can still coat and air-fry the pieces.

4. Coat the avocado slices by dredging them first in the flour, then the egg and then the breadcrumbs, pressing the crumbs on gently with your hands. Set the coated avocado fries on a tray and spray them on all sides with vegetable oil.

5. Air-fry the avocado fries, one layer at a time, at 400°F (205°C) for 6 minutes, turning them over halfway through the cooking time and spraying lightly again if necessary. When the fries are nicely browned on all sides, season with salt and remove.

6. While the avocado fries are air-frying, make the salsa fresca by combining everything in a food processor. Pulse several times until the salsa is a chunky purée. Serve the fries warm with the salsa on the side for dipping.

Fried Peaches

Servings: 4
Cooking Time: 8 Minutes
Ingredients:
- 2 egg whites
- 1 tablespoon water
- ¼ cup sliced almonds
- 2 tablespoons brown sugar
- ½ teaspoon almond extract
- 1 cup crisp rice cereal
- 2 medium, very firm peaches, peeled and pitted
- ¼ cup cornstarch
- oil for misting or cooking spray

Directions:
1. Preheat air fryer to 390°F (200°C).
2. Beat together egg whites and water in a shallow dish.
3. In a food processor, combine the almonds, brown sugar, and almond extract. Process until ingredients combine well and the nuts are finely chopped.
4. Add cereal and pulse just until cereal crushes. Pour crumb mixture into a shallow dish or onto a plate.
5. Cut each peach into eighths and place in a plastic bag or container with lid. Add cornstarch, seal, and shake to coat.
6. Remove peach slices from bag or container, tapping them hard to shake off the excess cornstarch. Dip in egg wash and roll in crumbs. Spray with oil.
7. Place in air fryer basket and cook for 5 minutes. Shake basket, separate any that have stuck together, and spritz a little oil on any spots that aren't browning.
8. Cook for 3 minutes longer, until golden brown and crispy.

Roasted Red Pepper Dip

Servings: 2
Cooking Time: 15 Minutes
Ingredients:
- 2 Medium-size red bell pepper(s)

- 1¾ cups (one 15-ounce can) Canned white beans, drained and rinsed
- 1 tablespoon Fresh oregano leaves, packed
- 3 tablespoons Olive oil
- 1 tablespoon Lemon juice
- ½ teaspoon Table salt
- ½ teaspoon Ground black pepper

Directions:
1. Preheat the air fryer to 400°F (205°C).
2. Set the pepper(s) in the basket and air-fry undisturbed for 15 minutes, until blistered and even blackened.
3. Use kitchen tongs to transfer the pepper(s) to a zip-closed plastic bag or small bowl. Seal the bag or cover the bowl with plastic wrap. Set aside for 20 minutes.
4. Peel each pepper, then stem it, cut it in half, and remove all its seeds and their white membranes.
5. Set the pieces of the pepper in a food processor. Add the beans, oregano, olive oil, lemon juice, salt, and pepper. Cover and process until smooth, stopping the machine at least once to scrape down the inside of the canister. Scrape the dip into a bowl and serve warm, or cover and refrigerate for up to 3 days (although the dip tastes best if it's allowed to come back to room temperature).

Cinnamon Honeyed Pretzel Bites

Servings: 6
Cooking Time: 40 Minutes
Ingredients:
- 1 ½ tsp quick-rise yeast
- 2 tsp light brown sugar
- 1 tsp vanilla extract
- ½ tsp lemon zest
- 2 ¼ cups flour
- ½ tsp salt
- ½ tbsp honey
- 1 tbsp cinnamon powder

Directions:
1. Preheat air fryer to 380°F (195°C). Stir ¾ cup warm water and yeast in a medium bowl. Sit for 5 minutes. Combine yeast water with 2 cups of flour, brown sugar, vanilla, lemon zest, cinnamon, salt, and honey. Stir until sticky dough forms. Sprinkle the rest of the flour on a flat work surface, then place the dough on the surface. Knead the dough for 2-3 minutes or until it comes together in a smooth ball. Divide the dough into 4 pieces. Roll each section into a log. Cut each log into 5 pieces. Arrange the dough pieces on the greased basket. Bake for 3 minutes, then use tongs to flip the pretzels. Cook for another 3-4 unti pretzels have browned. Serve warm and enjoy.

Home-style Buffalo Chicken Wings

Servings: 4
Cooking Time: 35 Minutes
Ingredients:
- 2 lb chicken wing portions
- 6 tbsp chili sauce
- 1 tsp dried oregano
- 1 tsp smoked paprika
- 1tsp garlic powder
- ½ tsp salt
- ¼ cup crumbled blue cheese
- 1/3 cup low-fat yogurt
- ½ tbsp lemon juice
- ½ tbsp white wine vinegar
- 2 celery stalks, cut into sticks
- 2 carrots, cut into sticks

Directions:
1. Add chicken with 1 tbsp of chili sauce, oregano, garlic, paprika, and salt to a large bowl. Toss to coat well, then set aside. In a small bowl, mash blue cheese and yogurt with a fork. Stir lemon juice and vinegar until smooth and blended. Refrigerate covered until it is time to serve.
2. Preheat air fryer to 300°F (150°C). Place the chicken in the greased frying basket and Air Fry for 22 minutes, flipping the chicken once until crispy and browned. Set aside in a clean bowl. Coat with the remaining tbsp of chili sauce. Serve with celery, carrot sticks and the blue cheese dip.

Crispy Tofu Bites

Servings: 4
Cooking Time: 20 Minutes
Ingredients:
- 1 pound Extra firm unflavored tofu
- Vegetable oil spray

Directions:
1. Wrap the piece of tofu in a triple layer of paper towels. Place it on a wooden cutting board and set a large pot on top of it to press out excess moisture. Set aside for 10 minutes.
2. Preheat the air fryer to 400°F (205°C).
3. Remove the pot and unwrap the tofu. Cut it into 1-inch cubes. Place these in a bowl and coat them generously with vegetable oil spray. Toss gently, then spray generously again before tossing, until all are glistening.
4. Gently pour the tofu pieces into the basket, spread them into as close to one layer as possible, and air-fry for 20 minutes, using kitchen tongs to gently rearrange the pieces at the 7- and 14-minute marks, until light brown and crisp.
5. Gently pour the tofu pieces onto a wire rack. Cool for 5 minutes before serving warm.

Fried Goat Cheese

Servings: 3

Cooking Time: 4 Minutes
Ingredients:
- 7 ounces 1- to 1½-inch-diameter goat cheese log
- 2 Large egg(s)
- 1¾ cups Plain dried bread crumbs (gluten-free, if a concern)
- Vegetable oil spray

Directions:
1. Slice the goat cheese log into ½-inch-thick rounds. Set these flat on a small cutting board, a small baking sheet, or a large plate. Freeze uncovered for 30 minutes.
2. Preheat the air fryer to 400°F (205°C).
3. Set up and fill two shallow soup plates or small pie plates on your counter: one in which you whisk the egg(s) until uniform and the other for the bread crumbs.
4. Take the goat cheese rounds out of the freezer. With clean, dry hands, dip one round in the egg(s) to coat it on all sides. Let the excess egg slip back into the rest, then dredge the round in the bread crumbs, turning it to coat all sides, even the edges. Repeat this process—egg, then bread crumbs—for a second coating. Coat both sides of the round and its edges with vegetable oil spray, then set it aside. Continue double-dipping, double-dredging, and spraying the remaining rounds.
5. Place the rounds in one layer in the basket. Air-fry undisturbed for 4 minutes, or until lightly browned and crunchy. Do not overcook. Some of the goat cheese may break through the crust. A few little breaks are fine but stop the cooking before the coating reaches structural failure.
6. Remove the basket from the machine and set aside for 3 minutes. Use a nonstick-safe spatula, and maybe a flatware fork for balance, to transfer the rounds to a wire rack. Cool for 5 minutes more before serving.

Hungarian Spiralized Fries

Servings: 4
Cooking Time: 30 Minutes
Ingredients:
- 2 russet potatoes, peeled
- 1 tbsp olive oil
- ½ tsp chili powder
- ½ tsp garlic powder
- ½ tsp Hungarian paprika
- Salt and pepper to taste

Directions:
1. Preheat the air fryer to 400°F (205°C). Using the spiralizer, cut the potatoes into 5-inch lengths and add them to a large bowl. Pour cold water, cover, and set aside for 30 minutes. Drain and dry with a kitchen towel, then toss back in the bowl. Drizzle the potatoes with olive oil and season with salt, pepper, chili, garlic, and paprika. Toss well. Put the potatoes in the frying basket and Air Fry for 10-12 minutes, shaking the basket once until the potatoes are golden and crispy. Serve warm and enjoy!

Mediterranean Potato Skins

Servings: 4
Cooking Time: 50 Minutes
Ingredients:
- 2 russet potatoes
- 3 tbsp olive oil
- Salt and pepper to taste
- 2 tbsp rosemary, chopped
- 10 Kalamata olives, diced
- ¼ cup crumbled feta
- 2 tbsp chopped dill

Directions:
1. Preheat air fryer to 380°F (195°C). Poke 2-3 holes in the potatoes with a fork. Drizzle them with some olive oil and sprinkle with salt. Put the potatoes into the frying basket and Bake for 30 minutes. When the potatoes are ready, remove them from the fryer and slice in half. Scoop out the flesh of the potatoes with a spoon, leaving a ½-inch layer of potato inside the skins, and set the skins aside.
2. Combine the scooped potato middles with the remaining olive oil, salt, black pepper, and rosemary in a medium bowl. Mix until well combined. Spoon the potato filling into the potato skins, spreading it evenly over them. Top with olives, dill and feta. Put the loaded potato skins back into the air fryer and Bake for 15 minutes. Enjoy!

Grilled Cheese Sandwich Deluxe

Servings: 4
Cooking Time: 6 Minutes
Ingredients:
- 8 ounces Brie
- 8 slices oat nut bread
- 1 large ripe pear, cored and cut into ½-inch-thick slices
- 2 tablespoons butter, melted

Directions:
1. Spread a quarter of the Brie on each of four slices of bread.
2. Top Brie with thick slices of pear, then the remaining 4 slices of bread.
3. Lightly brush both sides of each sandwich with melted butter.
4. Cooking 2 at a time, place sandwiches in air fryer basket and cook at 360°F (180°C) for 6minutes or until cheese melts and outside looks golden brown.

Crispy Curried Sweet Potato Fries

Servings: 4
Cooking Time: 20 Minutes
Ingredients:

- ½ cup sour cream
- ½ cup peach chutney
- 3 tsp curry powder
- 2 sweet potatoes, julienned
- 1 tbsp olive oil
- Salt and pepper to taste

Directions:
1. Preheat air fryer to 390°F (200°C). Mix together sour cream, peach chutney, and 1 ½ tsp curry powder in a small bowl. Set aside. In a medium bowl, add sweet potatoes, olive oil, the rest of the curry powder, salt, and pepper. Toss to coat. Place the potatoes in the frying basket. Bake for about 6 minutes, then shake the basket once. Cook for an additional 4 -6 minutes or until the potatoes are golden and crispy. Serve the fries hot in a basket along with the chutney sauce for dipping.

Potato Chips

Servings: 2
Cooking Time: 15 Minutes
Ingredients:
- 2 medium potatoes
- 2 teaspoons extra-light olive oil
- oil for misting or cooking spray
- salt and pepper

Directions:
1. Peel the potatoes.
2. Using a mandoline or paring knife, shave potatoes into thin slices, dropping them into a bowl of water as you cut them.
3. Dry potatoes as thoroughly as possible with paper towels or a clean dish towel. Toss potato slices with the oil to coat completely.
4. Spray air fryer basket with cooking spray and add potato slices.
5. Stir and separate with a fork.
6. Cook 390°F (200°C) for 5minutes. Stir and separate potato slices. Cook 5 more minutes. Stir and separate potatoes again. Cook another 5minutes.
7. Season to taste.

Cheesy Zucchini Chips

Servings: 4
Cooking Time: 35 Minutes
Ingredients:
- 1 lb thin zucchini chips
- 2 eggs
- ½ cup bread crumbs
- ½ cup grated Pecorino cheese
- Salt and pepper to taste
- ½ cup mayonnaise
- ½ tbsp olive oil

- ½ lemon. juiced
- 1 tsp garlic powder
- Salt and pepper to taste

Directions:

1. Preheat air fryer to 350°F（175°C）. Beat eggs in a small bowl, then set aside. In another small bowl, stir together bread crumbs, Pecorino, salt, and pepper. Dip zucchini slices into the egg mixture, then in the crumb mixture. Place them in the greased frying basket and Air Fry for 10 minutes. Remove and set aside to cool. Mix the mayonnaise, olive oil, lemon juice, garlic, salt, and pepper in a bowl to make aioli. Serve aioli with chips and enjoy.

Maple Loaded Sweet Potatoes

Servings: 4
Cooking Time: 45 Minutes

Ingredients:

- 4 sweet potatoes
- 2 tbsp butter
- 2 tbsp maple syrup
- 1 tsp cinnamon
- 1 tsp lemon zest
- ½ tsp vanilla extract

Directions:

1. Preheat air fryer to 390°F（200°C）. Poke three holes on the top of each of the sweet potatoes using a fork. Arrange in air fryer and Bake for 40 minutes. Remove and let cool for 5 minutes. While the sweet potatoes cool, melt butter and maple syrup together in the microwave for 15-20 seconds. Remove from microwave and stir in cinnamon, lemon zest, and vanilla. When the sweet potatoes are cool, cut open and drizzle the cinnamon butter mixture over each and serve immediately.

Fried Gyoza

Servings: 18
Cooking Time: 6 Minutes

Ingredients:

- 5 ounces Lean ground pork
- 2½ tablespoons Very thinly sliced scallion
- 1 tablespoon plus 2 teaspoons Minced peeled fresh ginger
- 1¼ teaspoons Toasted sesame oil
- ⅛ teaspoon Table salt
- ⅛ teaspoon Ground black pepper
- 18 Round gyoza or square wonton wrappers (thawed, if necessary)
- Vegetable oil spray

Directions:

1. Preheat the air fryer to 350°F（175°C）.
2. Mix the ground pork, scallion, ginger, sesame oil, salt, and pepper in a bowl until well combined.

3. Set a bowl of water on a clean, dry surface or next to a clean, dry cutting board. Set one gyoza or wonton wrapper on that surface. Dip your clean finger in the water and run it around the perimeter of the gyoza wrapper or the edge of the wonton wrapper. Put about 1 ½ teaspoons of the meat mixture in the center of the wrapper.
4. For the gyoza wrapper, fold the wrapper in half to close, pressing the edge to seal, then wet the outside of the edge of both sides of the seam and pleat it into little ridges to seal.
5. For the wonton wrapper, fold it in half lengthwise to make a rectangle, then seal the sides together, flattening the packet a bit as you do.
6. Set the filled wrapper aside and continue making more in the same way. When done, generously coat them on all sides with vegetable oil spray.
7. Place the gyoza in the basket in one layer and air-fry undisturbed for 6 minutes, or until browned and crisp at the edges.
8. Use kitchen tongs or a nonstick-safe spatula to gently transfer the gyoza to a wire rack. Cool for only 2 or 3 minutes before serving hot.

Crunchy Tortellini Bites

Servings: 5
Cooking Time: 10 Minutes

Ingredients:

- 10 ounces (about 2½ cups) Cheese tortellini
- ⅓ cup Yellow cornmeal
- ⅓ cup Seasoned Italian-style dried bread crumbs
- ⅓ cup (about 1 ounce) Finely grated Parmesan cheese
- 1 Large egg
- Olive oil spray

Directions:

1. Bring a large pot of water to a boil over high heat. Add the tortellini and cook for 3 minutes. Drain in a colander set in the sink, then spread out the tortellini on a large baking sheet and cool for 15 minutes.
2. Preheat the air fryer to 400°F（205°C）.
3. Mix the cornmeal, bread crumbs, and cheese in a large zip-closed plastic bag.
4. Whisk the egg in a medium bowl until uniform. Add the tortellini and toss well to coat, even along the inside curve of the pasta. Use a slotted spoon or kitchen tongs to transfer 5 or 6 tortellini to the plastic bag, seal, and shake gently to coat thoroughly and evenly. Set the coated tortellini aside on a cutting board and continue coating the rest in the same way.
5. Generously coat the tortellini on all sides with the olive oil spray, then set them in one layer in the basket. Air-fry undisturbed for 10 minutes, gently tossing the basket and rearranging the tortellini at the 4- and 7-minute marks, until brown and crisp.
6. Pour the contents of the basket onto a wire rack. Cool for 5 minutes before serving.

Potato Chips With Sour Cream And Onion Dip

Servings: 2
Cooking Time: 20 Minutes

Ingredients:

- 2 large potatoes (Yukon Gold or russet)
- vegetable or olive oil in a spray bottle
- sea salt and freshly ground black pepper
- Sour Cream and Onion Dip:
- ½ cup sour cream
- 1 tablespoon olive oil
- 2 scallions, white part only minced
- ¼ teaspoon salt
- freshly ground black pepper
- a squeeze of lemon juice (about ¼ teaspoon)

Directions:

1. Wash the potatoes well, but leave the skins on. Slice them into ⅛-inch thin slices, using a mandolin or food processor. Rinse the potatoes under cold water until the water runs clear and then let them soak in a bowl of cold water for at least 10 minutes. Drain and dry the potato slices really well in a single layer on a clean kitchen towel.

2. Preheat the air fryer to 300°F（150°C）. Spray the potato chips with the oil so that both sides are evenly coated, or rub the slices between your hands with some oil if you don't have a spray bottle.

3. Air-fry in two batches at 300°F（150°C）for 20 minutes, shaking the basket a few times during the cooking process so the chips crisp and brown more evenly. Season the finished chips with sea salt and freshly ground black pepper while they are still hot.

4. While the chips are air-frying, make the sour cream and onion dip by mixing together the sour cream, olive oil, scallions, salt, pepper and lemon juice. Serve the chips warm or at room temperature along with the dip.

Avocado Fries

Servings: 8
Cooking Time: 8 Minutes

Ingredients:

- 2 medium avocados, firm but ripe
- 1 large egg
- ½ teaspoon garlic powder
- ¼ teaspoon cayenne pepper
- ¼ teaspoon salt
- ¾ cup almond flour
- ½ cup finely grated Parmesan cheese
- ½ cup gluten-free breadcrumbs

Directions:

1. Preheat the air fryer to 370°F（185°C）.

2. Rinse the outside of the avocado with water. Slice the avocado in half, slice it in half again, and then slice it in half once more to get 8 slices. Remove the outer skin. Repeat for the other avocado. Set the avocado slices aside.

3. In a small bowl, whisk the egg, garlic powder, cayenne pepper, and salt in a small bowl. Set aside.

4. In a separate bowl, pour the almond flour.

5. In a third bowl, mix the Parmesan cheese and breadcrumbs.

6. Carefully roll the avocado slices in the almond flour, then dip them in the egg wash, and coat them in the cheese and breadcrumb topping. Repeat until all 16 fries are coated.

7. Liberally spray the air fryer basket with olive oil spray and place the avocado fries into the basket, leaving a little space around the sides between fries. Depending on the size of your air fryer, you may need to cook these in batches.

8. Cook fries for 8 minutes, or until the outer coating turns light brown.

9. Carefully remove, repeat with remaining slices, and then serve warm.

Vegetable Side Dishes Recipes

Sage & Thyme Potatoes

Servings: 4
Cooking Time: 30 Minutes
Ingredients:

- 2 red potatoes, peeled and cubed
- ¼ cup olive oil
- 1 tsp dried sage
- ½ tsp dried thyme
- ½ tsp salt
- 2 tbsp grated Parmesan

Directions:

1. Preheat air fryer to 360°F (180°C). Coat the red potatoes with olive oil, sage, thyme and salt in a bowl. Pour the potatoes into the air frying basket and Roast for 10 minutes. Stir the potatoes and sprinkle the Parmesan over the top. Continue roasting for 8 more minutes. Serve hot.

Green Peas With Mint

Servings: 4
Cooking Time: 5 Minutes
Ingredients:

- 1 cup shredded lettuce
- 1 10-ounce package frozen green peas, thawed
- 1 tablespoon fresh mint, shredded
- 1 teaspoon melted butter

Directions:

1. Lay the shredded lettuce in the air fryer basket.
2. Toss together the peas, mint, and melted butter and spoon over the lettuce.
3. Cook at 360°F (180°C) for 5minutes, until peas are warm and lettuce wilts.

Almond-crusted Zucchini Fries

Servings:2
Cooking Time: 30 Minutes
Ingredients:

- ½ cup grated Pecorino cheese
- 1 zucchini, cut into fries
- 1 tsp salt
- 1 egg
- 1 tbsp almond milk
- ½ cup almond flour

Directions:

. Preheat air fryer to 370ºF (185°C). Distribute zucchini fries evenly over a paper towel, sprinkle with salt, and let sit for 10 minutes to pull out moisture. Pat them dry with paper towels. In a bowl, beat egg and almond milk. In another bowl, combine almond flour and Pecorino cheese. Dip fries in egg mixture and then dredge them in flour mixture. Place zucchini fries in the lightly greased frying basket and Air Fry for 10 minutes, flipping once. Serve.

Fried Okra

Servings: 4
Cooking Time: 8 Minutes
Ingredients:

- 1 pound okra
- 1 large egg
- 1 tablespoon milk
- 1 teaspoon salt, divided
- ½ teaspoon black pepper, divided
- ¼ teaspoon paprika
- ¼ teaspoon thyme
- ½ cup cornmeal
- ½ cup all-purpose flour

Directions:

1. Preheat the air fryer to 400°F (205°C).
2. Cut the okra into ½-inch rounds.
3. In a medium bowl, whisk together the egg, milk, ½ teaspoon of the salt, and ¼ teaspoon of black pepper. Place the okra into the egg mixture and toss until well coated.
4. In a separate bowl, mix together the remaining ½ teaspoon of salt, the remaining ¼ teaspoon of black pepper, the paprika, the thyme, the cornmeal, and the flour. Working in small batches, dredge the egg-coated okra in the cornmeal mixture until all the okra has been breaded.
5. Place a single layer of okra in the air fryer basket and spray with cooking spray. Cook for 4 minutes, toss to check for crispness, and cook another 4 minutes. Repeat in batches, as needed.

Brown Rice And Goat Cheese Croquettes

Servings: 3
Cooking Time: 8 Minutes
Ingredients:

- ¾ cup Water
- 6 tablespoons Raw medium-grain brown rice, such as brown Arborio
- ½ cup Shredded carrot
- ¼ cup Walnut pieces
- 3 tablespoons (about 1½ ounces) Soft goat cheese
- 1 tablespoon Pasteurized egg substitute, such as Egg Beaters (gluten-free, if a concern)
- ¼ teaspoon Dried thyme
- ¼ teaspoon Table salt

- ¼ teaspoon Ground black pepper
- Olive oil spray

Directions:

1. Combine the water, rice, and carrots in a small saucepan set over medium-high heat. Bring to a boil, stirring occasionally. Cover, reduce the heat to very low, and simmer very slowly for 45 minutes, or until the water has been absorbed and the rice is tender. Set aside, covered, for 10 minutes.

2. Scrape the contents of the saucepan into a food processor. Cool for 10 minutes.

3. Preheat the air fryer to 400°F（205°C）.

4. Put the nuts, cheese, egg substitute, thyme, salt, and pepper into the food processor. Cover and pulse to a coarse paste, stopping the machine at least once to scrape down the inside of the canister.

5. Uncover the food processor; scrape down and remove the blade. Using wet, clean hands, form the mixture into two 4-inch-diameter patties for a small batch, three 4-inch-diameter patties for a medium batch, or four 4-inch-diameter patties for a large one. Generously coat both sides of the patties with olive oil spray.

6. Set the patties in the basket with as much air space between them as possible. Air-fry undisturbed for 8 minutes, or until brown and crisp.

7. Use a nonstick-safe spatula to transfer the croquettes to a wire rack. Cool for 5 minutes before serving.

Fingerling Potatoes

Servings: 4
Cooking Time: 15 Minutes

Ingredients:

- 1 pound fingerling potatoes
- 1 tablespoon light olive oil
- ½ teaspoon dried parsley
- ½ teaspoon lemon juice
- coarsely ground sea salt

Directions:

1. Cut potatoes in half lengthwise.
2. In a large bowl, combine potatoes, oil, parsley, and lemon juice. Stir well to coat potatoes.
3. Place potatoes in air fryer basket and cook at 360°F（180°C）for 15 minutes or until lightly browned and tender inside.
4. Sprinkle with sea salt before serving.

Garlicky Bell Pepper Mix

Servings: 4
Cooking Time: 30 Minutes

Ingredients:

- 2 tbsp vegetable oil
- ½ tsp dried cilantro
- 1 red bell pepper

- 1 yellow bell pepper
- 1 orange bell pepper
- 1 green bell pepper
- Salt and pepper to taste
- 1 head garlic

Directions:

1. Preheat air fryer to 330°F（165°C）. Slice the peppers into 1-inch strips. Transfer them to a large bowl along with 1 tbsp of vegetable oil. Toss to coat. Season with cilantro, salt, and pepper. Cut the top of a garlic head and place it cut-side up on an oiled square of aluminium foil. Drizzle with vegetable oil and wrap completely in the foil.

2. Roast the wrapped garlic in the air fryer for 15 minutes. Next, add the pepper strips and roast until the peppers are tender and the garlic is soft, 6-8 minutes. Transfer the peppers to a serving dish. Remove the garlic and unwrap the foil carefully. Once cooled, squeeze the cloves out of the garlic head and mix into the peppers' dish. Serve.

Spicy Bean Stuffed Potatoes

Servings: 4
Cooking Time: 60 Minutes

Ingredients:

- 1 lb russet potatoes, scrubbed and perforated with a fork
- 1 can diced green chilies, including juice
- 1/3 cup grated Mexican cheese blend
- 1 green bell pepper, diced
- 1 yellow bell pepper, diced
- ¼ cup torn iceberg lettuce
- 2 tsp olive oil
- 2 tbsp sour cream
- ½ tsp chili powder
- 2-3 jalapeños, sliced
- 1 red bell pepper, chopped
- Salt and pepper to taste
- 1/3 cup canned black beans
- 4 grape tomatoes, sliced
- ¼ cup chopped parsley

Directions:

1. Preheat air fryer at 400°F（205°C）. Brush olive oil over potatoes. Place them in the frying basket and Bake for 45 minutes, turning at 30 minutes mark. Let cool on a cutting board for 10 minutes until cool enough to handle. Slice each potato lengthwise and scoop out all but a ¼" layer of potato to form 4 boats.

2. Mash potato flesh, sour cream, green chilies, cheese, chili powder, jalapeños, green, yellow, and red peppers, salt, and pepper in a bowl until smooth. Fold in black beans. Divide between potato skin boats. Place potato boats in the frying basket and Bake for 2 minutes. Remove them to a serving plate. Top each boat with lettuce, tomatoes, and parsley. Sprinkle tops with salt and serve.

Pecorino Dill Muffins

Servings:4
Cooking Time: 25 Minutes
Ingredients:
- ¼ cup grated Pecorino cheese
- 1 cup flour
- 1 tsp dried dill
- ⅛ tsp salt
- ¼ tsp onion powder
- 2 tsp baking powder
- 1 egg
- ¼ cup Greek yogurt

Directions:
1. Preheat air fryer to 350ºF (175°C). In a bowl, combine dry the ingredients. Set aside. In another bowl, whisk the wet ingredients. Add the wet ingredients to the dry ingredients and combine until blended.
2. Transfer the batter to 6 silicone muffin cups lightly greased with olive oil. Place muffin cups in the frying basket and Bake for 12 minutes. Serve right away.

Five-spice Roasted Sweet Potatoes

Servings: 4
Cooking Time: 12 Minutes
Ingredients:
- ½ teaspoon ground cinnamon
- ¼ teaspoon ground cumin
- ¼ teaspoon paprika
- 1 teaspoon chile powder
- ⅛ teaspoon turmeric
- ½ teaspoon salt (optional)
- freshly ground black pepper
- 2 large sweet potatoes, peeled and cut into ¾-inch cubes (about 3 cups)
- 1 tablespoon olive oil

Directions:
1. In a large bowl, mix together cinnamon, cumin, paprika, chile powder, turmeric, salt, and pepper to taste.
2. Add potatoes and stir well.
3. Drizzle the seasoned potatoes with the olive oil and stir until evenly coated.
4. Place seasoned potatoes in the air fryer baking pan or an ovenproof dish that fits inside your air fryer basket.
5. Cook for 6minutes at 390°F (200°C), stop, and stir well.
6. Cook for an additional 6minutes.

Perfect French Fries

Servings: 3
Cooking Time: 37 Minutes
Ingredients:
- 1 pound Large russet potato(es)

- Vegetable oil or olive oil spray
- ½ teaspoon Table salt

Directions:
1. Cut each potato lengthwise into ¼-inch-thick slices. Cut each of these lengthwise into ¼-inch-thick matchsticks.
2. Set the potato matchsticks in a big bowl of cool water and soak for 5 minutes. Drain in a colander set in the sink, then spread the matchsticks out on paper towels and dry them very well.
3. Preheat the air fryer to 225°F (160°C) (or 230°F (165°C), if that's the closest setting).
4. When the machine is at temperature, arrange the matchsticks in an even layer (if overlapping but not compact) in the basket. Air-fry for 20 minutes, tossing and rearranging the fries twice.
5. Pour the contents of the basket into a big bowl. Increase the air fryer's temperature to 325°F (160°C) (or 330°F (165°C), if that's the closest setting).
6. Generously coat the fries with vegetable or olive oil spray. Toss well, then coat them again to make sure they're covered on all sides, tossing (and maybe spraying) a couple of times to make sure.
7. When the machine is at temperature, pour the fries into the basket and air-fry for 12 minutes, tossing and rearranging the fries at least twice.
8. Increase the machine's temperature to 375°F (190°C) (or 380°F (195°C) or 390°F (200°C), if one of these is the closest setting). Air-fry for 5 minutes more (from the moment you raise the temperature), tossing and rearranging the fries at least twice to keep them from burning and to make sure they all get an even measure of the heat, until brown and crisp.
9. Pour the contents of the basket into a serving bowl. Toss the fries with the salt and serve hot.

Buttery Radish Wedges

Servings:2
Cooking Time: 20 Minutes
Ingredients:
- 2 tbsp butter, melted
- 2 cloves garlic, minced
- ¼ tsp salt
- 20 radishes, quartered
- 2 tbsp feta cheese crumbles
- 1 tbsp chopped parsley

Directions:
1. Preheat air fryer to 370ºF (185°C). Mix the butter, garlic, and salt in a bowl. Stir in radishes. Place the radish wedges in the frying basket and Roast for 10 minutes, shaking once. Transfer to a large serving dish and stir in feta cheese. Scatter with parsley and serve.

Jerk Rubbed Corn On The Cob

Servings: 4
Cooking Time: 6 Minutes
Ingredients:
- 1 teaspoon ground allspice
- 1 teaspoon dried thyme
- ½ teaspoon ground ginger
- ½ teaspoon ground cinnamon
- ¼ teaspoon ground nutmeg
- ⅛ teaspoon ground cayenne pepper
- 1 teaspoon salt
- 2 tablespoons butter, melted
- 4 ears of corn, husked

Directions:
1. Preheat the air fryer to 380°F（195°C）.
2. Combine all the spices in a bowl. Brush the corn with the melted butter and then sprinkle the spices generously on all sides of each ear of corn.
3. Transfer the ears of corn to the air fryer basket. It's ok if they are crisscrossed on top of each other. Air-fry at 380°F（195°C）for 6 minutes, rotating the ears as they cook.
4. Brush more butter on at the end and sprinkle with any remaining spice mixture.

Herbed Baby Red Potato Hasselback

Servings: 4
Cooking Time: 35 Minutes
Ingredients:
- 6 baby red potatoes, scrubbed
- 3 tsp shredded cheddar cheese
- 1 tbsp olive oil
- 2 tbsp butter, melted
- 1 tbsp chopped thyme
- Salt and pepper to taste
- 3 tsp sour cream
- ¼ cup chopped parsley

Directions:
1. Preheat air fryer at 350ºF（175°C）. Make slices in the width of each potato about ¼-inch apart without cutting through. Rub potato slices with olive oil, both outside and in between slices. Place potatoes in the frying basket and Air Fry for 20 minutes, tossing once, brush with melted butter, and scatter with thyme. Remove them to a large serving dish. Sprinkle with salt, black pepper and top with a dollop of cheddar cheese, sour cream. Scatter with parsley to serve.

Roasted Broccoli And Red Bean Salad

Servings: 3

Cooking Time: 14 Minutes
Ingredients:
- 3 cups (about 1 pound) 1- to 1½-inch fresh broccoli florets (not frozen)
- 1½ tablespoons Olive oil spray
- 1¼ cups Canned red kidney beans, drained and rinsed
- 3 tablespoons Minced yellow or white onion
- 2 tablespoons plus 1 teaspoon Red wine vinegar
- ¾ teaspoon Dried oregano
- ¼ teaspoon Table salt
- ¼ teaspoon Ground black pepper

Directions:
1. Preheat the air fryer to 375°F（190°C）.
2. Put the broccoli florets in a big bowl, coat them generously with olive oil spray, then toss to coat all surfaces, even down into the crannies, spraying them a couple of times more.
3. Pour the florets into the basket, spreading them into as close to one layer as you can. Air-fry for 12 minutes, tossing and rearranging the florets twice so that any touching or covered parts are eventually exposed to the air currents, until light browned but still a bit firm. (If the machine is at 360°F（180°C）, you may need to add 2 minutes to the cooking time.)
4. Dump the contents of the basket onto a large cutting board. Cool for a minute or two, then chop the florets into small bits. Scrape these into a bowl and add the kidney beans, onion, vinegar, oregano, salt, and pepper. Toss well and serve warm or at room temperature.

Southern Okra Chips

Servings: 2
Cooking Time: 20 Minutes
Ingredients:
- 2 eggs
- ¼ cup whole milk
- ¼ cup bread crumbs
- ¼ cup cornmeal
- 1 tbsp Cajun seasoning
- Salt and pepper to taste
- ⅛ tsp chili pepper
- ½ lb okra, sliced
- 1 tbsp butter, melted

Directions:
1. Preheat air fryer at 400ºF（205°C）. Beat the eggs and milk in a bowl. In another bowl, combine the remaining ingredients, except okra and butter. Dip okra chips in the egg mixture, then dredge them in the breadcrumbs mixture. Place okra chips in the greased frying basket and Roast for 7 minutes, shake once and brush with melted butter. Serve right away.

Mushrooms

Servings: 4
Cooking Time: 12 Minutes
Ingredients:
- 8 ounces whole white button mushrooms
- ½ teaspoon salt
- ⅛ teaspoon pepper
- ¼ teaspoon garlic powder
- ¼ teaspoon onion powder
- 5 tablespoons potato starch
- 1 egg, beaten
- ¾ cup panko breadcrumbs
- oil for misting or cooking spray

Directions:
1. Place mushrooms in a large bowl. Add the salt, pepper, garlic and onion powders, and stir well to distribute seasonings.
2. Add potato starch to mushrooms and toss in bowl until well coated.
3. Dip mushrooms in beaten egg, roll in panko crumbs, and mist with oil or cooking spray.
4. Place mushrooms in air fryer basket. You can cook them all at once, and it's okay if a few are stacked.
5. Cook at 390°F (200°C) for 5minutes. Shake basket, then continue cooking for 7 more minutes, until golden brown and crispy.

Moroccan Cauliflower

Servings: 6
Cooking Time: 15 Minutes
Ingredients:
- 1 tablespoon curry powder
- 2 teaspoons smoky paprika
- ½ teaspoon ground cumin
- ½ teaspoon salt
- 1 head cauliflower, cut into bite-size pieces
- ¼ cup red wine vinegar
- 2 tablespoons extra-virgin olive oil
- 2 tablespoons chopped parsley

Directions:
1. Preheat the air fryer to 370°F (185°C).
2. In a large bowl, mix the curry powder, paprika, cumin, and salt. Add the cauliflower and stir to coat. Pour the red wine vinegar over the top and continue stirring.
3. Place the cauliflower into the air fryer basket; drizzle olive oil over the top.
4. Cook the cauliflower for 5 minutes, toss, and cook another 5 minutes. Raise the temperature to 400°F (205°C) and continue cooking for 4 to 6 minutes, or until crispy.

Savory Brussels Sprouts

Servings: 4

Cooking Time: 15 Minutes
Ingredients:
- 1 lb Brussels sprouts, quartered
- 2 tbsp balsamic vinegar
- 1 tbsp olive oil
- 1 tbsp honey
- Salt and pepper to taste
- 1 ½ tbsp lime juice
- Parsley for sprinkling

Directions:
1. Preheat air fryer at 350°F (175°C). Combine all ingredients in a bowl. Transfer them to the frying basket. Air Fry for 10 minutes, tossing once. Top with lime juice and parsley.

Provence French Fries

Servings: 4
Cooking Time: 25 Minutes
Ingredients:
- 2 russet potatoes
- 1 tbsp olive oil
- 1 tbsp herbs de Provence

Directions:
1. Preheat air fryer to 400°F (205°C). Slice the potatoes lengthwise into ½-inch thick strips. In a bowl, whisk the olive oil and herbs de Provence. Toss in the potatoes to coat. Arrange them in a single and Air Fry for 18-20 minutes, shaking once, until crispy. Serve warm.

Roasted Fennel Salad

Servings: 3
Cooking Time: 20 Minutes
Ingredients:
- 3 cups (about ¾ pound) Trimmed fennel (see the headnote), roughly chopped
- 1½ tablespoons Olive oil
- ¼ teaspoon Table salt
- ¼ teaspoon Ground black pepper
- 1½ tablespoons White balsamic vinegar (see here)

Directions:
1. Preheat the air fryer to 400°F (205°C).
2. Toss the fennel, olive oil, salt, and pepper in a large bowl until the fennel is well coated in the oil.
3. When the machine is at temperature, pour the fennel into the basket, spreading it out into as close to one layer as possible. Air-fry for 20 minutes, tossing and rearranging the fennel pieces twice so that any covered or touching parts get exposed to the air currents, until golden at the edges and softened.
4. Pour the fennel into a serving bowl. Add the vinegar while hot. Toss well, then cool a couple of minutes before serving. Or serve at room temperature.

Buttery Stuffed Tomatoes

Servings: 6
Cooking Time: 15 Minutes
Ingredients:
- 3 8-ounce round tomatoes
- ½ cup plus 1 tablespoon Plain panko bread crumbs (gluten-free, if a concern)
- 3 tablespoons (about ½ ounce) Finely grated Parmesan cheese
- 3 tablespoons Butter, melted and cooled
- 4 teaspoons Stemmed and chopped fresh parsley leaves
- 1 teaspoon Minced garlic
- ¼ teaspoon Table salt
- Up to ¼ teaspoon Red pepper flakes
- Olive oil spray

Directions:
1. Preheat the air fryer to 375°F（190°C）.
2. Cut the tomatoes in half through their "equators" (that is, not through the stem ends). One at a time, gently squeeze the tomato halves over a trash can, using a clean finger to gently force out the seeds and most of the juice inside, working carefully so that the tomato doesn't lose its round shape or get crushed.
3. Stir the bread crumbs, cheese, butter, parsley, garlic, salt, and red pepper flakes in a bowl until the bread crumbs are moistened and the parsley is uniform throughout the mixture. Pile this mixture into the spaces left in the tomato halves. Press gently to compact the filling. Coat the tops of the tomatoes with olive oil spray.
4. Place the tomatoes cut side up in the basket. They may touch each other. Air-fry for 15 minutes, or until the filling is lightly browned and crunchy.
5. Use nonstick-safe spatula and kitchen tongs for balance to gently transfer the stuffed tomatoes to a platter or a cutting board. Cool for a couple of minutes before serving.

Rich Baked Sweet Potatoes

Servings: 2
Cooking Time: 55 Minutes
Ingredients:
- 1 lb sweet potatoes, scrubbed and perforated with a fork
- 2 tsp olive oil
- Salt and pepper to taste
- 2 tbsp butter
- 3 tbsp honey

Directions:
1. Preheat air fryer at 400ºF（205°C）. Mix olive oil, salt, black pepper, and honey. Brush with the prepared mix over both sweet potatoes. Place them in the frying basket and Bake for 45 minutes, turning at 30 minutes mark. Let cool on a cutting board for 10 minutes until cool enough to handle. Slice each potato lengthwise. Press ends of one potato together to open up the slices. Top with butter to serve.

Vegetable Roast

Servings: 6
Cooking Time: 20 Minutes
Ingredients:
- 2 tbsp dill, chopped
- 2 zucchini, cubed
- 1 red bell pepper, diced
- 2 garlic cloves, sliced
- 2 tbsp olive oil
- ½ tsp salt
- ½ tsp red pepper flakes

Directions:
1. Preheat air fryer to 380°F（195°C）. Combine the zucchini, bell pepper, red pepper flakes, dill and garlic with olive oil and salt in a bowl. Pour the mixture into the frying basket and Roast for 14-16 minutes, shaking once. Serve warm.

Summer Watermelon And Cucumber Salad

Servings: 4
Cooking Time: 15 Minutes
Ingredients:
- ½ red onion, sliced into half-moons
- 2 tbsp crumbled goat cheese
- 10 chopped basil leaves
- 4 cups watermelon cubes
- ½ cucumber, sliced
- 4 tsp olive oil
- Salt and pepper to taste
- 3 cups arugula
- 1 tsp balsamic vinegar
- 1 tsp honey
- 1 tbsp chopped mint

Directions:
1. Preheat air fryer at 375ºF（190°C）. Toss watermelon, cucumber, onion, 2 tsp of olive oil, salt, and pepper in a bowl. Place it in the frying basket and Air Fry for 4 minutes, tossing once. In a salad bowl, whisk the arugula, balsamic vinegar, honey, and the remaining olive oil until the arugula is coated. Add in watermelon mixture. Scatter with goat cheese, basil leaves and mint to serve.

Corn Au Gratin

Servings: 4

Cooking Time: 20 Minutes

Ingredients:
- ½ cup grated cheddar
- 3 tbsp flour
- 2 cups yellow corn
- 1 egg, beaten
- ¼ cup milk
- ½ cup heavy cream
- Salt and pepper to taste
- 2 tbsp butter, cubed

Directions:
1. Preheat air fryer to 320°F（160°C）. Mix flour, corn, egg, milk, and heavy cream in a medium bowl. Stir in cheddar cheese, salt and pepper. Pour into the prepared baking pan. Top with butter. Bake for 15 minutes. Serve warm.

Tandoori Cauliflower

Servings: 4

Cooking Time: 10 Minutes

Ingredients:
- ½ cup Plain full-fat yogurt (not Greek yogurt)
- 1½ teaspoons Yellow curry powder, purchased or homemade (see the headnote)
- 1½ teaspoons Lemon juice
- ¾ teaspoon Table salt (optional)
- 4½ cups (about 1 pound 2 ounces) 2-inch cauliflower florets

Directions:
1. Preheat the air fryer to 400°F（205°C）.
2. Whisk the yogurt, curry powder, lemon juice, and salt (if using) in a large bowl until uniform. Add the florets and stir gently to coat the florets well and evenly. Even better, use your clean, dry hands to get the yogurt mixture down into all the nooks of the florets.
3. When the machine is at temperature, transfer the florets to the basket, spreading them gently into as close to one layer as you can. Air-fry for 10 minutes, tossing and rearranging the florets twice so that any covered or touching parts are exposed to the air currents, until lightly browned and tender if still a bit crunchy.
4. Pour the contents of the basket onto a wire rack. Cool for at least 5 minutes before serving, or serve at room temperature.

The Ultimate Mac`n`cheese

Servings: 4

Cooking Time: 35 Minutes

Ingredients:
- ¼ cup shredded sharp cheddar cheese

- ¼ cup grated Swiss cheese
- ¼ cup grated Parmesan
- ½ lb cooked elbow macaroni
- 3 tbsp butter, divided
- 1 sweet onion, diced
- 2 tsp red chili
- 1 tbsp flour
- 4 oz mascarpone cheese
- ¼ cup whole milk
- ¼ cup bread crumbs

Directions:
1. Melt 2 tbsp of butter in a skillet over -high heat for 30 seconds. Add in onions and red chili and stir-fry for 3 minutes until they´re translucent. Stir in flour until the sauce thickens. Stir in all cheeses and milk, then mix in macaroni. Spoon macaroni mixture into a greased cake pan. Preheat air fryer at 375°F（190°C）. Mix the breadcrumbs and the remaining butter in a bowl. Scatter over pasta mixture. Place cake pan in the frying basket and Bake for 15 minutes. Let sit for 10 minutes before serving.

Curried Fruit

Servings: 6

Cooking Time: 20 Minutes

Ingredients:
- 1 cup cubed fresh pineapple
- 1 cup cubed fresh pear (firm, not overly ripe)
- 8 ounces frozen peaches, thawed
- 1 15-ounce can dark, sweet, pitted cherries with juice
- 2 tablespoons brown sugar
- 1 teaspoon curry powder

Directions:
1. Combine all ingredients in large bowl. Stir gently to mix in the sugar and curry.
2. Pour into air fryer baking pan and cook at 360°F（180°C）for 10minutes.
3. Stir fruit and cook 10 more minutes.
4. Serve hot.

Grits Casserole

Servings: 4

Cooking Time: 30 Minutes

Ingredients:
- 10 fresh asparagus spears, cut into 1-inch pieces
- 2 cups cooked grits, cooled to room temperature
- 1 egg, beaten
- 2 teaspoons Worcestershire sauce
- ½ teaspoon garlic powder
- ¼ teaspoon salt
- 2 slices provolone cheese (about 1½ ounces)
- oil for misting or cooking spray

Directions:

1. Mist asparagus spears with oil and cook at 390°F (200°C) for 5minutes, until crisp-tender.
2. In a medium bowl, mix together the grits, egg, Worcestershire, garlic powder, and salt.
3. Spoon half of grits mixture into air fryer baking pan and top with asparagus.
4. Tear cheese slices into pieces and layer evenly on top of asparagus.
5. Top with remaining grits.
6. Bake at 360°F (180°C) for 25 minutes. The casserole will rise a little as it cooks. When done, the top will have browned lightly with just a hint of crispiness.

Cinnamon Roasted Pumpkin

Servings: 2
Cooking Time: 25 Minutes
Ingredients:
- 1 lb pumpkin, halved crosswise and seeded
- 1 tsp coconut oil
- 1 tsp sugar
- ½ tsp ground nutmeg
- 1 tsp ground cinnamon

Directions:
1. Prepare the pumpkin by rubbing coconut oil on the cut sides. In a small bowl, combine sugar, nutmeg and cinnamon. Sprinkle over the pumpkin. Preheat air fryer to 325°F (160°C). Put the pumpkin in the greased frying basket, cut sides up. Bake until the squash is soft in the center, 15 minutes. Test with a knife to ensure softness. Serve.

Roasted Bell Peppers With Garlic & Dill

Servings: 4
Cooking Time: 30 Minutes
Ingredients:
- 4 bell peppers, seeded and cut into fourths
- 1 tsp olive oil
- 4 garlic cloves, minced
- ½ tsp dried dill

Directions:
1. Preheat air fryer to 350°F (175°C). Add the peppers to the frying basket, spritz with olive oil, shake, and Roast for 15 minutes. Season with garlic and dill, then cook for an additional 3-5 minutes. The veggies should be soft. Serve.

Hasselbacks

Servings: 4
Cooking Time: 41 Minutes
Ingredients:
- 2 large potatoes (approx. 1 pound each)
- oil for misting or cooking spray

- salt, pepper, and garlic powder
- 1½ ounces sharp Cheddar cheese, sliced very thin
- ¼ cup chopped green onions
- 2 strips turkey bacon, cooked and crumbled
- light sour cream for serving (optional)

Directions:
1. Preheat air fryer to 390°F (200°C).
2. Scrub potatoes. Cut thin vertical slices ¼-inch thick crosswise about three-quarters of the way down so that bottom of potato remains intact.
3. Fan potatoes slightly to separate slices. Mist with oil and sprinkle with salt, pepper, and garlic powder to taste. Potatoes will be very stiff, but try to get some of the oil and seasoning between the slices.
4. Place potatoes in air fryer basket and cook for 40 minutes or until centers test done when pierced with a fork.
5. Top potatoes with cheese slices and cook for 30 seconds to 1 minute to melt cheese.
6. Cut each potato in half crosswise, and sprinkle with green onions and crumbled bacon. If you like, add a dollop of sour cream before serving.

Fried Corn On The Cob

Servings: 2
Cooking Time: 10 Minutes
Ingredients:
- 1½ tablespoons Regular or low-fat mayonnaise (not fat-free; gluten-free, if a concern)
- 1½ teaspoons Minced garlic
- ¼ teaspoon Table salt
- ¾ cup Plain panko bread crumbs (gluten-free, if a concern)
- 3 4-inch lengths husked and de-silked corn on the cob
- Vegetable oil spray

Directions:
1. Preheat the air fryer to 400°F (205°C).
2. Stir the mayonnaise, garlic, and salt in a small bowl until well combined. Spread the panko on a dinner plate.
3. Brush the mayonnaise mixture over the kernels of a piece of corn on the cob. Set the corn in the bread crumbs, then roll, pressing gently, to coat it. Lightly coat with vegetable oil spray. Set it aside, then coat the remaining piece(s) of corn in the same way.
4. Set the coated corn on the cob in the basket with as much air space between the pieces as possible. Air-fry undisturbed for 10 minutes, or until brown and crisp along the coating.
5. Use kitchen tongs to gently transfer the pieces of corn to a wire rack. Cool for 5 minutes before serving.

Lemony Green Bean Sautée

Servings: 6
Cooking Time: 15 Minutes
Ingredients:

- 1 tbsp cilantro, chopped
- 1 lb green beans, trimmed
- ½ red onion, sliced
- 2 tbsp olive oil
- Salt and pepper to taste
- 1 tbsp grapefruit juice
- 6 lemon wedges

Directions:

1. Preheat air fryer to 360°F（180°C）. Coat the green beans, red onion, olive oil, salt, pepper, cilantro and grapefruit juice in a bowl. Pour the mixture into the air fryer and Bake for 5 minutes. Stir well and cook for 5 minutes more. Serve with lemon wedges. Enjoy!

Canadian Bacon & Cheese Sandwich

Servings: 1
Cooking Time: 30 Minutes
Ingredients:
- 1 English muffin, halved
- 1 egg
- 1 Canadian bacon slice
- 1 slice provolone cheese

Directions:
1.   Preheat air fryer to 350°F (175°C). Put the muffin, crusty side up, in the frying basket. Place a slice of bacon next to the muffins and Bake for 5 minutes. Flip the bacon and muffins, and lay a slice of provolone cheese on top of the muffins. Beat the egg in a small heatproof bowl.
2.   Add the bowl in the frying basket next to the bacon and muffins and Bake for 15 minutes, or until the cheese melts, bacon is crispy and eggs set. Remove the muffin to a plate, layer a slice of bacon, then the egg and top with the second toasted muffin.

Cajun Breakfast Potatoes

Servings: 4
Cooking Time: 20 Minutes
Ingredients:
- 1 pound roasting potatoes (like russet), scrubbed clean
- 1 tablespoon vegetable oil
- 2 teaspoons paprika
- ½ teaspoon garlic powder
- ¼ teaspoon onion powder
- ¼ teaspoon ground cumin
- 1 teaspoon thyme
- 1 teaspoon sea salt
- ½ teaspoon black pepper

Directions:
1.   Cut the potatoes into 1-inch cubes.
2.   In a large bowl, toss the cut potatoes with vegetable oil.
3.   Sprinkle paprika, garlic powder, onion powder, cumin, thyme, salt, and pepper onto the potatoes, and toss to coat well.
4.   Preheat the air fryer to 400°F (205°C) for 4 minutes.
5.   Add the potatoes to the air fryer basket and bake for 10 minutes. Stir or toss the potatoes and continue baking for an additional 5 minutes. Stir or toss again and continue baking for an additional 5 minutes or until the desired crispness is achieved.

Almond Cranberry Granola

Servings: 12
Cooking Time: 9 Minutes
Ingredients:
- 2 tablespoons sesame seeds
- ¼ cup chopped almonds
- ¼ cup sunflower seeds
- ½ cup unsweetened shredded coconut
- 2 tablespoons unsalted butter, melted or at least softened
- 2 tablespoons coconut oil
- ⅓ cup honey
- 2½ cups oats
- ¼ teaspoon sea salt
- ½ cup dried cranberries

Directions:
1.   In a large mixing bowl, stir together the sesame seeds, almonds, sunflower seeds, coconut, butter, coconut oil, honey, oats, and salt.
2.   Line the air fryer basket with parchment paper. Punch 8 to 10 holes into the parchment paper with a fork so air can circulate. Pour the granola mixture onto the parchment paper
3.   Air fry the granola at 350°F (175°C) for 9 minutes, stirring every 3 minutes.
4.   When cooking is complete, stir in the dried cranberries and allow the mixture to cool. Store in an airtight container up to 2 weeks or freeze for 6 months.

Sweet Potato-cinnamon Toast

Servings: 6
Cooking Time: 8 Minutes
Ingredients:
- 1 small sweet potato, cut into ⅜-inch slices
- oil for misting
- ground cinnamon

Directions:
1.   Preheat air fryer to 390°F (200°C).
2.   Spray both sides of sweet potato slices with oil. Sprinkl both sides with cinnamon to taste.
3.   Place potato slices in air fryer basket in a single layer.
4.   Cook for 4minutes, turn, and cook for 4 more minutes or until potato slices are barely fork tender.

Quesadillas

Servings: 4
Cooking Time: 12 Minutes
Ingredients:
- 4 eggs
- 2 tablespoons skim milk
- salt and pepper
- oil for misting or cooking spray
- 4 flour tortillas
- 4 tablespoons salsa
- 2 ounces Cheddar cheese, grated
- ½ small avocado, peeled and thinly sliced

Directions:
1. Preheat air fryer to 270°F (185°C).
2. Beat together eggs, milk, salt, and pepper.
3. Spray a 6 x 6-inch air fryer baking pan lightly with cooking spray and add egg mixture.
4. Cook 9minutes, stirring every 1 to 2minutes, until eggs are scrambled to your liking. Remove and set aside.
5. Spray one side of each tortilla with oil or cooking spray. Flip over.
6. Divide eggs, salsa, cheese, and avocado among the tortillas, covering only half of each tortilla.
7. Fold each tortilla in half and press down lightly.
8. Place 2 tortillas in air fryer basket and cook at 390°F (200°C) for 3minutes or until cheese melts and outside feels slightly crispy. Repeat with remaining two tortillas.
9. Cut each cooked tortilla into halves or thirds.

Bacon, Broccoli And Swiss Cheese Bread Pudding

Servings: 2
Cooking Time: 48 Minutes
Ingredients:
- ½ pound thick cut bacon, cut into ¼-inch pieces
- 3 cups brioche bread or rolls, cut into ½-inch cubes
- 3 eggs
- 1 cup milk
- ½ teaspoon salt
- freshly ground black pepper
- 1 cup frozen broccoli florets, thawed and chopped
- 1½ cups grated Swiss cheese

Directions:
1. Preheat the air fryer to 400°F (205°C).
2. Air-fry the bacon for 6 minutes until crispy, shaking the basket a few times while it cooks to help it cook evenly. Remove the bacon and set it aside on a paper towel.
3. Air-fry the brioche bread cubes for 2 minutes to dry and toast lightly. (If your brioche is a few days old and slightly stale, you can omit this step.)
4. Butter a 6- or 7-inch cake pan. Combine all the ingredients in a large bowl and toss well. Transfer the mixture to the buttered cake pan, cover with aluminum foil

and refrigerate the bread pudding overnight, or for at least 8 hours.
5. Remove the casserole from the refrigerator an hour before you plan to cook, and let it sit on the countertop to come to room temperature.
6. Preheat the air fryer to 330°F (165°C). Transfer the covered cake pan, to the basket of the air fryer, lowering the dish into the basket using a sling made of aluminum foil (fold a piece of aluminum foil into a strip about 2-inches wide by 24-inches long). Fold the ends of the aluminum foil over the top of the dish before returning the basket to the air fryer. Air-fry for 20 minutes. Remove the foil and air-fry for an additional 20 minutes. If the top starts to brown a little too much before the custard has set, simply return the foil to the pan. The bread pudding has cooked through when a skewer inserted into the center comes out clean.

Apple Fritters

Servings: 6
Cooking Time: 12 Minutes
Ingredients:
- 1 cup all-purpose flour
- 1½ teaspoons baking powder
- ¼ teaspoon salt
- 2 tablespoon brown sugar
- 1 teaspoon vanilla extract
- ¾ cup plain Greek yogurt
- 1 tablespoon cinnamon
- 1 large Granny Smith apple, cored, peeled, and finely chopped
- ¼ cup chopped walnuts
- ½ cup powdered sugar
- 1 tablespoon milk

Directions:
1. Preheat the air fryer to 320°F (160°C).
2. In a medium bowl, combine the flour, baking powder, and salt.
3. In a large bowl, add the brown sugar, vanilla, yogurt, cinnamon, apples, and walnuts. Mix the dry ingredients into the wet, using your hands to combine, until all the ingredients are mixed together. Knead the mixture in the bowl about 4 times.
4. Lightly spray the air fryer basket with olive oil spray.
5. Divide the batter into 6 equally sized balls; then lightly flatten them and place inside the basket. Repeat until all the fritters are formed.
6. Place the basket in the air fryer and cook for 6 minutes, flip, and then cook another 6 minutes.
7. While the fritters are cooking, in a small bowl, mix the powdered sugar with the milk. Set aside.
8. When the cooking completes, remove the air fryer basket and allow the fritters to cool on a wire rack. Drizzle with the homemade glaze and serve.

Wild Blueberry Lemon Chia Bread

Servings: 6
Cooking Time: 27 Minutes

Ingredients:

- ¼ cup extra-virgin olive oil
- ⅓ cup plus 1 tablespoon cane sugar
- 1 large egg
- 3 tablespoons fresh lemon juice
- 1 tablespoon lemon zest
- ⅔ cup milk
- 1 cup all-purpose flour
- ¾ teaspoon baking powder
- ⅛ teaspoon salt
- 2 tablespoons chia seeds
- 1 cup frozen wild blueberries
- ⅓ cup powdered sugar
- 2 teaspoons milk

Directions:

1. Preheat the air fryer to 310°F（155°C）.
2. In a medium bowl, mix the olive oil with the sugar. Whisk in the egg, lemon juice, lemon zest, and milk; set aside.
3. In a small bowl, combine the all-purpose flour, baking powder, and salt.
4. Slowly mix the dry ingredients into the wet ingredients. Stir in the chia seeds and wild blueberries.
5. Liberally spray a 7-inch springform pan with olive-oil spray. Pour the batter into the pan and place the pan in the air fryer. Bake for 25 to 27 minutes, or until a toothpick inserted in the center comes out clean.
6. Remove and let cool on a wire rack for 10 minutes prior to removing from the pan.
7. Meanwhile, in a small bowl, mix the powdered sugar with the milk to create the glaze.
8. Slice and serve with a drizzle of the powdered sugar glaze.

Hashbrown Potatoes Lyonnaise

Servings: 4
Cooking Time: 33 Minutes

Ingredients:

- 1 Vidalia (or other sweet) onion, sliced
- 1 teaspoon butter, melted
- 1 teaspoon brown sugar
- 2 large russet potatoes (about 1 pound), sliced ½-inch thick
- 1 tablespoon vegetable oil
- salt and freshly ground black pepper

Directions:

1. Preheat the air fryer to 370°F（185°C）.
2. Toss the sliced onions, melted butter and brown sugar together in the air fryer basket. Air-fry for 8 minutes, shaking the basket occasionally to help the onions cook evenly.
3. While the onions are cooking, bring a 3-quart saucepan of salted water to a boil on the stovetop. Par-cook the potatoes in boiling water for 3 minutes. Drain the potatoes and pat them dry with a clean kitchen towel.
4. Add the potatoes to the onions in the air fryer basket and drizzle with vegetable oil. Toss to coat the potatoes with the oil and season with salt and freshly ground black pepper.
5. Increase the air fryer temperature to 400°F（205°C）and air-fry for 22 minutes tossing the vegetables a few times during the cooking time to help the potatoes brown evenly. Season to taste again with salt and freshly ground black pepper and serve warm.

Eggless Mung Bean Tart

Servings: 2
Cooking Time: 20 Minutes

Ingredients:

- 2 tsp soy sauce
- 1 tsp lime juice
- 1 large garlic clove, minced or pressed
- ½ tsp red chili flakes
- ½ cup mung beans, soaked
- Salt and pepper to taste
- ½ minced shallot
- 1 green onion, chopped

Directions:

1. Preheat the air fryer to 390°F（200°C）. Add the soy sauce, lime juice, garlic, and chili flakes to a bowl and stir. Set aside.Place the drained beans in a blender along with ½ cup of water, salt, and pepper. Blend until smooth. Stir in shallot and green onion, but do not blend.
2. Pour the batter into a greased baking pan. Bake for 15 minutes in the air fryer until golden. A knife inserted in the center should come out clean. Once cooked, cut the "quiche" into quarters. Drizzle with sauce and serve.

Favorite Blueberry Muffins

Servings: 8
Cooking Time: 25 Minutes

Ingredients:

- 1 cup all-purpose flour
- ½ tsp baking soda
- 1/3 cup granulated sugar
- ¼ tsp salt
- 1 tbsp lemon juice
- 1 tsp lemon zest
- ¼ cup milk

- ½ tsp vanilla extract
- 1 egg
- 1 tbsp vegetable oil
- ¼ cup halved blueberries
- 1 tbsp powdered sugar

Directions:

1. Preheat air fryer at 375ºF（190°C）. Combine dry ingredients in a bowl. Mix ¼ cup of fresh milk with 1 tsp of lemon juice and leave for 10 minutes. Put it in another bowl with the wet ingredients. Pour wet ingredients into dry ingredients and gently toss to combine. Fold in blueberries. Spoon mixture into 8 greased silicone cupcake liners and Bake them in the fryer for 6-8 minutes. Let cool onto a cooling rack. Serve right away sprinkled with powdered sugar.

Blueberry French Toast Sticks

Servings: 4

Cooking Time: 20 Minutes

Ingredients:

- 3 bread slices, cut into strips
- 1 tbsp butter, melted
- 2 eggs
- 1 tbsp milk
- 1 tbsp sugar
- ½ tsp vanilla extract
- 1 cup fresh blueberries
- 1 tbsp lemon juice

Directions:

1. Preheat air fryer to 380°F（195°C）. After laying the bread strips on a plate, sprinkle some melted butter over each piece. Whisk the eggs, milk, vanilla, and sugar, then dip the bread in the mix. Place on a wire rack to let the batter drip. Put the bread strips in the air fryer and Air Fry for 5-7 minutes. Use tongs to flip them once and cook until golden. With a fork, smash the blueberries and lemon juice together. Spoon the blueberries sauce over the French sticks. Serve immediately.

Thai Turkey Sausage Patties

Servings:4

Cooking Time: 30 Minutes

Ingredients:

- 12 oz turkey sausage
- 1 tsp onion powder
- 1 tsp dried coriander
- ¼ tsp Thai curry paste
- ¼ tsp red pepper flakes
- Salt and pepper to taste

Directions:

1. Preheat air fryer to 350°F（175°C）. Place the sausage, onion, coriander, curry paste, red flakes, salt, and black pepper in a large bowl and mix well. Form into eight patties. Arrange the patties on the greased frying basket and Air Fry for 10 minutes, flipping once halfway through. Once the patties are cooked, transfer to a plate and serve hot.

Cinnamon Pear Oat Muffins

Servings: 6

Cooking Time: 30 Minutes + Cooling Time

Ingredients:

- ½ cup apple sauce
- 1 large egg
- 1/3 cup brown sugar
- 2 tbsp butter, melted
- ½ cup milk
- 11/3 cups rolled oats
- 1 tsp ground cinnamon
- ½ tsp baking powder
- Pinch of salt
- ½ cup diced peeled pears

Directions:

1. Preheat the air fryer to 350°F（175°C）. Place the apple sauce, egg, brown sugar, melted butter, and milk into a bowl and mix to combine. Stir in the oats, cinnamon, baking powder, and salt and mix well, then fold in the pears.

2. Grease 6 silicone muffin cups with baking spray, then spoon the batter in equal portions into the cups. Put the muffin cups in the frying basket and Bake for 13-18 minutes or until set. Leave to cool for 15 minutes. Serve.

Cinnamon Biscuit Rolls

Servings: 12

Cooking Time: 5 Minutes

Ingredients:

- Dough
- ¼ cup warm water (105–115°F)（40 - 45°C）
- 1 teaspoon active dry yeast
- 1 tablespoon sugar
- ½ cup buttermilk, lukewarm
- 2 cups flour, plus more for dusting
- 1 teaspoon baking powder
- ½ teaspoon salt
- 3 tablespoons cold butter
- Filling
- 1 tablespoon butter, melted
- 1 teaspoon cinnamon
- 2 tablespoons sugar
- Icing
- ⅔ cup powdered sugar
- ¼ teaspoon vanilla

- 2–3 teaspoons milk

Directions:

1. Dissolve yeast and sugar in warm water. Add buttermilk, stir, and set aside.

2. In a large bowl, sift together flour, baking powder, and salt. Using knives or a pastry blender, cut in butter until mixture is well combined and crumbly.

3. Pour in buttermilk mixture and stir with fork until a ball of dough forms.

4. Knead dough on a lightly floured surface for 5minutes. Roll into an 8 x 11-inch rectangle.

5. For the filling, spread the melted butter over the dough.

6. In a small bowl, stir together the cinnamon and sugar, then sprinkle over dough.

7. Starting on a long side, roll up dough so that you have a roll about 11 inches long. Cut into 12 slices with a serrated knife and sawing motion so slices remain round.

8. Place rolls on a plate or cookie sheet about an inch apart and let rise for 30minutes.

9. For icing, mix the powdered sugar, vanilla, and milk. Stir and add additional milk until icing reaches a good spreading consistency.

10. Preheat air fryer to 360°F（180°C）.

11. Place 6 cinnamon rolls in basket and cook 5 minutes or until top springs back when lightly touched. Repeat to cook remaining 6 rolls.

12. Spread icing over warm rolls and serve.

Mini Everything Bagels

Servings: 4
Cooking Time: 6 Minutes

Ingredients:

- 1 cup all-purpose flour
- 2 teaspoons baking powder
- ½ teaspoon salt
- 1 cup plain Greek yogurt
- 1 egg, whisked
- 1 teaspoon sesame seeds
- 1 teaspoon dehydrated onions
- ½ teaspoon poppy seeds
- ½ teaspoon garlic powder
- ½ teaspoon sea salt flakes

Directions:

1. In a large bowl, mix together the flour, baking powder, and salt. Make a well in the dough and add in the Greek yogurt. Mix with a spoon until a dough forms.

2. Place the dough onto a heavily floured surface and knead for 3 minutes. You may use up to 1 cup of additional flour as you knead the dough, if necessary.

3. Cut the dough into 8 pieces and roll each piece into a 6-inch, snakelike piece. Touch the ends of each piece together so it closes the circle and forms a bagel shape. Brush the tops of the bagels with the whisked egg.

4. In a small bowl, combine the sesame seeds, dehydrated onions, poppy seeds, garlic powder, and sea salt flakes. Sprinkle the seasoning on top of the bagels.

5. Preheat the air fryer to 360°F（180°C）. Using a bench scraper or flat-edged spatula, carefully place the bagels into the air fryer basket. Spray the bagel tops with cooking spray. Air-fry the bagels for 6 minutes or until golden brown. Allow the bread to cool at least 10 minutes before slicing for serving.

Meaty Omelet

Servings: 4
Cooking Time: 20 Minutes

Ingredients:

- 6 eggs
- ½ cup grated Swiss cheese
- 3 breakfast sausages, sliced
- 8 bacon strips, sliced
- Salt and pepper to taste

Directions:

1. Preheat air fryer to 360°F（180°C）. In a bowl, beat the eggs and stir in Swiss cheese, sausages and bacon. Transfer the mixture to a baking dish and set in the fryer. Bake for 15 minutes or until golden and crisp. Season and serve.

All-in-one Breakfast Toast

Servings: 1
Cooking Time: 10 Minutes

Ingredients:

- 1 strip of bacon, diced
- 1 slice of 1-inch thick bread (such as Texas Toast or hand-sliced bread)
- 1 tablespoon softened butter (optional)
- 1 egg
- salt and freshly ground black pepper
- ¼ cup grated Colby or Jack cheese

Directions:

1. Preheat the air fryer to 400°F（200°C）.

2. Air-fry the bacon for 3 minutes, shaking the basket once or twice while it cooks. Remove the bacon to a paper towel lined plate and set aside.

3. Use a sharp paring knife to score a large circle in the middle of the slice of bread, cutting halfway through, but not all the way through to the cutting board. Press down on the circle in the center of the bread slice to create an indentation. If using, spread the softened butter on the edges and in the hole of the bread.

4. Transfer the slice of bread, hole side up, to the air fryer basket. Crack the egg into the center of the bread, and season with salt and pepper.

5. Air-fry at 380°F (195°C) for 5 minutes. Sprinkle the grated cheese around the edges of the bread leaving the center of the yolk uncovered, and top with the cooked bacon. Press the cheese and bacon into the bread lightly to help anchor it to the bread and prevent it from blowing around in the air fryer.

6. Air-fry for one or two more minutes (depending on how you like your egg cooked), just to melt the cheese and finish cooking the egg. Serve immediately.

Parma Ham & Egg Toast Cups

Servings: 4
Cooking Time: 25 Minutes
Ingredients:

- 4 crusty rolls
- 4 Gouda cheese thin slices
- 5 eggs
- 2 tbsp heavy cream
- ½ tsp dried thyme
- 3 Parma ham slices, chopped
- Salt and pepper to taste

Directions:

1. Preheat air fryer to 330°F (165°C). Slice off the top of the rolls, then tear out the insides with your fingers, leaving about ½-inch of bread to make a shell. Press one cheese slice inside the roll shell until it takes the shape of the roll.

2. Beat eggs with heavy cream in a medium bowl. Next, mix in the remaining ingredients. Spoon egg mixture into the rolls lined with cheese. Place rolls in the greased frying basket and Bake until eggs are puffy and brown, 8-12 minutes. Serve warm.

Mascarpone Iced Cinnamon Rolls

Servings: 6
Cooking Time: 40 Minutes
Ingredients:

- ¼ cup mascarpone cheese, softened
- 9 oz puff pastry sheet
- 3 tbsp light brown sugar
- 2 tsp ground cinnamon
- 2 tsp butter, melted
- ¼ tsp vanilla extract
- ¼ tsp salt
- 2 tbsp milk
- 1 tbsp lemon zest
- ¼ cup confectioners' sugar

Directions:

1. Preheat air fryer to 320°F (160°C). Mix the brown sugar and cinnamon in a small bowl. Unroll the pastry sheet on its paper and brush it with melted butter. Then sprinkle with cinnamon sugar. Roll up the dough tightly, then cut into rolls about 1-inch wide. Put into a greased baking pan with the spiral side showing. Put the pan into the air fryer and Bake until golden brown, 18-20 minutes. Set aside to cool for 5-10 minutes.

2. Meanwhile, add the mascarpone cheese, vanilla, and salt in a small bowl, whisking until smooth and creamy. Add the confectioners' sugar and continue whisking until fully blended. Pour and mix in 1 tsp of milk at a time until the glaze is pourable but still with some thickness. Spread the glaze over the warm cinnamon rolls and scatter with lemon zest. Serve and enjoy!

Crunchy French Toast Sticks

Servings: 2
Cooking Time: 9 Minutes
Ingredients:

- 2 eggs, beaten
- ¾ cup milk
- ½ teaspoon vanilla extract
- ½ teaspoon ground cinnamon
- 1½ cups crushed crunchy cinnamon cereal, or any cereal flakes
- 4 slices Texas Toast (or other bread that you can slice into 1-inch thick slices)
- maple syrup, for serving
- vegetable oil or melted butter

Directions:

1. Combine the eggs, milk, vanilla and cinnamon in a shallow bowl. Place the crushed cereal in a second shallow bowl.

2. Trim the crusts off the slices of bread and cut each slice into 3 sticks. Dip the sticks of bread into the egg mixture, turning them over to coat all sides. Let the bread sticks absorb the egg mixture for ten seconds or so, but don't let them get too wet. Roll the bread sticks in the cereal crumbs, pressing the cereal gently onto all sides so that it adheres to the bread.

3. Preheat the air fryer to 400°F (205°C).

4. Spray or brush the air fryer basket with oil or melted butter. Place the coated sticks in the basket. It's ok to stack a few on top of the others in the opposite direction.

5. Air-fry for 9 minutes. Turn the sticks over a couple of times during the cooking process so that the sticks crisp evenly. Serve warm with the maple syrup or some berries.

Effortless Toffee Zucchini Bread

Servings: 6
Cooking Time: 30 Minutes
Ingredients:

- 1 cup flour
- ½ tsp baking soda
- ½ cup granulated sugar
- ¼ tsp ground cinnamon
- ¼ tsp nutmeg
- ¼ tsp salt
- 1/3 cup grated zucchini
- 1 egg
- 1 tbsp olive oil
- 1 tsp vanilla extract
- 2 tbsp English toffee bits
- 2 tbsp mini chocolate chips
- 1/2 cup chopped walnuts

Directions:

1. Preheat air fryer at 375ºF (190°C). Combine the flour, baking soda, toffee bits, sugar, cinnamon, nutmeg, salt, zucchini, egg, olive oil, vanilla and chocolate chips in a bowl. Add the walnuts to the batter and mix until evenly distributed.
2. Pour the mixture into a greased cake pan. Place the pan in the fryer and Bake for 20 minutes. Let sit for 10 minutes until slightly cooled before slicing. Serve immediately.

Oat Muffins With Blueberries

Servings: 6
Cooking Time: 25 Minutes
Ingredients:

- ¾ cup old-fashioned rolled oats
- 1 ½ cups flour
- ½ cup evaporated cane sugar
- 1 tbsp baking powder
- 1 tsp ground cinnamon
- ¼ tsp ground chia seeds
- ¼ tsp ground sesame seeds
- ½ tsp salt
- 1 cup vanilla almond milk
- 4 tbsp butter, softened
- 2 eggs
- 1 tsp vanilla extract
- 1 cup blueberries
- 2 tbsp powdered sugar

Directions:

1. Preheat air fryer to 350°F (175°C). Combine flour oats, sugar, baking powder, chia seeds, sesame seeds, cinnamon, and salt in a bowl. Mix the almond milk, butter, eggs, and vanilla in another bowl until smooth. Pour in dry ingredients and stir to combine. Fold in blueberries. Fill 12 silicone muffin cups about halfway and place them in the frying basket. Bake for 12-15 minutes until just browned, and a toothpick in the center comes out clean. Cool for 5 minutes. Serve topped with powdered sugar.

Bread Boat Eggs

Servings: 4
Cooking Time: 10 Minutes
Ingredients:

- 4 pistolette rolls
- 1 teaspoon butter
- ¼ cup diced fresh mushrooms
- ½ teaspoon dried onion flakes
- 4 eggs
- ½ teaspoon salt
- ¼ teaspoon dried dill weed
- ¼ teaspoon dried parsley
- 1 tablespoon milk

Directions:

1. Cut a rectangle in the top of each roll and scoop out center, leaving ½-inch shell on the sides and bottom.
2. Place butter, mushrooms, and dried onion in air fryer baking pan and cook for 1 minute. Stir and cook 3 more minutes.
3. In a medium bowl, beat together the eggs, salt, dill, parsley, and milk. Pour mixture into pan with mushrooms.
4. Cook at 390°F (200°C) for 2 minutes. Stir. Continue cooking for 3 or 4 minutes, stirring every minute, until eggs are scrambled to your liking.
5. Remove baking pan from air fryer and fill rolls with scrambled egg mixture.
6. Place filled rolls in air fryer basket and cook at 390°F (200°C) for 2 to 3 minutes or until rolls are lightly browned.

Breakfast Chimichangas

Servings: 4
Cooking Time: 8 Minutes
Ingredients:

- Four 8-inch flour tortillas
- ½ cup canned refried beans
- 1 cup scrambled eggs
- ½ cup grated cheddar or Monterey jack cheese
- 1 tablespoon vegetable oil
- 1 cup salsa

Directions:

1. Lay the flour tortillas out flat on a cutting board. In the center of each tortilla, spread 2 tablespoons refried beans. Next, add ¼ cup eggs and 2 tablespoons cheese to each tortilla.

2. To fold the tortillas, begin on the left side and fold to the center. Then fold the right side into the center. Next fold the bottom and top down and roll over to completely seal the chimichanga. Using a pastry brush or oil mister, brush the tops of the tortilla packages with oil.

3. Preheat the air fryer to 400°F (205°C) for 4 minutes. Place the chimichangas into the air fryer basket, seam side down, and air fry for 4 minutes. Using tongs, turn over the chimichangas and cook for an additional 2 to 3 minutes or until light golden brown.

Zucchini Walnut Bread

Servings: 6
Cooking Time: 30 Minutes
Ingredients:
- ¾ cup all-purpose flour
- ½ teaspoon baking soda
- 1 teaspoon ground cinnamon
- ⅛ teaspoon salt
- 1 large egg
- ⅓ cup packed brown sugar
- ¼ cup canola oil
- 1 teaspoon vanilla extract
- ⅓ cup milk
- 1 medium zucchini, shredded (about 1⅓ cups)
- ⅓ cup chopped walnuts

Directions:
1. Preheat the air fryer to 320°F (160°C).
2. In a medium bowl, mix together the flour, baking soda, cinnamon, and salt.
3. In a large bowl, whisk together the egg, brown sugar, oil, vanilla, and milk. Stir in the zucchini.
4. Slowly fold the dry ingredients into the wet ingredients. Stir in the chopped walnuts. Then pour the batter into two 4-inch oven-safe loaf pans.
5. Bake for 30 minutes or until a toothpick inserted into the center comes out clean. Let cool before slicing.
6. NOTE: Store tightly wrapped on the counter for up to 5 days, in the refrigerator for up to 10 days, or in the freezer for 3 months.

Pesto Egg & Ham Sandwiches

Servings: 2
Cooking Time: 20 Minutes
Ingredients:
- 4 sandwich bread slices
- 2 tbsp butter, melted
- 4 eggs, scrambled
- 4 deli ham slices
- 2 Colby cheese slices
- 4 tsp basil pesto sauce
- ¼ tsp red chili flakes
- ¼ sliced avocado

Directions:
1. Preheat air fryer at 370ºF (185°C). Brush 2 pieces of bread with half of the butter and place them, butter side down, into the frying basket. Divide eggs, chili flakes, sliced avocado, ham, and cheese on each bread slice.
2. Spread pesto on the remaining bread slices and place them, pesto side-down, onto the sandwiches. Brush the remaining butter on the tops of the sandwiches and Bake for 6 minutes, flipping once. Serve immediately.

Sugar-dusted Beignets

Servings: 4
Cooking Time: 30 Minutes
Ingredients:
- 1 tsp fast active dry yeast
- 1/3 cup buttermilk
- 3 tbsp brown sugar
- 1 egg
- ½ tsp brandy
- 1 ½ cups flour
- 3 tbsp chopped dried plums
- 3 tbsp golden raisins
- 2 tbsp butter, melted
- 2 tbsp powdered sugar

Directions:
1. Combine the yeast with 3 tbsp of water and leave it until frothy, about 5 minutes. Add the buttermilk, brown sugar, brandy, and egg and stir. Add the flour and stir again. Use your hands to mix the plums and raisins into the dough. Leave the mix in the bowl for 15 minutes.
2. Preheat air fryer to 330°F (165°C). Shape the dough in a square, then slice it into 16 pieces. Make 16 balls, then drizzle butter over the balls. Put the balls in the air fryer in a single layer, making sure they don't touch. Air Fry for 5-8 minutes until they puff up and are golden. Repeat until all balls are cooked. Toss in powdered sugar and serve.

Orange Trail Oatmeal

Servings: 4
Cooking Time: 20 Minutes
Ingredients:
- 1 ½ cups quick-cooking oats
- 1/3 cup light brown sugar
- 1 egg
- 1 tsp orange zest
- 1 tbsp orange juice
- 2 tbsp whole milk
- 2 tbsp honey
- 2 tbsp butter, melted
- 2 tsp dried cranberries
- 1 tsp dried blueberries

- 1/8 tsp ground nutmeg
- Salt to taste
- ¼ cup pecan pieces

Directions:

1. Preheat air fryer at 325ºF（160°C）. Combine the oats, sugar, egg, orange zest, orange juice, milk, honey, butter, dried cranberries, dried blueberries, nutmeg, salt, and pecan in a bowl. Press mixture into a greased cake pan. Place cake pan in the frying basket and Roast for 8 minutes. Let cool onto for 5 minutes before slicing. Serve.

Banana-blackberry Muffins

Servings: 6
Cooking Time: 20 Minutes

Ingredients:

- 1 ripe banana, mashed
- ½ cup milk
- 1 tsp apple cider vinegar
- 1 tsp vanilla extract
- 2 tbsp ground flaxseed
- 2 tbsp coconut sugar
- ¾ cup flour
- 1 tsp baking powder
- ½ tsp baking soda
- ¾ cup blackberries

Directions:

1. Preheat air fryer to 350°F（175°C）. Place the banana in a bowl. Stir in milk, apple vinegar, vanilla extract, flaxseed, and coconut sugar until combined. In another bowl, combine flour, baking powder, and baking soda. Pour it into the banana mixture and toss to combine. Divide the batter between 6 muffin molds and top each with blackberries, pressing slightly. Bake for 16 minutes until golden brown and a toothpick comes out clean. Serve cooled.

Scones

Servings: 9
Cooking Time: 8 Minutes Per Batch

Ingredients:

- 2 cups self-rising flour, plus ¼ cup for kneading
- ⅓ cup granulated sugar
- ¼ cup butter, cold
- 1 cup milk

Directions:

1. Preheat air fryer at 360°F（180°C）.
2. In large bowl, stir together flour and sugar.
3. Cut cold butter into tiny cubes, and stir into flour mixture with fork.
4. Stir in milk until soft dough forms.
5. Sprinkle ¼ cup of flour onto wax paper and place dough on top. Knead lightly by folding and turning the dough about 6 to 8 times.

6. Pat dough into a 6 x 6-inch square.
7. Cut into 9 equal squares.
8. Place all squares in air fryer basket or as many as will fit in a single layer, close together but not touching.
9. Cook at 360°F（180°C）for 8 minutes. When done, scones will be lightly browned on top and will spring back when pressed gently with a dull knife.
10. Repeat steps 8 and 9 to cook remaining scones.

Home-style Pumpkin Crumble

Servings: 6
Cooking Time: 60 Minutes + Chilling Time

Ingredients:

- ¾ cup canned pumpkin puree
- ½ cup whole-wheat flour
- 5 tbsp sugar
- ¼ tsp baking soda
- ¼ tsp baking powder
- 1 tsp pumpkin pie spice
- ⅛ tsp ground cinnamon
- ⅛ tsp ground nutmeg
- ⅛ tsp salt
- 1 tbsp orange zest
- 1 tbsp butter, melted
- 1 egg
- ¾ tsp vanilla extract
- 2 tbsp light brown sugar
- ½ tbsp cornflour
- ⅛ tsp ground cinnamon
- ½ tbsp cold butter

Directions:

1. Combine all dry ingredients in a bowl with a whisk. In a large bowl, combine pumpkin puree, butter, egg, and vanilla. Beat these ingredients in a mixer at medium speed until thick. Slowly add 1/3 cup of the flour mixture to the pumpkin mixture at a low speed until it is combined. Pour batter into a greased baking dish.
2. Prepare the crumb topping by combining brown sugar, cornflour, and cinnamon in a small bowl. Using a fork, cut in the cold butter until the mixture is coarse and crumbly. Sprinkle over the batter evenly.
3. Preheat air fryer to 300°F（150°C）. Put the pan in the frying basket. Bake until a toothpick in the center comes out clean, 40-45 minutes. Allow to cool for 30 minutes before cutting and serving.

Zucchini Hash Browns

Servings: 4
Cooking Time: 20 Minutes
Ingredients:
- 2 shredded zucchinis
- 2 tbsp nutritional yeast
- 1 tsp allspice
- 1 egg white

Directions:
1. Preheat air fryer to 400°F (205°C). Combine zucchinis, nutritional yeast, allspice, and egg white in a bowl. Make 4 patties out of the mixture. Cut 4 pieces of parchment paper, put a patty on each foil, and fold in all sides to create a rectangle. Using a spatula, flatten them and spread them.
2. Then unwrap each foil and remove the hash browns onto the fryer and Air Fry for 12 minutes until golden brown and crispy, turning once. Serve right away.

Cheesy Egg Bites

Servings: 6
Cooking Time: 35 Minutes
Ingredients:
- ½ cup shredded Muenster cheese
- 5 eggs, beaten
- 3 tbsp sour cream
- ½ tsp dried oregano
- Salt and pepper to taste
- 1/3 cup minced bell pepper
- 3 tbsp minced scallions

Directions:
1. Preheat the air fryer to 325°F (160°C). Make a foil sling: Fold an 18-inch-long piece of heavy-duty aluminum foil lengthwise into thirds. Combine the eggs, sour cream, oregano, salt, and pepper in a bowl. Add the bell peppers, scallions, and cheese and stir. Add the mixture to 6 egg bite cups, making sure to get some of the solids in each cup.
2. Put the egg bite pan on the sling you made and lower it into the fryer. Leave the foil in but bend down the edges so they fit. Bake the bites for 10-15 minutes or until a toothpick inserted into the center comes out clean. Remove the egg bite pan using the foil sling. Cool for 5 minutes, then turn the pan upside down over a plate to remove the egg bites. Serve warm.

Strawberry Streusel Muffins

Servings: 12
Cooking Time: 14 Minutes
Ingredients:
- 1¾ cups all-purpose flour
- ½ cup granulated sugar
- 2 teaspoons baking powder
- ¼ teaspoon baking soda
- ½ teaspoon salt
- ½ cup plain yogurt
- ½ cup milk
- ¼ cup vegetable oil
- 2 large eggs
- 1 teaspoon vanilla extract
- ½ cup freeze-dried strawberries
- 2 tablespoons brown sugar
- ¼ cup oats
- 2 tablespoons butter

Directions:
1. Preheat the air fryer to 330°F (165°C).
2. In a large bowl, whisk together the flour, sugar, baking powder, baking soda, and salt; set aside.
3. In a separate bowl, whisk together the yogurt, milk, vegetable oil, eggs, and vanilla extract.
4. Make a well in the dry ingredients; then pour the wet ingredients into the well of the dry ingredients. Using a rubber spatula, mix the ingredients for 1 minute or until slightly lumpy. Fold in the strawberries.
5. In a small bowl, use your fingers to mix together the brown sugar, oats, and butter until coarse crumbles appear. Divide the mixture in half.
6. Using silicone muffin liners, fill 6 muffin liners two-thirds full.
7. Crumble half of the streusel topping onto the first batch of muffins.
8. Carefully place the muffin liners in the air fryer basket and bake for 14 minutes (or until the tops are browned and a toothpick inserted in the center comes out clean). Carefully remove the muffins from the basket and repeat with the remaining batter and topping.
9. Serve warm.

Coconut & Peanut Rice Cereal

Servings: 4
Cooking Time: 15 Minutes
Ingredients:
- 4 cups rice cereal
- 1 cup coconut shreds
- 2 tbsp peanut butter
- 1 tsp vanilla extract
- ¼ cup honey
- 1 tbsp light brown sugar
- 2 tsp ground cinnamon
- ¼ cup hazelnut flour
- Salt to taste

Directions:
1. Preheat air fryer at 350°F (175°C). Combine the rice cereal, coconut shreds, peanut butter, vanilla extract, honey, brown sugar, cinnamon, hazelnut flour, and salt in a bowl. Press mixture into a greased cake pan. Place cake pan in the frying basket and Air Fry for 5 minutes, stirring once. Let cool completely for 10 minutes before crumbling. Store it into an airtight container up to 5 days.

Green Egg Quiche

Servings: 4
Cooking Time: 30 Minutes
Ingredients:
- 1 cup broccoli florets
- 2 cups baby spinach
- 2 garlic cloves, minced
- ¼ tsp ground nutmeg
- 1 tbsp olive oil
- Salt and pepper to taste
- 4 eggs
- 2 scallions, chopped
- 1 red onion, chopped
- 1 tbsp sour cream
- ½ cup grated fontina cheese

Directions:
1. Preheat air fryer to 375°F (190°C). Combine broccoli, spinach, onion, garlic, nutmeg, olive oil, and salt in a medium bowl, tossing to coat. Arrange the broccoli in a single layer in the parchment-lined frying basket and cook for 5 minutes. Remove and set to the side.
2. Use the same medium bowl to whisk eggs, salt, pepper, scallions, and sour cream. Add the roasted broccoli and ¼ cup fontina cheese until all ingredients are well combined. Pour the mixture into a greased baking dish and top with cheese. Bake in the air fryer for 15-18 minutes until the center is set. Serve and enjoy.

Shakshuka Cups

Servings: 4
Cooking Time: 25 Minutes
Ingredients:
- 2 tbsp tomato paste
- ½ cup chicken broth
- 4 tomatoes, diced
- 2 garlic cloves, minced
- ½ tsp dried oregano
- ½ tsp dried coriander
- ½ tsp dried basil
- ¼ tsp red pepper flakes
- ¼ tsp paprika
- 4 eggs
- Salt and pepper to taste
- 2 scallions, diced
- ½ cup grated cheddar cheese
- ½ cup Parmesan cheese
- 4 bread slices, toasted

Directions:
1. Preheat air fryer to 350°F (175°C). Combine the tomato paste, chicken broth, tomatoes, garlic, oregano, coriander, basil, red pepper flakes, and paprika. Pour the mixture evenly into greased ramekins. Bake in the air fryer for 5 minutes. Carefully remove the ramekins and crack one egg in each ramekin, then season with salt and pepper. Top with scallions, grated cheese, and Parmesan cheese. Return the ramekins to the frying basket and bake for 3-5 minutes until the eggs are set, and the cheese is melted. Serve with toasted bread immediately.

Spring Vegetable Omelet

Servings: 4
Cooking Time: 20 Minutes
Ingredients:
- ¼ cup chopped broccoli, lightly steamed
- ½ cup grated cheddar cheese
- 6 eggs
- ¼ cup steamed kale
- 1 green onion, chopped
- Salt and pepper to taste

Directions:
1. Preheat air fryer to 360°F (180°C). In a bowl, beat the eggs. Stir in kale, broccoli, green onion, and cheddar cheese. Transfer the mixture to a greased baking dish and Bake in the fryer for 15 minutes until golden and crisp. Season to taste and serve immediately.

Southern Sweet Cornbread

Servings: 6
Cooking Time: 17 Minutes
Ingredients:
- cooking spray
- ½ cup white cornmeal
- ½ cup flour
- 2 teaspoons baking powder
- ½ teaspoon salt
- 4 teaspoons sugar
- 1 egg
- 2 tablespoons oil
- ½ cup milk

Directions:
1. Preheat air fryer to 360°F (180°C).
2. Spray air fryer baking pan with nonstick cooking spray.
3. In a medium bowl, stir together the cornmeal, flour, baking powder, salt, and sugar.
4. In a small bowl, beat together the egg, oil, and milk. Stir into dry ingredients until well combined.
5. Pour batter into prepared baking pan.
6. Cook at 360°F (180°C) for 17 minutes or until toothpick inserted in center comes out clean or with crumbs clinging.

Hole In One

Servings: 1
Cooking Time: 7 Minutes
Ingredients:

- 1 slice bread
- 1 teaspoon soft butter
- 1 egg
- salt and pepper
- 1 tablespoon shredded Cheddar cheese
- 2 teaspoons diced ham

Directions:

1. Place a 6 x 6-inch baking dish inside air fryer basket and preheat fryer to 330°F (165°C).
2. Using a 2½-inch-diameter biscuit cutter, cut a hole in center of bread slice.
3. Spread softened butter on both sides of bread.
4. Lay bread slice in baking dish and crack egg into the hole. Sprinkle egg with salt and pepper to taste.
5. Cook for 5minutes.
6. Turn toast over and top it with shredded cheese and diced ham.
7. Cook for 2 more minutes or until yolk is done to your liking.

Veggie & Feta Scramble Bowls

Servings: 2
Cooking Time: 25 Minutes
Ingredients:

- 1 russet potato, cubed
- 1 bell pepper, cut into strips
- ½ feta, cubed
- 1 tbsp nutritional yeast
- ½ tsp garlic powder
- ½ tsp onion powder
- ¼ tsp ground turmeric
- 1 tbsp apple cider vinegar

Directions:

1. Preheat air fryer to 400°F (205°C). Put in potato cubes and bell pepper strips and Air Fry for 10 minutes. Combine the feta, nutritional yeast, garlic, onion, turmeric, and apple vinegar in a small pan. Fit a trivet in the fryer, lay the pan on top, and Air Fry for 5 more minutes until potatoes are tender and feta cheese cooked. Share potatoes and bell peppers into 2 bowls and top with feta scramble. Serve.

Honey Donuts

Servings: 6
Cooking Time: 25 Minutes + Chilling Time
Ingredients:

- 1 refrigerated puff pastry sheet
- 2 tsp flour
- 2 ½ cups powdered sugar
- 3 tbsp honey
- 2 tbsp milk
- 2 tbsp butter, melted
- ½ tsp vanilla extract
- ½ tsp ground cinnamon
- Pinch of salt

Directions:

1. Preheat the air fryer to 325°F (160°C). Dust a clean work surface with flour and lay the puff pastry on it, then cut crosswise into five 3-inch wide strips. Cut each strip into thirds for 15 squares. Lay round parchment paper in the bottom of the basket, then add the pastry squares in a single layer.
2. Make sure none are touching. Bake for 13-18 minutes or until brown, then leave on a rack to cool. Repeat for all dough. Combine the sugar, honey, milk, butter, vanilla, cinnamon, and salt in a small bowl and mix with a wire whisk until combined. Dip the top half of each donut in the glaze, turn the donut glaze side up, and return to the wire rack. Let cool until the glaze sets, then serve.

Sweet Potato & Mushroom Hash

Servings: 6
Cooking Time: 35 Minutes
Ingredients:

- 2 peeled sweet potatoes, cubed
- 4 oz baby Bella mushrooms, diced
- ½ red bell pepper, diced
- ½ red onion, diced
- 2 tbsp olive oil
- 1 garlic clove, minced
- Salt and pepper to taste
- ½ tbsp chopped marjoram

Directions:

1. Preheat air fryer to 380°F (195°C). Place all ingredients in a large bowl and toss until the vegetables are well coated. Pour the vegetables into the frying basket. Bake for 8-10 minutes, then shake the vegetables. Cook for 8-10 more minutes. Serve and enjoy!

Chicken Scotch Eggs

Servings:4

Cooking Time: 25 Minutes

Ingredients:

- 1 lb ground chicken
- 2 tsp Dijon mustard
- 2 tsp grated yellow onion
- 1 tbsp chopped chives
- 1 tbsp chopped parsley
- ⅛ tsp ground nutmeg
- 1 lemon, zested
- Salt and pepper to taste
- 4 hard-boiled eggs, peeled
- 1 egg, beaten
- 1 cup bread crumbs
- 2 tsp olive oil

Directions:

1. Preheat air fryer to 350ºF（175°C）. In a bowl, mix the ground chicken, mustard, onion, chives, parsley, nutmeg, salt, lemon zest and pepper. Shape into 4 oval balls and form the balls evenly around the boiled eggs. Submerge them in the beaten egg and dip in the crumbs. Brush with olive oil. Place the scotch eggs in the frying basket and Air Fry for 14 minutes, flipping once. Serve hot.

Beef , pork & Lamb Recipes

Paprika Fried Beef

Servings: 4
Cooking Time: 30 Minutes
Ingredients:
- Celery salt to taste
- 4 beef cube steaks
- ½ cup milk
- 1 cup flour
- 2 tsp paprika
- 1 egg
- 1 cup bread crumbs
- 2 tbsp olive oil

Directions:
1. Preheat air fryer to 350°F (175°C). Place the cube steaks in a zipper sealed bag or between two sheets of cling wrap. Gently pound the steaks until they are slightly thinner. Set aside. In a bowl, mix together milk, flour, paprika, celery salt, and egg until just combined. In a separate bowl, mix together the crumbs and olive oil. Take the steaks and dip them into the buttermilk batter, shake off some of the excess, and return to a plate for 5 minutes. Next, dip the steaks in the bread crumbs, patting the crumbs into both sides. Air Fry the steaks until the crust is crispy and brown, 12-16 minutes. Serve warm.

Leftover Roast Beef Risotto

Servings: 4
Cooking Time: 30 Minutes
Ingredients:
- ½ chopped red bell pepper
- ½ chopped cooked roast beef
- 3 tbsp grated Parmesan
- 2 tsp butter, melted
- 1 shallot, finely chopped
- 3 garlic cloves, minced
- ¾ cup short-grain rice
- 1¼ cups beef broth

Directions:
1. Preheat air fryer to 390°F (200°C). Add the melted butter, shallot, garlic, and red bell pepper to a baking pan and stir to combine. Air Fry for 2 minutes, or until the vegetables are crisp-tender. Remove from the air fryer and stir in the rice, broth, and roast beef. Put the cooking pan back into the fryer and Bake for 18-22 minutes, stirring once during cooking until the rice is al dente and the beef is cooked through. Sprinkle with Parmesan and serve.

Albóndigas

Servings: 4
Cooking Time: 15 Minutes

Ingredients:
- 1 pound Lean ground pork
- 3 tablespoons Very finely chopped trimmed scallions
- 3 tablespoons Finely chopped fresh cilantro leaves
- 3 tablespoons Plain panko bread crumbs (gluten-free, if a concern)
- 3 tablespoons Dry white wine, dry sherry, or unsweetened apple juice
- 1½ teaspoons Minced garlic
- 1¼ teaspoons Mild smoked paprika
- ¾ teaspoon Dried oregano
- ¾ teaspoon Table salt
- ¼ teaspoon Ground black pepper
- Olive oil spray

Directions:
1. Preheat the air fryer to 400°F (205°C).
2. Mix the ground pork, scallions, cilantro, bread crumbs, wine or its substitute, garlic, smoked paprika, oregano, salt, and pepper in a bowl until the herbs and spices are evenly distributed in the mixture.
3. Lightly coat your clean hands with olive oil spray, then form the ground pork mixture into balls, using 2 tablespoons for each one. Spray your hands frequently so that the meat mixture doesn't stick.
4. Set the balls in the basket so that they're not touching, even if they're close together. Air-fry undisturbed for 15 minutes, or until well browned and an instant-read meat thermometer inserted into one or two balls registers 165°F (75°C).
5. Use a nonstick-safe spatula and kitchen tongs for balance to gently transfer the fragile balls to a wire rack to cool for 5 minutes before serving.

Canadian-style Rib Eye Steak

Servings: 2
Cooking Time: 15 Minutes
Ingredients:
- 2 tsp Montreal steak seasoning
- 1 ribeye steak
- 1 tbsp butter, halved
- 1 tsp chopped parsley
- ½ tsp fresh rosemary

Directions:
1. Preheat air fryer at 400°F (205°C). Sprinkle ribeye with steak seasoning and rosemary on both sides. Place it in the basket and Bake for 10 minutes, turning once. Remove it to a cutting board and top with butter halves. Let rest for 5 minutes and scatter with parsley. Serve immediately.

Aromatic Pork Tenderloin

Servings: 6
Cooking Time: 65 Minutes
Ingredients:

- 1 pork tenderloin
- 2 tbsp olive oil
- 2 garlic cloves, minced
- 1 tsp dried sage
- 1 tsp dried marjoram
- 1 tsp dried thyme
- 1 tsp paprika
- Salt and pepper to taste

Directions:

1. Preheat air fryer to 360°F (180°C). Drizzle oil over the tenderloin, then rub garlic, sage, marjoram, thyme, paprika, salt and pepper all over. Place the tenderloin in the greased frying basket and Bake for 45 minutes. Flip the pork and cook for another 15 minutes. Check the temperature for doneness. Let the cooked tenderloin rest for 10 minutes before slicing. Serve and enjoy!

Smokehouse-style Beef Ribs

Servings: 3
Cooking Time: 25 Minutes
Ingredients:

- ¼ teaspoon Mild smoked paprika
- ¼ teaspoon Garlic powder
- ¼ teaspoon Onion powder
- ¼ teaspoon Table salt
- ¼ teaspoon Ground black pepper
- 3 10- to 12-ounce beef back ribs (not beef short ribs)

Directions:

1. Preheat the air fryer to 350°F (175°C).
2. Mix the smoked paprika, garlic powder, onion powder, salt, and pepper in a small bowl until uniform. Massage and pat this mixture onto the ribs.
3. When the machine is at temperature, set the ribs in the basket in one layer, turning them on their sides if necessary, sort of like they're spooning but with at least ¼ inch air space between them. Air-fry for 25 minutes, turning once, until deep brown and sizzling.
4. Use kitchen tongs to transfer the ribs to a wire rack. Cool for 5 minutes before serving.

Mini Meatloaves With Pancetta

Servings: 4
Cooking Time: 40 Minutes
Ingredients:

- ¼ cup grated Parmesan

- 1/3 cup quick-cooking oats
- 2 tbsp milk
- 3 tbsp ketchup
- 3 tbsp Dijon mustard
- 1 egg
- 1 tsp dried oregano
- Salt and pepper to taste
- 1 lb lean ground beef
- 4 pancetta slices, uncooked

Directions:

1. Preheat the air fryer to 375°F (190°C). Combine the oats, milk, 1 tbsp of ketchup, 1 tbsp of mustard, the egg, oregano, Parmesan cheese, salt, and pepper, and mix. Add the beef and mix with your hands, then form 4 mini loaves. Wrap each mini loaf with pancetta, covering the meat.
2. Combine the remaining ketchup and mustard and set aside. Line the frying basket with foil and poke holes in it, then set the loaves in the basket. Brush with the ketchup/mustard mix. Bake for 17-22 minutes or until cooked and golden. Serve and enjoy!

Boneless Ribeyes

Servings: 2
Cooking Time: 10-15 Minutes
Ingredients:

- 2 8-ounce boneless ribeye steaks
- 4 teaspoons Worcestershire sauce
- ½ teaspoon garlic powder
- pepper
- 4 teaspoons extra virgin olive oil
- salt

Directions:

1. Season steaks on both sides with Worcestershire sauce. Use the back of a spoon to spread evenly.
2. Sprinkle both sides of steaks with garlic powder and coarsely ground black pepper to taste.
3. Drizzle both sides of steaks with olive oil, again using the back of a spoon to spread evenly over surfaces.
4. Allow steaks to marinate for 30minutes.
5. Place both steaks in air fryer basket and cook at 390°F (200°C) for 5minutes.
6. Turn steaks over and cook until done:
7. Medium rare: additional 5 minutes
8. Medium: additional 7 minutes
9. Well done: additional 10 minutes
10. Remove steaks from air fryer basket and let sit 5minute Salt to taste and serve.

Honey Mustard Pork Roast

Servings:4
Cooking Time: 50 Minutes
Ingredients:

- 1 boneless pork loin roast
- 2 tbsp Dijon mustard
- 2 tsp olive oil
- 1 tsp honey
- 1 garlic clove, minced
- Salt and pepper to taste
- 1 tsp dried rosemary

Directions:

1. Preheat air fryer to 350ºF（175°C）. Whisk all ingredients in a bowl. Massage into loin on all sides. Place the loin in the frying basket and Roast for 40 minutes, turning once. Let sit onto a cutting board for 5 minutes before slicing. Serve.

Cal-mex Chimichangas

Servings: 4
Cooking Time: 30 Minutes
Ingredients:

- 1 can diced tomatoes with chiles
- 1 cup shredded cheddar
- ½ cup chopped onions
- 2 garlic cloves, minced
- 1 lb ground beef
- 2 tbsp taco seasoning
- Salt and pepper to taste
- 4 flour tortillas
- ½ cup Pico de Gallo

Directions:

1. Warm the olive oil in a skillet over medium heat and stir-fry the onion and garlic for 3 minutes or until fragrant. Add ground beef, taco seasoning, salt and pepper. Stir and break up the beef with a spoon. Cook for 3-4 minutes or until it is browned. Stir in diced tomatoes with chiles. Scoop ½ cup of beef onto each tortilla. Form chimichangas by folding the sides of the tortilla into the middle, then roll up from the bottom. Use a toothpick to secure the chimichanga.
2. Preheat air fryer to 400°F（205°C）. Lightly spray the chimichangas with cooking oil. Place the first batch in the fryer and Bake for 8 minutes. Transfer to a serving dish and top with shredded cheese and pico de gallo.

Kentucky-style Pork Tenderloin

Servings:2
Cooking Time: 30 Minutes
Ingredients:

- 1 lb pork tenderloin, halved crosswise

- 1 tbsp smoked paprika
- 2 tsp ground cumin
- 1 tsp garlic powder
- 1 tsp shallot powder
- ¼ tsp chili pepper
- Salt and pepper to taste
- 1 tsp Italian seasoning
- 2 tbsp butter, melted
- 1 tsp Worcestershire sauce

Directions:

1. Preheat air fryer to 350ºF（175°C）. In a shallow bowl, combine all spices. Set aside. In another bowl, whisk butter and Worcestershire sauce and brush over pork tenderloin. Sprinkle with the seasoning mix. Place pork in the lightly greased frying basket and Air Fry for 16 minutes, flipping once. Let sit onto a cutting board for 5 minutes before slicing. Serve immediately.

Honey Pork Links

Servings:4
Cooking Time: 20 Minutes
Ingredients:

- 12 oz ground mild pork sausage, removed from casings
- 1 tsp rubbed sage
- 2 tbsp honey
- ⅛ tsp cayenne pepper
- ⅛ tsp paprika
- Salt and pepper to taste

Directions:

1. Preheat air fryer to 400ºF（205°C）. Remove the sausage from the casings. Transfer to a bowl and add the remaining ingredients. Mix well. Make 8 links out of the mixture. Add the links to the frying basket and Air Fry for 8-10 minutes, flipping once. Serve right away.

Santorini Steak Bowls

Servings:2
Cooking Time: 15 Minutes
Ingredients:

- 5 pitted Kalamata olives, halved
- 1 cucumber, diced
- 2 tomatoes, diced
- 1 tbsp apple cider vinegar
- 2 tsp olive oil
- ¼ cup feta cheese crumbles
- ½ tsp Greek oregano
- ½ tsp dried dill
- ¼ tsp garlic powder
- ⅛ tsp ground nutmeg
- Salt and pepper to taste
- 1 (¾-lb) strip steak

Directions:

1. In a large bowl, combine cucumber, tomatoes, vinegar, olive oil, olives, and feta cheese. Let chill covered in the fridge until ready to use. Preheat air fryer to 400°F (205°C). Combine all spices in a bowl, then coat strip steak with this mixture. Add steak in the lightly greased frying basket and Air Fry for 10 minutes or until you reach your desired doneness, flipping once. Let sit onto a cutting board for 5 minutes. Thinly slice against the grain and divide between 2 bowls. Top with the cucumber mixture. Serve.

Extra Crispy Country-style Pork Riblets

Servings: 3
Cooking Time: 30 Minutes
Ingredients:

- ⅓ cup Tapioca flour
- 2½ tablespoons Chile powder
- ¾ teaspoon Table salt (optional)
- 1¼ pounds Boneless country-style pork ribs, cut into 1½-inch chunks
- Vegetable oil spray

Directions:

1. Preheat the air fryer to 375°F (190°C).
2. Mix the tapioca flour, chile powder, and salt (if using) in a large bowl until well combined. Add the country-style rib chunks and toss well to coat thoroughly.
3. When the machine is at temperature, gently shake off any excess tapioca coating from the chunks. Generously coat them on all sides with vegetable oil spray. Arrange the chunks in the basket in one (admittedly fairly tight) layer. The pieces may touch. Air-fry for 30 minutes, rearranging the pieces at the 10- and 20-minute marks to expose any touching bits, until very crisp and well browned.
4. Gently pour the contents of the basket onto a wire rack. Cool for 5 minutes before serving.

Beef & Barley Stuffed Bell Peppers

Servings: 4
Cooking Time: 30 Minutes
Ingredients:

- 1 cup pulled cooked roast beef
- 4 bell peppers, tops removed
- 1 onion, chopped
- ½ cup grated carrot
- 2 tsp olive oil
- 2 tomatoes, chopped
- 1 cup cooked barley
- 1 tsp dried marjoram

Directions:

1. Preheat air fryer to 400°F (205°C). Cut the tops of the bell peppers, then remove the stems. Put the onion, carrots, and olive oil in a baking pan and cook for 2-4 minutes. The veggies should be crispy but soft. Put the veggies in a bowl, toss in the tomatoes, barley, roast beef, and marjoram, and mix to combine. Spoon the veggie mix into the cleaned bell peppers and put them in the frying basket. Bake for 12-16 minutes or until the peppers are tender. Serve warm.

Pork Cutlets With Aloha Salsa

Servings: 4
Cooking Time: 9 Minutes
Ingredients:

- Aloha Salsa
- 1 cup fresh pineapple, chopped in small pieces
- ¼ cup red onion, finely chopped
- ¼ cup green or red bell pepper, chopped
- ½ teaspoon ground cinnamon
- 1 teaspoon low-sodium soy sauce
- ⅛ teaspoon crushed red pepper
- ⅛ teaspoon ground black pepper
- 2 eggs
- 2 tablespoons milk
- ¼ cup flour
- ¼ cup panko breadcrumbs
- 4 teaspoons sesame seeds
- 1 pound boneless, thin pork cutlets (⅜- to ½-inch thick)
- lemon pepper and salt
- ¼ cup cornstarch
- oil for misting or cooking spray

Directions:

1. In a medium bowl, stir together all ingredients for salsa. Cover and refrigerate while cooking pork.
2. Preheat air fryer to 390°F (200°C).
3. Beat together eggs and milk in shallow dish.
4. In another shallow dish, mix together the flour, panko, and sesame seeds.
5. Sprinkle pork cutlets with lemon pepper and salt to taste. Most lemon pepper seasoning contains salt, so go easy adding extra.
6. Dip pork cutlets in cornstarch, egg mixture, and then panko coating. Spray both sides with oil or cooking spray.
7. Cook cutlets for 3minutes. Turn cutlets over, spraying both sides, and continue cooking for 6 minutes or until well done.
8. Serve fried cutlets with salsa on the side.

Stress-free Beef Patties

Servings: 2
Cooking Time: 30 Minutes
Ingredients:
- ½ lb ground beef
- 1 ½ tbsp ketchup
- 1 ½ tbsp tamari
- ½ tsp jalapeño powder
- ½ tsp mustard powder
- Salt and pepper to taste

Directions:
1. Preheat air fryer to 350°F（175°C）.Add the beef, ketchup, tamari, jalapeño, mustard salt, and pepper in a bowl and mix until evenly combined. Shape into 2 patties, then place them on the greased frying basket. Air Fry for 18-20 minutes, turning once. Serve and enjoy!

Provençal Grilled Rib-eye

Servings: 4
Cooking Time: 25 Minutes
Ingredients:
- 4 ribeye steaks
- 1 tbsp herbs de Provence
- Salt and pepper to taste

Directions:
1. Preheat air fryer to 360°F（180°C）. Season the steaks with herbs, salt and pepper. Place them in the greased frying basket and cook for 8-12 minutes, flipping once. Use a thermometer to check for doneness and adjust time as needed. Let the steak rest for a few minutes and serve.

Mustard-crusted Rib-eye

Servings: 2
Cooking Time: 9 Minutes
Ingredients:
- Two 6-ounce rib-eye steaks, about 1-inch thick
- 1 teaspoon coarse salt
- ½ teaspoon coarse black pepper
- 2 tablespoons Dijon mustard

Directions:
1. Rub the steaks with the salt and pepper. Then spread the mustard on both sides of the steaks. Cover with foil and let the steaks sit at room temperature for 30 minutes.
2. Preheat the air fryer to 390°F（200°C）.
3. Cook the steaks for 9 minutes. Check for an internal temperature of 140°F（60°C）and immediately remove the steaks and let them rest for 5 minutes before slicing.

Better-than-chinese-take-out Sesame Beef

Servings: 4

Cooking Time: 14 Minutes
Ingredients:
- 1¼ pounds Beef flank steak
- 2½ tablespoons Regular or low-sodium soy sauce or gluten-free tamari sauce
- 2 tablespoons Toasted sesame oil
- 2½ teaspoons Cornstarch
- 1 pound 2 ounces (about 4½ cups) Frozen mixed vegetables for stir-fry, thawed, seasoning packet discarded
- 3 tablespoons Unseasoned rice vinegar (see here)
- 3 tablespoons Thai sweet chili sauce
- 2 tablespoons Light brown sugar
- 2 tablespoons White sesame seeds
- 2 teaspoons Water
- Vegetable oil spray
- 1½ tablespoons Minced peeled fresh ginger
- 1 tablespoon Minced garlic

Directions:
1. Set the flank steak on a cutting board and run your clean fingers across it to figure out which way the meat's fibers are running. (Usually, they run the long way from end to end, or perhaps slightly at an angle lengthwise along the cut.) Cut the flank steak into three pieces parallel to the meat's grain. Then cut each of these pieces into ½-inch-wide strips against the grain.
2. Put the meat strips in a large bowl. For a small batch, add 2 teaspoons of the soy or tamari sauce, 2 teaspoons of the sesame oil, and ½ teaspoon of the cornstarch; for a medium batch, add 1 tablespoon of the soy or tamari sauce, 1 tablespoon of the sesame oil, and 1 teaspoon of the cornstarch; and for a large batch, add 1½ tablespoons of the soy or tamari sauce, 1½ tablespoons of the sesame oil, and 1½ teaspoons of the cornstarch. Toss well until the meat is thoroughly coated in the marinade. Set aside at room temperature.
3. Preheat the air fryer to 400°F（205°C）.
4. When the machine is at temperature, place the beef strips in the basket in as close to one layer as possible. The strips will overlap or even cover each other. Air-fry for 10 minutes, tossing and rearranging the strips three times so that the covered parts get exposed, until browned and even a little crisp. Pour the strips into a clean bowl.
5. Spread the vegetables in the basket and air-fry undisturbed for 4 minutes, just until they are heated through and somewhat softened. Pour these into the bowl with the meat strips. Turn off the air fryer.
6. Whisk the rice vinegar, sweet chili sauce, brown sugar, sesame seeds, the remaining soy sauce, and the remaining sesame oil in a small bowl until well combined. For a small batch, whisk the remaining 1 teaspoon cornstarch with the water in a second small bowl to make a smooth slurry; for medium batch, whisk the remaining 1½ teaspoons cornstarch with the water in a second small bowl to make a

smooth slurry; and for a large batch, whisk the remaining 2 teaspoons cornstarch with the water in a second small bowl to make a smooth slurry.

7.   Generously coat the inside of a large wok with vegetable oil spray, then set the wok over high heat for a few minutes. Add the ginger and garlic; stir-fry for 10 seconds or so, just until fragrant. Add the meat and vegetables; stir-fry for 1 minute to heat through.

8.   Add the rice vinegar mixture and continue stir-frying until the sauce is bubbling, less than 1 minute. Add the cornstarch slurry and stir-fry until the sauce has thickened, just a few seconds. Remove the wok from the heat and serve hot.

Apple Cornbread Stuffed Pork Loin With Apple Gravy

Servings: 4
Cooking Time: 61 Minutes
Ingredients:

- 4 strips of bacon, chopped
- 1 Granny Smith apple, peeled, cored and finely chopped
- 2 teaspoons fresh thyme leaves
- ¼ cup chopped fresh parsley
- 2 cups cubed cornbread
- ½ cup chicken stock
- salt and freshly ground black pepper
- 1 (2-pound) boneless pork loin
- kitchen twine
- Apple Gravy:
- 2 tablespoons butter
- 1 shallot, minced
- 1 Granny Smith apple, peeled, cored and finely chopped
- 3 sprigs fresh thyme
- 2 tablespoons flour
- 1 cup chicken stock
- ½ cup apple cider
- salt and freshly ground black pepper, to taste

Directions:

1.   Preheat the air fryer to 400°F（205°C）.

2.   Add the bacon to the air fryer and air-fry for 6 minutes until crispy. While the bacon is cooking, combine the apple, fresh thyme, parsley and cornbread in a bowl and toss well. Moisten the mixture with the chicken stock and season to taste with salt and freshly ground black pepper. Add the cooked bacon to the mixture.

3.   Butterfly the pork loin by holding it flat on the cutting board with one hand, while slicing into the pork loin parallel to the cutting board with the other. Slice into the longest side of the pork loin, but stop before you cut all the way through. You should then be able to open the pork loin up like a book, making it twice as wide as it was when you started. Season

the inside of the pork with salt and freshly ground black pepper.

4.   Spread the cornbread mixture onto the butterflied pork loin, leaving a one-inch border around the edge of the pork. Roll the pork loin up around the stuffing to enclose the stuffing, and tie the rolled pork in several places with kitchen twine or secure with toothpicks. Try to replace any stuffing that falls out of the roast as you roll it, by stuffing it into the ends of the rolled pork. Season the outside of the pork with salt and freshly ground black pepper.

5.   Preheat the air fryer to 360°F（180°C）.

6.   Place the stuffed pork loin into the air fryer, seam side down. Air-fry the pork loin for 15 minutes at 360°F （180°C）. Turn the pork loin over and air-fry for an additional 15 minutes. Turn the pork loin a quarter turn and air-fry for an additional 15 minutes. Turn the pork loin over again to expose the fourth side, and air-fry for an additional 10 minutes. The pork loin should register 155°F（70°C） on an instant read thermometer when it is finished.

7.   While the pork is cooking, make the apple gravy. Preheat a saucepan over medium heat on the stovetop and melt the butter. Add the shallot, apple and thyme sprigs and sauté until the apple starts to soften and brown a little. Add the flour and stir for a minute or two. Whisk in the stock and apple cider vigorously to prevent the flour from forming lumps. Bring the mixture to a boil to thicken and season to taste with salt and pepper.

8.   Transfer the pork loin to a resting plate and loosely tent with foil, letting the pork rest for at least 5 minutes before slicing and serving with the apple gravy poured over the top.

Pork Cutlets With Almond-lemon Crust

Servings: 3
Cooking Time: 14 Minutes
Ingredients:

- ¾ cup Almond flour
- ¾ cup Plain dried bread crumbs (gluten-free, if a concern)
- 1½ teaspoons Finely grated lemon zest
- 1¼ teaspoons Table salt
- ¾ teaspoon Garlic powder
- ¾ teaspoon Dried oregano
- 1 Large egg white(s)
- 2 tablespoons Water
- 3 6-ounce center-cut boneless pork loin chops (about ¾ inch thick)
- Olive oil spray

Directions:

1.   Preheat the air fryer to 375°F（190°C）.

2. Mix the almond flour, bread crumbs, lemon zest, salt, garlic powder, and dried oregano in a large bowl until well combined.

3. Whisk the egg white(s) and water in a shallow soup plate or small pie plate until uniform.

4. Dip a chop in the egg white mixture, turning it to coat all sides, even the ends. Let any excess egg white mixture slip back into the rest, then set it in the almond flour mixture. Turn it several times, pressing gently to coat it evenly. Generously coat the chop with olive oil spray, then set aside to dip and coat the remaining chop(s).

5. Set the chops in the basket with as much air space between them as possible. Air-fry undisturbed for 12 minutes, or until browned and crunchy. You may need to add 2 minutes to the cooking time if the machine is at 360°F (180°C).

6. Use kitchen tongs to transfer the chops to a wire rack. Cool for a few minutes before serving.

Delicious Juicy Pork Meatballs

Servings:4
Cooking Time: 35 Minutes
Ingredients:

- ¼ cup grated cheddar cheese
- 1 lb ground pork
- 1 egg
- 1 tbsp Greek yogurt
- ½ tsp onion powder
- ¼ cup chopped parsley
- 2 tbsp bread crumbs
- ¼ tsp garlic powder
- Salt and pepper to taste

Directions:

1. Preheat air fryer to 350ºF (175°C). In a bowl, combine the ground pork, egg, yogurt, onion, parsley, cheddar cheese, bread crumbs, garlic, salt, and black pepper. Form mixture into 16 meatballs. Place meatballs in the lightly greased frying basket and Air Fry for 8-10 minutes, flipping once. Serve.

Barbecue-style London Broil

Servings: 5
Cooking Time: 17 Minutes
Ingredients:

- ¾ teaspoon Mild smoked paprika
- ¾ teaspoon Dried oregano
- ¾ teaspoon Table salt
- ¾ teaspoon Ground black pepper
- ¼ teaspoon Garlic powder
- ¼ teaspoon Onion powder
- 1½ pounds Beef London broil (in one piece)

- Olive oil spray

Directions:

1. Preheat the air fryer to 400°F (205°C).

2. Mix the smoked paprika, oregano, salt, pepper, garlic powder, and onion powder in a small bowl until uniform.

3. Pat and rub this mixture across all surfaces of the beef. Lightly coat the beef on all sides with olive oil spray.

4. When the machine is at temperature, lay the London broil flat in the basket and air-fry undisturbed for 8 minutes for the small batch, 10 minutes for the medium batch, or 12 minutes for the large batch for medium-rare, until an instant-read meat thermometer inserted into the center of the meat registers 130°F (55°C) (not USDA-approved). Add 1, 2, or 3 minutes, respectively (based on the size of the cut) for medium, until an instant-read meat thermometer registers 135°F (55°C) (not USDA-approved). Or add 3, 4, or 5 minutes respectively for medium, until an instant-read meat thermometer registers 145°F (60°C) (USDA-approved).

5. Use kitchen tongs to transfer the London broil to a cutting board. Let the meat rest for 10 minutes. It needs a long time for the juices to be reincorporated into the meat's fibers. Carve it against the grain into very thin (less than ¼-inch-thick) slices to serve.

Balsamic Short Ribs

Servings: 2
Cooking Time: 30 Minutes
Ingredients:

- 1/8 tsp Worcestershire sauce
- ¼ cup olive oil
- ¼ cup balsamic vinegar
- ¼ cup chopped basil leaves
- ¼ cup chopped oregano
- 1 tbsp honey
- ¼ cup chopped fresh sage
- 3 cloves garlic, quartered
- ½ tsp salt
- 1 lb beef short ribs

Directions:

1. Add all ingredients, except for the short ribs, to a plastic resealable bag and shake to combine. Reserve 2 tbsp of balsamic mixture in a small bowl. Place short ribs in the plastic bag and massage into ribs. Seal the bag and let marinate in the fridge for 30 minutes up to overnight.

2. Preheat air fryer at 325ºF (160°C). Place short ribs in the frying basket and Bake for 16 minutes, turn once and brush with extra sauce. Serve warm.

Sage Pork With Potatoes

Servings: 4
Cooking Time: 30 Minutes
Ingredients:

- 2 cups potatoes
- 2 tsp olive oil
- 1 lb pork tenderloin, cubed
- 1 onion, chopped
- 1 red bell pepper, chopped
- 2 garlic cloves, minced
- ½ tsp dried sage
- ½ tsp fennel seeds, crushed
- 2 tbsp chicken broth

Directions:

1. Preheat air fryer to 370°F (185°C). Add the potatoes and olive oil to a bowl and toss to coat. Transfer them to the frying basket and Air Fry for 15 minutes. Remove the bowl. Add the pork, onion, red bell pepper, garlic, sage, and fennel seeds, to the potatoes, add chicken broth and stir gently. Return the bowl to the frying basket and cook for 10 minutes. Be sure to shake the basket at least once. The pork should be cooked through and the potatoes soft and crispy. Serve immediately.

Spicy Hoisin Bbq Pork Chops

Servings: 2
Cooking Time: 12 Minutes
Ingredients:

- 3 tablespoons hoisin sauce
- ¼ cup honey
- 1 tablespoon soy sauce
- 3 tablespoons rice vinegar
- 2 tablespoons brown sugar
- 1½ teaspoons grated fresh ginger
- 1 to 2 teaspoons Sriracha sauce, to taste
- 2 to 3 bone-in center cut pork chops, 1-inch thick (about 1¼ pounds)
- chopped scallions, for garnish

Directions:

1. Combine the hoisin sauce, honey, soy sauce, rice vinegar, brown sugar, ginger, and Sriracha sauce in a small saucepan. Whisk the ingredients together and bring the mixture to a boil over medium-high heat on the stovetop. Reduce the heat and simmer the sauce until it has reduced in volume and thickened slightly – about 10 minutes.
2. Preheat the air fryer to 400°F (205°C).
3. Place the pork chops into the air fryer basket and pour half the hoisin BBQ sauce over the top. Air-fry for 6 minutes. Then, flip the chops over, pour the remaining hoisin BBQ sauce on top and air-fry for 6 more minutes, depending on the thickness of the pork chops. The internal temperature of the pork chops should be 155°F (70°C) when tested with an instant read thermometer.

4. Let the pork chops rest for 5 minutes before serving. You can spoon a little of the sauce from the bottom drawer of the air fryer over the top if desired. Sprinkle with chopped scallions and serve.

Mushroom & Quinoa-stuffed Pork Loins

Servings: 3
Cooking Time: 25 Minutes
Ingredients:

- 3 boneless center-cut pork loins, pocket cut in each loin
- ½ cup diced white mushrooms
- 1 tsp vegetable oil
- 3 bacon slices, diced
- ½ onion, peeled and diced
- 1 cup baby spinach
- Salt and pepper to taste
- ½ cup cooked quinoa
- ½ cup mozzarella cheese

Directions:

1. Warm the oil in a skillet over medium heat. Add the bacon and cook for 3 minutes until the fat is rendered but not crispy. Add in onion and mushrooms and stir-fry for 3 minutes until the onions are translucent. Stir in spinach, salt, and pepper and cook for 1 minute until the spinach wilts. Set aside and toss in quinoa.
2. Preheat air fryer at 350°F (175°C). Stuff quinoa mixture into each pork loin and sprinkle with mozzarella cheese. Place them in the frying basket and Air Fry for 11 minutes. Let rest onto a cutting board for 5 minutes before serving.

Red Curry Flank Steak

Servings: 4
Cooking Time: 18 Minutes
Ingredients:

- 3 tablespoons red curry paste
- ¼ cup olive oil
- 2 teaspoons grated fresh ginger
- 2 tablespoons soy sauce
- 2 tablespoons rice wine vinegar
- 3 scallions, minced
- 1½ pounds flank steak
- fresh cilantro (or parsley) leaves

Directions:

1. Mix the red curry paste, olive oil, ginger, soy sauce, rice vinegar and scallions together in a bowl. Place the flank steak in a shallow glass dish and pour half the marinade over the steak. Pierce the steak several times with a fork or meat tenderizer to let the marinade penetrate the meat. Turn the steak over, pour the remaining marinade over the top and pierce the steak several times again. Cover and marinate the steak in the refrigerator for 6 to 8 hours.

2. When you are ready to cook, remove the steak from the refrigerator and let it sit at room temperature for 30 minutes.
3. Preheat the air fryer to 400°F (205°C).
4. Cut the flank steak in half so that it fits more easily into the air fryer and transfer both pieces to the air fryer basket. Pour the marinade over the steak. Air-fry for 18 minutes, depending on your preferred degree of doneness of the steak (12 minutes = medium rare). Flip the steak over halfway through the cooking time.
5. When your desired degree of doneness has been reached, remove the steak to a cutting board and let it rest for 5 minutes before slicing. Thinly slice the flank steak against the grain of the meat. Transfer the slices to a serving platter, pour any juice from the bottom of the air fryer over the sliced flank steak and sprinkle the fresh cilantro on top.

Pork Loin

Servings: 8
Cooking Time: 50 Minutes
Ingredients:
- 1 tablespoon lime juice
- 1 tablespoon orange marmalade
- 1 teaspoon coarse brown mustard
- 1 teaspoon curry powder
- 1 teaspoon dried lemongrass
- 2-pound boneless pork loin roast
- salt and pepper
- cooking spray

Directions:
1. Mix together the lime juice, marmalade, mustard, curry powder, and lemongrass.
2. Rub mixture all over the surface of the pork loin. Season to taste with salt and pepper.
3. Spray air fryer basket with nonstick spray and place pork roast diagonally in basket.
4. Cook at 360°F (180°C) for approximately 50 minutes, until roast registers 130°F (55°C) on a meat thermometer.
5. Wrap roast in foil and let rest for 10minutes before slicing.

Country-style Pork Ribs(1)

Servings: 4
Cooking Time: 30 Minutes
Ingredients:
- 2 tbsp cornstarch
- 2 tbsp olive oil
- 1 tsp mustard powder
- ½ tsp thyme
- ½ tsp garlic powder
- 1 tsp paprika
- Salt and pepper to taste
- 12 country-style pork ribs

Directions:

1. Preheat air fryer to 400°F (205°C). Mix together cornstarch, olive oil, mustard powder, thyme, garlic powder, paprika, salt, and pepper in a bowl. Rub the seasoned mixture onto the ribs. Put the ribs into the frying basket. Bake for 14-16 minutes, flipping once until the ribs are crisp. Serve.

Mongolian Beef

Servings: 4
Cooking Time: 15 Minutes
Ingredients:
- 1½ pounds flank steak, thinly sliced
- on the bias into ¼-inch strips
- Marinade
- 2 tablespoons soy sauce*
- 1 clove garlic, smashed
- big pinch crushed red pepper flakes
- Sauce
- 1 tablespoon vegetable oil
- 2 cloves garlic, minced
- 1 tablespoon finely grated fresh ginger
- 3 dried red chili peppers
- ¾ cup soy sauce*
- ¾ cup chicken stock
- 5 to 6 tablespoons brown sugar (depending on how sweet you want the sauce)
- ½ cup cornstarch, divided
- 1 bunch scallions, sliced into 2-inch pieces

Directions:
1. Marinate the beef in the soy sauce, garlic and red pepper flakes for one hour.
2. In the meantime, make the sauce. Preheat a small saucepan over medium heat on the stovetop. Add the oil, garlic, ginger and dried chili peppers and sauté for just a minute or two. Add the soy sauce, chicken stock and brown sugar and continue to simmer for a few minutes. Dissolve 3 tablespoons of cornstarch in 3 tablespoons of water and stir this into the saucepan. Stir the sauce over medium heat until it thickens. Set this aside.
3. Preheat the air fryer to 400°F (205°C).
4. Remove the beef from the marinade and transfer it to a zipper sealable plastic bag with the remaining cornstarch. Shake it around to completely coat the beef and transfer the coated strips of beef to a baking sheet or plate, shaking off any excess cornstarch. Spray the strips with vegetable oil on all sides and transfer them to the air fryer basket.
5. Air-fry at 400°F (205°C) for 15 minutes, shaking the basket to toss and rotate the beef strips throughout the cooking process. Add the scallions for the last 4 minutes of the cooking. Transfer the hot beef strips and scallions to a bowl and toss with the sauce (warmed on the stovetop if necessary), coating all the beef strips with the sauce. Serve warm over white rice.

Greek Pork Chops

Servings: 4
Cooking Time: 30 Minutes
Ingredients:
- 3 tbsp grated Halloumi cheese
- 4 pork chops
- 1 tsp Greek seasoning
- Salt and pepper to taste
- ¼ cup all-purpose flour
- 2 tbsp bread crumbs

Directions:
1. Preheat air fryer to 380°F（195°C）. Season the pork chops with Greek seasoning, salt and pepper. In a shallow bowl, add flour. In another shallow bowl, combine the crumbs and Halloumi. Dip the chops in the flour, then in the bread crumbs. Place them in the fryer and spray with cooking oil. Bake for 12-14 minutes, flipping once. Serve warm.

Sloppy Joes

Servings: 4
Cooking Time: 17 Minutes
Ingredients:
- oil for misting or cooking spray
- 1 pound very lean ground beef
- 1 teaspoon onion powder
- ⅓ cup ketchup
- ¼ cup water
- ½ teaspoon celery seed
- 1 tablespoon lemon juice
- 1½ teaspoons brown sugar
- 1¼ teaspoons low-sodium Worcestershire sauce
- ½ teaspoon salt (optional)
- ½ teaspoon vinegar
- ⅛ teaspoon dry mustard
- hamburger or slider buns

Directions:
1. Spray air fryer basket with nonstick cooking spray or olive oil.
2. Break raw ground beef into small chunks and pile into basket.
3. Cook at 390°F（200°C）for 5minutes. Stir to break apart and cook 3minutes. Stir and cook 4 minutes longer or until meat is well done.
4. Remove meat from air fryer, drain, and use a knife and fork to crumble into small pieces.
5. Give your air fryer basket a quick rinse to remove any bits of meat.
6. Place all the remaining ingredients except the buns in a 6 x 6-inch baking pan and mix together.
7. Add meat and stir well.

8. Cook at 330°F（165°C）for 5minutes. Stir and cook for 2minutes.
9. Scoop onto buns.

Garlic And Oregano Lamb Chops

Servings: 4
Cooking Time: 17 Minutes
Ingredients:
- 1½ tablespoons Olive oil
- 1 tablespoon Minced garlic
- 1 teaspoon Dried oregano
- 1 teaspoon Finely minced orange zest
- ¾ teaspoon Fennel seeds
- ¾ teaspoon Table salt
- ¾ teaspoon Ground black pepper
- 6 4-ounce, 1-inch-thick lamb loin chops

Directions:
1. Mix the olive oil, garlic, oregano, orange zest, fennel seeds, salt, and pepper in a large bowl. Add the chops and toss well to coat. Set aside as the air fryer heats, tossing one more time.
2. Preheat the air fryer to 400°F（205°C）.
3. Set the chops bone side down in the basket (that is, so they stand up on their bony edge) with as much air space between them as possible. Air-fry undisturbed for 14 minutes for medium-rare, or until an instant-read meat thermometer inserted into the thickest part of a chop (without touching bone) registers 132°F（55°C）(not USDA-approved). Or air-fry undisturbed for 17 minutes for well done, or until an instant-read meat thermometer registers 145°F（60°C）(USDA-approved).
4. Use kitchen tongs to transfer the chops to a wire rack. Cool for 5 minutes before serving.

Grilled Pork & Bell Pepper Salad

Servings: 4
Cooking Time: 25 Minutes
Ingredients:
- 1 cup sautéed button mushrooms, sliced
- 2 lb pork tenderloin, sliced
- 1 tsp olive oil
- 1 tsp dried marjoram
- 6 tomato wedges
- 6 green olives
- 6 cups mixed salad greens
- 1 red bell pepper, sliced
- 1/3 cup vinaigrette dressing

Directions:

1. Preheat air fryer to 400°F（205°C）. Combine the pork and olive oil, making sure the pork is well-coated. Season with marjoram. Lay the pork in the air fryer. Grill for 4-6 minutes, turning once until the pork is cooked through.

2. While the pork is cooking, toss the salad greens, red bell pepper, tomatoes, olives, and mushrooms into a bowl. Lay the pork slices on top of the salad, season with vinaigrette, and toss. Serve while the pork is still warm.

Skirt Steak Fajitas

Servings: 4
Cooking Time: 30 Minutes
Ingredients:

- 2 tablespoons olive oil
- ¼ cup lime juice
- 1 clove garlic, minced
- ½ teaspoon ground cumin
- ½ teaspoon hot sauce
- ½ teaspoon salt
- 2 tablespoons chopped fresh cilantro
- 1 pound skirt steak
- 1 onion, sliced
- 1 teaspoon chili powder
- 1 red pepper, sliced
- 1 green pepper, sliced
- salt and freshly ground black pepper
- 8 flour tortillas
- shredded lettuce, crumbled Queso Fresco (or grated Cheddar cheese), sliced black olives, diced tomatoes, sour cream and guacamole for serving

Directions:

1. Combine the olive oil, lime juice, garlic, cumin, hot sauce, salt and cilantro in a shallow dish. Add the skirt steak and turn it over several times to coat all sides. Pierce the steak with a needle-style meat tenderizer or paring knife. Marinate the steak in the refrigerator for at least 3 hours, or overnight. When you are ready to cook, remove the steak from the refrigerator and let it sit at room temperature for 30 minutes.

2. Preheat the air fryer to 400°F（205°C）.

3. Toss the onion slices with the chili powder and a little olive oil and transfer them to the air fryer basket. Air-fry at 400°F（205°C）for 5 minutes. Add the red and green peppers to the air fryer basket with the onions, season with salt and pepper and air-fry for 8 more minutes, until the onions and peppers are soft. Transfer the vegetables to a dish and cover with aluminum foil to keep warm.

4. Place the skirt steak in the air fryer basket and pour the marinade over the top. Air-fry at 400°F（205°C）for 12 minutes. Flip the steak over and air-fry at 400°F（205°C）for an additional 5 minutes. (The time needed for your steak will depend on the thickness of the skirt steak. 17 minutes

should bring your steak to roughly medium.) Transfer the cooked steak to a cutting board and let the steak rest for a few minutes. If the peppers and onions need to be heated, return them to the air fryer for just 1 to 2 minutes.

5. Thinly slice the steak at an angle, cutting against the grain of the steak. Serve the steak with the onions and peppers, the warm tortillas and the fajita toppings on the side so that everyone can make their own fajita.

Bacon, Blue Cheese And Pear Stuffed Pork Chops

Servings: 3
Cooking Time: 24 Minutes
Ingredients:

- 4 slices bacon, chopped
- 1 tablespoon butter
- ½ cup finely diced onion
- ⅓ cup chicken stock
- 1½ cups seasoned stuffing cubes
- 1 egg, beaten
- ½ teaspoon dried thyme
- ½ teaspoon salt
- ⅛ teaspoon black pepper
- 1 pear, finely diced
- ⅓ cup crumbled blue cheese
- 3 boneless center-cut pork chops (2-inch thick)
- olive oil
- salt and freshly ground black pepper

Directions:

1. Preheat the air fryer to 400°F（205°C）.

2. Place the bacon into the air fryer basket and air-fry for 6 minutes, stirring halfway through the cooking time. Remove the bacon and set it aside on a paper towel. Pour out the grease from the bottom of the air fryer.

3. To make the stuffing, melt the butter in a medium saucepan over medium heat on the stovetop. Add the onion and sauté for a few minutes, until it starts to soften. Add the chicken stock and simmer for 1 minute. Remove the pan from the heat and add the stuffing cubes. Stir until the stock has been absorbed. Add the egg, dried thyme, salt and freshly ground black pepper, and stir until combined. Fold in the diced pear and crumbled blue cheese.

4. Place the pork chops on a cutting board. Using the palm of your hand to hold the chop flat and steady, slice into the side of the pork chop to make a pocket in the center of the chop. Leave about an inch of chop uncut and make sure you don't cut all the way through the pork chop. Brush both sides of the pork chops with olive oil and season with salt and freshly ground black pepper. Stuff each pork chop with a third of the stuffing, packing the stuffing tightly inside the pocket.

5. Preheat the air fryer to 360°F（180°C）.

6. Spray or brush the sides of the air fryer basket with oil. Place the pork chops in the air fryer basket with the open stuffed edge of the pork chop facing the outside edges of the basket.

7. Air-fry the pork chops for 18 minutes, turning the pork chops over halfway through the cooking time. When the chops are done, let them rest for 5 minutes and then transfer to a serving platter.

Pork & Beef Egg Rolls

Servings: 8
Cooking Time: 8 Minutes
Ingredients:
- ¼ pound very lean ground beef
- ¼ pound lean ground pork
- 1 tablespoon soy sauce
- 1 teaspoon olive oil
- ½ cup grated carrots
- 2 green onions, chopped
- 2 cups grated Napa cabbage
- ¼ cup chopped water chestnuts
- ¼ teaspoon salt
- ¼ teaspoon garlic powder
- ¼ teaspoon black pepper
- 1 egg
- 1 tablespoon water
- 8 egg roll wraps
- oil for misting or cooking spray

Directions:
1. In a large skillet, brown beef and pork with soy sauce. Remove cooked meat from skillet, drain, and set aside.
2. Pour off any excess grease from skillet. Add olive oil, carrots, and onions. Sauté until barely tender, about 1 minute.
3. Stir in cabbage, cover, and cook for 1 minute or just until cabbage slightly wilts. Remove from heat.
4. In a large bowl, combine the cooked meats and vegetables, water chestnuts, salt, garlic powder, and pepper. Stir well. If needed, add more salt to taste.
5. Beat together egg and water in a small bowl.
6. Fill egg roll wrappers, using about ¼ cup of filling for each wrap. Roll up and brush all over with egg wash to seal. Spray very lightly with olive oil or cooking spray.
7. Place 4 egg rolls in air fryer basket and cook at 390°F (200°C) for 4minutes. Turn over and cook 4 more minutes, until golden brown and crispy.
8. Repeat to cook remaining egg rolls.

Lamb Chops In Currant Sauce

Servings: 4
Cooking Time: 30 Minutes
Ingredients:

- ½ cup chicken broth
- 2 tbsp red currant jelly
- 2 tbsp Dijon mustard
- 1 tbsp lemon juice
- ½ tsp dried thyme
- ½ tsp dried mint
- 8 lamb chops
- Salt and pepper to taste

Directions:
1. Preheat the air fryer to 375°F (190°C). Combine the broth, jelly, mustard, lemon juice, mint, and thyme and mix with a whisk until smooth. Sprinkle the chops with salt and pepper and brush with some of the broth mixture.
2. Set 4 chops in the frying basket in a single layer, then add a raised rack and lay the rest of the chops on top. Bake for 15-20 minutes. Then, lay them in a cake pan and add the chicken broth mix. Put in the fryer and Bake for 3-5 more minutes or until the sauce is bubbling and the chops are tender.

Broccoli & Mushroom Beef

Servings: 4
Cooking Time: 30 Minutes
Ingredients:
- 1 lb sirloin strip steak, cubed
- 1 cup sliced cremini mushrooms
- 2 tbsp potato starch
- ½ cup beef broth
- 1 tsp soy sauce
- 2 ½ cups broccoli florets
- 1 onion, chopped
- 1 tbsp grated fresh ginger
- 1 cup cooked quinoa

Directions:
1. Add potato starch, broth, and soy sauce to a bowl and mix, then add in the beef and coat thoroughly. Marinate for 5 minutes. Preheat air fryer to 400°F (205°C). Set aside the broth and move the beef to a bowl. Add broccoli, onion, mushrooms, and ginger and transfer the bowl to the air fryer. Bake for 12-15 minutes until the beef is golden brown and the veggies soft. Pour the reserved broth over the beef and cook for 2-3 more minutes until the sauce is bubbling. Serve warm over cooked quinoa.

Chicken Fried Steak

Servings: 4
Cooking Time: 15 Minutes
Ingredients:
- 2 eggs
- ½ cup buttermilk
- 1½ cups flour
- ¾ teaspoon salt

- ½ teaspoon pepper
- 1 pound beef cube steaks
- salt and pepper
- oil for misting or cooking spray

Directions:

1. Beat together eggs and buttermilk in a shallow dish.
2. In another shallow dish, stir together the flour, ½ teaspoon salt, and ¼ teaspoon pepper.
3. Season cube steaks with remaining salt and pepper to taste. Dip in flour, buttermilk egg wash, and then flour again.
4. Spray both sides of steaks with oil or cooking spray.
5. Cooking in 2 batches, place steaks in air fryer basket in single layer. Cook at 360°F（180°C）for 10minutes. Spray tops of steaks with oil and cook 5minutes or until meat is well done.
6. Repeat to cook remaining steaks.

Chipotle Pork Meatballs

Servings:4
Cooking Time: 35 Minutes
Ingredients:

- 1 lb ground pork
- 1 egg
- ¼ cup chipotle sauce
- ¼ cup grated celery
- ¼ cup chopped parsley
- ¼ cup chopped cilantro
- ¼ cup flour
- ¼ tsp salt

Directions:

1. Preheat air fryer to 350°F（175°C）. In a large bowl, combine the ground pork, egg, chipotle sauce, celery, parsley, cilantro, flour, and salt. Form mixture into 16 meatballs. Place the meatballs in the lightly greased frying basket and Air Fry for 8-10 minutes, flipping once. Serve immediately!

City "chicken"

Servings: 3
Cooking Time: 10 Minutes
Ingredients:

- 1 pound Pork tenderloin, cut into 2-inch cubes
- ½ cup All-purpose flour or tapioca flour
- 1 Large egg(s)
- 1 teaspoon Dried poultry seasoning blend
- 1¼ cups Plain panko bread crumbs (gluten-free, if a concern)
- Vegetable oil spray

Directions:

1. Preheat the air fryer to 350°F（175°C）.

2. Thread 3 or 4 pieces of pork on a 4-inch bamboo skewer. You'll need 2 or 3 skewers for a small batch, 3 or 4 for a medium, and up to 6 for a large batch.
3. Set up and fill three shallow soup plates or small pie plates on your counter: one for the flour; one for the egg(s), beaten with the poultry seasoning until foamy; and one for the bread crumbs.
4. Dip and roll one skewer into the flour, coating all sides of the meat. Gently shake off any excess flour, then dip and roll the skewer in the egg mixture. Let any excess egg mixture slip back into the rest, then set the skewer in the bread crumbs and roll it around, pressing gently, until the exterior surfaces of the meat are evenly coated. Generously coat the meat on the skewer with vegetable oil spray. Set aside and continue dredging, dipping, coating, and spraying the remaining skewers.
5. Set the skewers in the basket in one layer and air-fry undisturbed for 10 minutes, or until brown and crunchy.
6. Use kitchen tongs to transfer the skewers to a wire rack. Cool for a minute or two before serving.

Tasty Filet Mignon

Servings:2
Cooking Time: 30 Minutes
Ingredients:

- 2 filet mignon steaks
- ¼ tsp garlic powder
- Salt and pepper to taste
- 1 tbsp butter, melted

Directions:

1. Preheat air fryer to 370°F（185°C）. Sprinkle the steaks with salt, garlic and pepper on both sides. Place them in the greased frying basket and Air Fry for 12 minutes to yield a medium-rare steak, turning twice. Transfer steaks to a cutting board, brush them with butter and let rest 5 minutes before serving.

Natchitoches Meat Pies

Servings: 8
Cooking Time: 12 Minutes
Ingredients:

- Filling
- ½ pound lean ground beef
- ¼ cup finely chopped onion
- ¼ cup finely chopped green bell pepper
- ⅛ teaspoon salt
- ½ teaspoon garlic powder
- ½ teaspoon red pepper flakes
- 1 tablespoon low sodium Worcestershire sauce
- Crust
- 2 cups self-rising flour
- ¼ cup butter, finely diced

- 1 cup milk
- Egg Wash
- 1 egg
- 1 tablespoon water or milk
- oil for misting or cooking spray

Directions:

1. Mix all filling ingredients well and shape into 4 small patties.
2. Cook patties in air fryer basket at 390°F（200°C）for 10 to 12minutes or until well done.
3. Place patties in large bowl and use fork and knife to crumble meat into very small pieces. Set aside.
4. To make the crust, use a pastry blender or fork to cut the butter into the flour until well mixed. Add milk and stir until dough stiffens.
5. Divide dough into 8 equal portions.
6. On a lightly floured surface, roll each portion of dough into a circle. The circle should be thin and about 5 inches in diameter, but don't worry about getting a perfect shape. Uneven circles result in a rustic look that many people prefer.
7. Spoon 2 tablespoons of meat filling onto each dough circle.
8. Brush egg wash all the way around the edge of dough circle, about ½-inch deep.
9. Fold each circle in half and press dough with tines of a dinner fork to seal the edges all the way around.
10. Brush tops of sealed meat pies with egg wash.
11. Cook filled pies in a single layer in air fryer basket at 360°F（180°C）for 4minutes. Spray tops with oil or cooking spray, turn pies over, and spray bottoms with oil or cooking spray. Cook for an additional 2minutes.
12. Repeat previous step to cook remaining pies.

Barbecue Country-style Pork Ribs

Servings: 3
Cooking Time: 30 Minutes
Ingredients:

- 3 8-ounce boneless country-style pork ribs
- 1½ teaspoons Mild smoked paprika
- 1½ teaspoons Light brown sugar
- ¾ teaspoon Onion powder
- ¾ teaspoon Ground black pepper
- ¼ teaspoon Table salt
- Vegetable oil spray

Directions:

1. Preheat the air fryer to 350°F（175°C）. Set the ribs in a bowl on the counter as the machine heats.
2. Mix the smoked paprika, brown sugar, onion powder, pepper, and salt in a small bowl until well combined. Rub this mixture over all the surfaces of the country-style ribs.

Generously coat the country-style ribs with vegetable oil spray.

3. Set the ribs in the basket with as much air space between them as possible. Air-fry undisturbed for 30 minutes, or until browned and sizzling and an instant-read meat thermometer inserted into one rib registers at least 145°F（60°C）.
4. Use kitchen tongs to transfer the country-style ribs to a wire rack. Cool for 5 minutes before serving.

Italian Sausage & Peppers

Servings: 6
Cooking Time: 25 Minutes
Ingredients:

- 1 6-ounce can tomato paste
- ⅔ cup water
- 1 8-ounce can tomato sauce
- 1 teaspoon dried parsley flakes
- ½ teaspoon garlic powder
- ⅛ teaspoon oregano
- ½ pound mild Italian bulk sausage
- 1 tablespoon extra virgin olive oil
- ½ large onion, cut in 1-inch chunks
- 4 ounces fresh mushrooms, sliced
- 1 large green bell pepper, cut in 1-inch chunks
- 8 ounces spaghetti, cooked
- Parmesan cheese for serving

Directions:

1. In a large saucepan or skillet, stir together the tomato paste, water, tomato sauce, parsley, garlic, and oregano. Heat on stovetop over very low heat while preparing meat and vegetables.
2. Break sausage into small chunks, about ½-inch pieces. Place in air fryer baking pan.
3. Cook at 390°F（200°C）for 5minutes. Stir. Cook 7 minutes longer or until sausage is well done. Remove from pan, drain on paper towels, and add to the sauce mixture.
4. If any sausage grease remains in baking pan, pour it off or use paper towels to soak it up. (Be careful handling that hot pan!)
5. Place olive oil, onions, and mushrooms in pan and stir. Cook for 5minutes or just until tender. Using a slotted spoon transfer onions and mushrooms from baking pan into the sauce and sausage mixture.
6. Place bell pepper chunks in air fryer baking pan and cook for 8 minutes or until tender. When done, stir into sauce with sausage and other vegetables.
7. Serve over cooked spaghetti with plenty of Parmesan cheese.

Traditional Italian Beef Meatballs

Servings:4
Cooking Time: 35 Minutes
Ingredients:
- 1/3 cup grated Parmesan
- 1 lb ground beef
- 1 egg, beaten
- 2 tbsp tomato paste
- ½ tsp Italian seasonings
- ¼ cup ricotta cheese
- 3 cloves garlic, minced
- ¼ cup grated yellow onion
- Salt and pepper to taste
- ¼ cup almond flour
- ¼ cup chopped basil
- 2 cups marinara sauce

Directions:
1. Preheat air fryer to 400ºF (205°C). In a large bowl, combine ground beef, egg, tomato paste, Italian seasoning, ricotta cheese, Parmesan cheese, garlic, onion, salt, pepper, flour, and basil. Form mixture into 4 meatballs. Add them to the greased frying basket and Air Fry for 20 minutes. Warm the marinara sauce in a skillet over medium heat for 3 minutes. Add in cooked meatballs and roll them around in sauce for 2 minutes. Serve with sauce over the top.

Taco Pie With Meatballs

Servings: 4
Cooking Time: 40 Minutes + Cooling Time
Ingredients:
- 1 cup shredded quesadilla cheese
- 1 cup shredded Colby cheese
- 10 cooked meatballs, halved
- 1 cup salsa
- 1 cup canned refried beans
- 2 tsp chipotle powder
- ½ tsp ground cumin
- 4 corn tortillas

Directions:
1. Preheat the air fryer to 375°F (190°C). Combine the meatball halves, salsa, refried beans, chipotle powder, and cumin in a bowl. In a baking pan, add a tortilla and top with one-quarter of the meatball mixture. Sprinkle one-quarter of the cheeses on top and repeat the layers three more times, ending with cheese. Put the pan in the fryer. Bake for 15-20 minutes until the pie is bubbling and the cheese has melted. Let cool on a wire rack for 10 minutes. Run a knife around the edges of the pan and remove the sides of the pan, then cut into wedges to serve.

Berbere Beef Steaks

Servings: 4
Cooking Time: 45 Minutes
Ingredients:
- 1 chipotle pepper in adobo sauce, minced
- 1 lb skirt steak
- 2 tbsp chipotle sauce
- ¼ tsp Berbere seasoning
- Salt and pepper to taste

Directions:
1. Cut the steak into 4 equal pieces, then place them on a plate. Mix together chipotle pepper, adobo sauce, salt, pepper, and Berbere seasoning in a bowl. Spread the mixture on both sides of the steak. Chill for 2 hours.
2. Preheat air fryer to 390°F (200°C). Place the steaks in the frying basket and Bake for 5 minutes on each side for well-done meat. Allow the steaks to rest for 5 more minutes. To serve, slice against the grain.

Citrus Pork Lettuce Wraps

Servings:4
Cooking Time: 35 Minutes
Ingredients:
- Salt and white pepper to taste
- 1 tbsp cornstarch
- 1 tbsp red wine vinegar
- 2 tbsp orange marmalade
- 1 tsp pulp-free orange juice
- 2 tsp olive oil
- ¼ tsp chili pepper
- ¼ tsp ground ginger
- 1 lb pork loin, cubed
- 8 iceberg lettuce leaves

Directions:
1. Create a slurry by whisking cornstarch and 1 tbsp of water in a bowl. Set aside. Place a small saucepan over medium heat. Add the red wine vinegar, orange marmalade, orange juice, olive oil, chili pepper, and ginger and cook for 3 minutes, stirring continuously. Mix in the slurry and simmer for 1 more minute. Turn the heat off and let it thicken, about3 minutes.
2. Preheat air fryer to 350°F (175°C). Sprinkle the pork with salt and white pepper. Place them in the greased frying basket and Air Fry for 8-10 minutes until cooked through and browned, turning once. Transfer pork cubes to a bowl with the sauce and toss to coat. Serve in lettuce leaves.

Italian Meatballs

Servings: 4
Cooking Time: 12 Minutes

Ingredients:

- 12 ounces lean ground beef
- 4 ounces Italian sausage, casing removed
- ½ cup breadcrumbs
- 1 cup grated Parmesan cheese
- 1 egg
- 2 tablespoons milk
- 2 teaspoons Italian seasoning
- ½ teaspoon onion powder
- ½ teaspoon garlic powder
- Pinch of red pepper flakes

Directions:

1. In a large bowl, place all the ingredients and mix well. Roll out 24 meatballs.
2. Preheat the air fryer to 360°F（180°C）.
3. Place the meatballs in the air fryer basket and cook for 12 minutes, tossing every 4 minutes. Using a food thermometer, check to ensure the internal temperature of the meatballs is 165°F（75°C）.

Calzones South Of The Border

Servings: 8
Cooking Time: 8 Minutes

Ingredients:

- Filling
- ¼ pound ground pork sausage
- ½ teaspoon chile powder
- ¼ teaspoon ground cumin
- ⅛ teaspoon garlic powder
- ⅛ teaspoon onion powder
- ⅛ teaspoon oregano
- ½ cup ricotta cheese
- 1 ounce sharp Cheddar cheese, shredded
- 2 ounces Pepper Jack cheese, shredded
- 1 4-ounce can chopped green chiles, drained
- oil for misting or cooking spray
- salsa, sour cream, or guacamole
- Crust
- 2 cups white wheat flour, plus more for kneading and rolling
- 1 package (¼ ounce) RapidRise yeast
- 1 teaspoon salt
- ½ teaspoon chile powder
- ½ teaspoon ground cumin
- 1 cup warm water (115°F（45°C）to 125°F（50°C）)
- 2 teaspoons olive oil

Directions:

1. Crumble sausage into air fryer baking pan and stir in the filling seasonings: chile powder, cumin, garlic powder, onion powder, and oregano. Cook at 390°F（200°C）for 2minutes. Stir, breaking apart, and cook for 3 to 4minutes, until well done. Remove and set aside on paper towels to drain.
2. To make dough, combine flour, yeast, salt, chile powder, and cumin. Stir in warm water and oil until soft dough forms. Turn out onto lightly floured board and knead for 3 or 4minutes. Let dough rest for 10minutes.
3. Place the three cheeses in a medium bowl. Add cooked sausage and chiles and stir until well mixed.
4. Cut dough into 8 pieces.
5. Working with 4 pieces of the dough, press each into a circle about 5 inches in diameter. Top each dough circle with 2 heaping tablespoons of filling. Fold over into a half-moon shape and press edges together. Seal edges firmly to prevent leakage. Spray both sides with oil or cooking spray.
6. Place 4 calzones in air fryer basket and cook at 360°F（180°C）for 5minutes. Mist with oil or spray and cook for 3minutes, until crust is done and nicely browned.
7. While the first batch is cooking, press out the remaining dough, fill, and shape into calzones.
8. Spray both sides with oil or cooking spray and cook for 5minutes. If needed, mist with oil and continue cooking for 3 minutes longer. This second batch will cook a little faster than the first because your air fryer is already hot.
9. Serve plain or with salsa, sour cream, or guacamole.

Basil Cheese & Ham Stromboli

Servings: 6
Cooking Time: 30 Minutes

Ingredients:

- 1 can refrigerated pizza dough
- ½ cup shredded mozzarella
- ½ red bell pepper, sliced
- 2 tsp all-purpose flour
- 6 Havarti cheese slices
- 12 deli ham slices
- ½ tsp dried basil
- 1 tsp garlic powder
- ½ tsp oregano
- Black pepper to taste

Directions:

1. Preheat air fryer to 400°F（205°C）. Flour a flat work surface and roll out the pizza dough. Use a knife to cut into 6 equal-sized rectangles. On each rectangle, add 1 slice of Havarti, 1 tbsp of mozzarella, 2 slices of ham, and some red pepper slices. Season with basil, garlic, oregano, and black pepper. Fold one side of the dough over the filling to the opposite side. Press the edges with the back of a fork to seal them.Place one batch of stromboli in the fryer and lightly spray with cooking oil. Air Fry for 10 minutes. Serve and enjoy!

Crispy Pork Medallions With Radicchio And Endive Salad

Servings: 4
Cooking Time: 7 Minutes
Ingredients:

- 1 (8-ounce) pork tenderloin
- salt and freshly ground black pepper
- ¼ cup flour
- 2 eggs, lightly beaten
- ¾ cup cracker meal
- 1 teaspoon paprika
- 1 teaspoon dry mustard
- 1 teaspoon garlic powder
- 1 teaspoon dried thyme
- 1 teaspoon salt
- vegetable or canola oil, in spray bottle
- Vinaigrette
- ¼ cup white balsamic vinegar
- 2 tablespoons agave syrup (or honey or maple syrup)
- 1 tablespoon Dijon mustard
- juice of ½ lemon
- 2 tablespoons chopped chervil or flat-leaf parsley
- salt and freshly ground black pepper
- ½ cup extra-virgin olive oil
- Radicchio and Endive Salad
- 1 heart romaine lettuce, torn into large pieces
- ½ head radicchio, coarsely chopped
- 2 heads endive, sliced
- ½ cup cherry tomatoes, halved
- 3 ounces fresh mozzarella, diced
- salt and freshly ground black pepper

Directions:

1. Slice the pork tenderloin into 1-inch slices. Using a meat pounder, pound the pork slices into thin ½-inch medallions. Generously season the pork with salt and freshly ground black pepper on both sides.
2. Set up a dredging station using three shallow dishes. Place the flour in one dish and the beaten eggs in a second dish. Combine the cracker meal, paprika, dry mustard, garlic powder, thyme and salt in a third dish.
3. Preheat the air fryer to 400°F (205°C).
4. Dredge the pork medallions in flour first and then into the beaten egg. Let the excess egg drip off and coat both sides of the medallions with the cracker meal crumb mixture. Spray both sides of the coated medallions with vegetable or canola oil.
5. Air-fry the medallions in two batches at 400°F (205°C) for 5 minutes. Once you have air-fried all the medallions, flip them all over and return the first batch of medallions back into the air fryer on top of the second batch. Air-fry at 400°F (205°C) for an additional 2 minutes.
6. While the medallions are cooking, make the salad and dressing. Whisk the white balsamic vinegar, agave syrup, Dijon mustard, lemon juice, chervil, salt and pepper together in a small bowl. Whisk in the olive oil slowly until combined and thickened.
7. Combine the romaine lettuce, radicchio, endive, cherry tomatoes, and mozzarella cheese in a large salad bowl. Drizzle the dressing over the vegetables and toss to combine. Season with salt and freshly ground black pepper.
8. Serve the pork medallions warm on or beside the salad.

Crispy Pork Pork Escalopes

Servings: 4
Cooking Time: 20 Minutes
Ingredients:

- 4 pork loin steaks
- Salt and pepper to taste
- ¼ cup flour
- 2 tbsp bread crumbs

Directions:

1. Preheat air fryer to 380°F (195°C). Season pork with salt and pepper. In one shallow bowl, add flour. In another, add bread crumbs. Dip the steaks first in the flour, then in the crumbs. Place them in the fryer and spray with oil. Bake for 12-14 minutes, flipping once until crisp. Serve.

Beef And Spinach Braciole

Servings: 4
Cooking Time: 92 Minutes
Ingredients:

- 7-inch oven-safe baking pan or casserole
- ½ onion, finely chopped
- 1 teaspoon olive oil
- ⅓ cup red wine
- 2 cups crushed tomatoes
- 1 teaspoon Italian seasoning
- ½ teaspoon garlic powder
- ¼ teaspoon crushed red pepper flakes
- 2 tablespoons chopped fresh parsley
- 2 top round steaks (about 1½ pounds)
- salt and freshly ground black pepper
- 2 cups fresh spinach, chopped
- 1 clove minced garlic
- ½ cup roasted red peppers, julienned
- ½ cup grated pecorino cheese
- ¼ cup pine nuts, toasted and rough chopped
- 2 tablespoons olive oil

Directions:

1. Preheat the air fryer to 400°F (205°C).
2. Toss the onions and olive oil together in a 7-inch metal baking pan or casserole dish. Air-fry at 400°F (205°C) for 5 minutes, stirring a couple times during the cooking process.

Add the red wine, crushed tomatoes, Italian seasoning, garlic powder, red pepper flakes and parsley and stir. Cover the pan tightly with aluminum foil, lower the air fryer temperature to 350°F (175°C) and continue to air-fry for 15 minutes.

3. While the sauce is simmering, prepare the beef. Using a meat mallet, pound the beef until it is ¼-inch thick. Season both sides of the beef with salt and pepper. Combine the spinach, garlic, red peppers, pecorino cheese, pine nuts and olive oil in a medium bowl. Season with salt and freshly ground black pepper. Spread the mixture evenly over the steaks. Starting at one of the short ends, roll the beef around the filling, tucking in the sides as you roll to ensure the filling is completely enclosed. Secure the beef rolls with toothpicks.

4. Remove the baking pan with the sauce from the air fryer and set it aside. Preheat the air fryer to 400°F (205°C).

5. Brush or spray the beef rolls with a little olive oil and air-fry at 400°F (205°C) for 12 minutes, rotating the beef during the cooking process for even browning. When the beef is browned, submerge the rolls into the sauce in the baking pan, cover the pan with foil and return it to the air fryer. Air-fry at 250°F (120°C) for 60 minutes.

6. Remove the beef rolls from the sauce. Cut each roll into slices and serve with pasta, ladling some of the sauce overtop.

Balsamic London Broil

Servings: 4
Cooking Time: 25 Minutes
Ingredients:
- 2 ½ lb top round London broil steak
- ¼ cup coconut aminos
- 1 tbsp balsamic vinegar
- 1 tbsp olive oil
- 1 tbsp mustard
- 2 tsp maple syrup
- 2 garlic cloves, minced
- 1 tsp dried oregano
- Salt and pepper to taste
- ¼ tsp smoked paprika
- 2 tbsp red onions, chopped

Directions:
1. Whisk coconut aminos, mustard, vinegar, olive oil, maple oregano, syrup, oregano garlic, red onions, salt, pepper, and paprika in a small bowl. Put the steak in a shallow container and pour the marinade over the steak. Cover and let sit for 20 minutes.

2. Preheat air fryer to 400°F (205°C). Transfer the steak to the frying basket and bake for 5 minutes. Flip the steak and bake for another 4 to 6 minutes. Allow sitting for 5 minutes before slicing. Serve warm and enjoy.

Meat Loaves

Servings: 4
Cooking Time: 19 Minutes
Ingredients:
- Sauce
- ¼ cup white vinegar
- ¼ cup brown sugar
- 2 tablespoons Worcestershire sauce
- ½ cup ketchup
- Meat Loaves
- 1 pound very lean ground beef
- ⅔ cup dry bread (approx. 1 slice torn into small pieces)
- 1 egg
- ⅓ cup minced onion
- 1 teaspoon salt
- 2 tablespoons ketchup

Directions:
1. In a small saucepan, combine all sauce ingredients and bring to a boil. Remove from heat and stir to ensure that brown sugar dissolves completely.

2. In a large bowl, combine the beef, bread, egg, onion, salt, and ketchup. Mix well.

3. Divide meat mixture into 4 portions and shape each into a thick, round patty. Patties will be about 3 to 3½ inches in diameter, and all four should fit easily into the air fryer basket at once.

4. Cook at 360°F (180°C) for 18 minutes, until meat is well done. Baste tops of mini loaves with a small amount of sauce, and cook 1 minute.

5. Serve hot with additional sauce on the side.

Stuffed Pork Chops

Servings: 4
Cooking Time: 12 Minutes
Ingredients:
- 4 boneless pork chops
- ½ teaspoon salt
- ½ teaspoon black pepper
- ¼ teaspoon paprika
- 1 cup frozen spinach, defrosted and squeezed dry
- 2 cloves garlic, minced
- 2 ounces cream cheese
- ¼ cup grated Parmesan cheese
- 1 tablespoon extra-virgin olive oil

Directions:
1. Pat the pork chops with a paper towel. Make a slit in the side of each pork chop to create a pouch.

2. Season the pork chops with the salt, pepper, and paprika

3. In a small bowl, mix together the spinach, garlic, cream cheese, and Parmesan cheese.

4. Divide the mixture into fourths and stuff the pork chop pouches. Secure the pouches with toothpicks.

5.   Preheat the air fryer to 400°F (205°C).

6.   Place the stuffed pork chops in the air fryer basket and spray liberally with cooking spray. Cook for 6 minutes, flip and coat with more cooking spray, and cook another 6 minutes. Check to make sure the meat is cooked to an internal temperature of 145°F (60°C). Cook the pork chops in batches, as needed.

Cajun Pork Loin Chops

Servings: 4
Cooking Time: 25 Minutes
Ingredients:
- 8 thin boneless pork loin chops
- ¾ tsp Coarse sea salt
- 1 egg, beaten
- 1 tsp Cajun seasoning
- ½ cup bread crumbs
- 1 cucumber, sliced
- 1 tomato, sliced

Directions:
1.   Place the chops between two sheets of parchment paper. Pound the pork to ¼-inch thickness using a meat mallet or rolling pin. Season with sea salt. In a shallow bowl, beat the egg with 1 tsp of water and Cajun seasoning. In a second bowl, add the breadcrumbs. Dip the chops into the egg mixture, shake, and dip into the crumbs.

2.   Preheat air fryer to 400°F (205°C). Place the chops in the greased frying basket and Air Fry for 6-8 minutes, flipping once until golden and cooked through. Serve immediately with cucumber and tomato.

Oktoberfest Bratwursts

Servings:4
Cooking Time: 35 Minutes
Ingredients:
- ½ onion, cut into half-moons
- 1 lb pork bratwurst links
- 2 cups beef broth
- 1 cup beer
- 2 cups drained sauerkraut
- 2 tbsp German mustard

Directions:
1.   Pierce each bratwurst with a fork twice. Place them along with beef broth, beer, 1 cup of water, and onion in a saucepan over high heat and bring to a boil. Lower the heat and simmer for 15 minutes. Drain.

2.   Preheat air fryer to 400ºF (205°C). Place bratwursts and onion in the frying basket and Air Fry for 3 minutes. Flip bratwursts, add the sauerkraut and cook for 3 more minutes. Serve warm with mustard on the side.

Meatloaf With Tangy Tomato Glaze

Servings: 6
Cooking Time: 50 Minutes
Ingredients:
- 1 pound ground beef
- ½ pound ground pork
- ½ pound ground veal (or turkey)
- 1 medium onion, diced
- 1 small clove of garlic, minced
- 2 egg yolks, lightly beaten
- ½ cup tomato ketchup
- 1 tablespoon Worcestershire sauce
- ½ cup plain breadcrumbs*
- 2 teaspoons salt
- freshly ground black pepper
- ½ cup chopped fresh parsley, plus more for garnish
- 6 tablespoons ketchup
- 1 tablespoon balsamic vinegar
- 2 tablespoons brown sugar

Directions:
1.   Combine the meats, onion, garlic, egg yolks, ketchup, Worcestershire sauce, breadcrumbs, salt, pepper and fresh parsley in a large bowl and mix well.

2.   Preheat the air fryer to 350°F (175°C) and pour a little water into the bottom of the air fryer drawer. (This will help prevent the grease that drips into the bottom drawer from burning and smoking.)

3.   Transfer the meatloaf mixture to the air fryer basket, packing it down gently. Run a spatula around the meatloaf to create a space about ½-inch wide between the meat and the side of the air fryer basket.

4.   Air-fry at 350°F (175°C) for 20 minutes. Carefully invert the meatloaf onto a plate (remember to remove the basket from the air fryer drawer so you don't pour all the grease out) and slide it back into the air fryer basket to turn it over. Re-shape the meatloaf with a spatula if necessary. Air-fry for another 20 minutes at 350°F (175°C).

5.   Combine the ketchup, balsamic vinegar and brown sugar in a bowl and spread the mixture over the meatloaf. Air-fry for another 10 minutes, until an instant read thermometer inserted into the center of the meatloaf registers 160°F (70°C).

6.   Allow the meatloaf to rest for a few more minutes and then transfer it to a serving platter using a spatula. Slice the meatloaf, sprinkle a little chopped parsley on top if desired, and serve.

Thyme Steak Finger Strips

Servings: 2

Cooking Time: 25 Minutes

Ingredients:

- ½ lb top sirloin strips
- 1 cup breadcrumbs
- ½ tsp garlic powder
- ½ tsp steak seasoning
- 2 eggs, beaten
- Salt and pepper to taste
- ½ tbsp dried thyme

Directions:

1. Preheat air fryer to 350°F（175°C）. Put the breadcrumbs, garlic powder, steak seasoning, thyme, salt, and pepper in a bowl and stir to combine. Add in the sirloin steak strips and toss to coat all sides. Dip into the beaten eggs, then dip again into the dry ingredients. Lay the coated steak pieces on the greased frying basket in an even layer. Air Fry for 16-18 minutes, turning once. Serve and enjoy!

Dijon Shrimp Cakes

Servings: 4
Cooking Time: 30 Minutes
Ingredients:

- 1 cup cooked shrimp, minced
- ¾ cup saltine cracker crumbs
- 1 cup lump crabmeat
- 3 green onions, chopped
- 1 egg, beaten
- ¼ cup mayonnaise
- 2 tbsp Dijon mustard
- 1 tbsp lemon juice

Directions:

1. Preheat the air fryer to 375°F (190°C). Combine the crabmeat, shrimp, green onions, egg, mayonnaise, mustard, ¼ cup of cracker crumbs, and the lemon juice in a bowl and mix gently. Make 4 patties, sprinkle with the rest of the cracker crumbs on both sides, and spray with cooking oil. Line the frying basket with a round parchment paper with holes poked in it. Coat the paper with cooking spray and lay the patties on it. Bake for 10-14 minutes or until the patties are golden brown. Serve warm.

Cheesy Tuna Tower

Servings:2
Cooking Time: 15 Minutes
Ingredients:

- ½ cup grated mozzarella
- 1 can tuna in water
- ¼ cup mayonnaise
- 2 tsp yellow mustard
- 1 tbsp minced dill pickle
- 1 tbsp minced celery
- 1 tbsp minced green onion
- Salt and pepper to taste
- 4 tomato slices
- 8 avocado slices

Directions:

1. Preheat air fryer to 350ºF (175°C). In a bowl, combine tuna, mayonnaise, mustard, pickle, celery, green onion, salt, and pepper. Cut a piece of parchment paper to fit the bottom of the frying basket. Place tomato slices on paper in a single layer and top with 2 avocado slices. Share tuna salad over avocado slices and top with mozzarella cheese. Place the towers in the frying basket and Bake for 4 minutes until the cheese starts to brown. Serve warm.

Rich Salmon Burgers With Broccoli Slaw

Servings: 4
Cooking Time: 25 Minutes
Ingredients:

- 1 lb salmon fillets
- 1 egg
- ¼ cup dill, chopped
- 1 cup bread crumbs
- Salt to taste
- ½ tsp cayenne pepper
- 1 lime, zested
- 1 tsp fish sauce
- 4 buns
- 3 cups chopped broccoli
- ½ cup shredded carrots
- ¼ cup sunflower seeds
- 2 garlic cloves, minced
- 1 cup Greek yogurt

Directions:

1. Preheat air fryer to 360°F (180°C). Blitz the salmon fillets in your food processor until they are finely chopped. Remove to a large bowl and add egg, dill, bread crumbs, salt, and cayenne. Stir to combine. Form the mixture into 4 patties. Put them into the frying basket and Bake for 10 minutes, flipping once. Combine broccoli, carrots, sunflower seeds, garlic, salt, lime, fish sauce, and Greek yogurt in a bowl. Serve the salmon burgers onto buns with broccoli slaw. Enjoy!

Southern Shrimp With Cocktail Sauce

Servings: 2
Cooking Time: 20 Minutes
Ingredients:

- ½ lb raw shrimp, tail on, deveined and shelled
- 1 cup ketchup
- 2 tbsp prepared horseradish
- 1 tbsp lemon juice
- ½ tsp Worcestershire sauce
- 1/8 tsp chili powder
- Salt and pepper to taste
- 1/3 cup flour
- 2 tbsp cornstarch
- ¼ cup milk
- 1 egg
- ½ cup bread crumbs
- 1 tbsp Cajun seasoning

- 1 lemon, cut into pieces

Directions:

1. In a small bowl, whisk the ketchup, horseradish, lemon juice, Worcestershire sauce, chili powder, salt, and pepper. Let chill covered in the fridge until ready to use. Preheat air fryer at 375°F (190°C). In a bowl, mix the flour, cornstarch, and salt. In another bowl, beat the milk and egg and in a third bowl, combine breadcrumbs and Cajun seasoning.

2. Roll the shrimp in the flour mixture, shake off excess flour. Then, dip in the egg, shake off excess egg. Finally, dredge in the breadcrumbs mixture. Place shrimp in the greased frying basket and Air Fry for 8 minutes, flipping once. Serve with cocktail sauce and lemon slices.

Bacon-wrapped Scallops

Servings: 4
Cooking Time: 8 Minutes

Ingredients:

- 16 large scallops
- 8 bacon strips
- ½ teaspoon black pepper
- ¼ teaspoon smoked paprika

Directions:

1. Pat the scallops dry with a paper towel. Slice each of the bacon strips in half. Wrap 1 bacon strip around 1 scallop and secure with a toothpick. Repeat with the remaining scallops. Season the scallops with pepper and paprika.

2. Preheat the air fryer to 350°F (175°C).

3. Place the bacon-wrapped scallops in the air fryer basket and cook for 4 minutes, shake the basket, cook another 3 minutes, shake the basket, and cook another 1 to 3 to minutes. When the bacon is crispy, the scallops should be cooked through and slightly firm, but not rubbery. Serve immediately.

The Best Oysters Rockefeller

Servings: 2
Cooking Time: 30 Minutes

Ingredients:

- 4 tsp grated Parmesan
- 2 tbsp butter
- 1 sweet onion, minced
- 1 clove garlic, minced
- 1 cup baby spinach
- ⅛ tsp Tabasco hot sauce
- ½ tsp lemon juice
- ½ tsp lemon zest
- ¼ cup bread crumbs
- 12 oysters, on the half shell

Directions:

1. Melt butter in a skillet over medium heat. Stir in onion, garlic, and spinach and stir-fry for 3 minutes until the onion is translucent. Mix in Parmesan cheese, hot sauce, lemon juice, lemon zest, and bread crumbs. Divide this mixture between the tops of oysters.

2. Preheat air fryer to 400°F (205°C). Place oysters in the frying basket and Air Fry for 6 minutes. Serve immediately.

Fried Oysters

Servings: 12
Cooking Time: 8 Minutes

Ingredients:

- 1½ cups All-purpose flour
- 1½ cups Yellow cornmeal
- 1½ tablespoons Cajun dried seasoning blend (for a homemade blend, see here)
- 1¼ cups, plus more if needed Amber beer, pale ale, or IPA
- 12 Large shucked oysters, any liquid drained off
- Vegetable oil spray

Directions:

1. Preheat the air fryer to 400°F (205°C).

2. Whisk ⅔ cup of the flour, ½ cup of the cornmeal, and the seasoning blend in a bowl until uniform. Set aside.

3. Whisk the remaining ⅓ cup flour and the remaining ½ cup cornmeal with the beer in a second bowl, adding more beer in dribs and drabs until the mixture is the consistency of pancake batter.

4. Using a fork, dip a shucked oyster in the beer batter, coating it thoroughly. Gently shake off any excess batter, then set the oyster in the dry mixture and turn gently to coat well and evenly. Set the coated oyster on a cutting board and continue dipping and coating the remainder of the oysters.

5. Coat the oysters with vegetable oil spray, then set them in the basket with as much air space between them as possible. Air-fry undisturbed for 8 minutes, or until lightly browned and crisp.

6. Use a nonstick-safe spatula to transfer the oysters to a wire rack. Cool for a couple of minutes before serving.

Potato-wrapped Salmon Fillets

Servings: 3
Cooking Time: 8 Minutes

Ingredients:

- 1 Large 1-pound elongated yellow potato(es), peeled
- 3 6-ounce, 1½-inch-wide, quite thick skinless salmon fillets
- Olive oil spray
- ¼ teaspoon Table salt
- ¼ teaspoon Ground black pepper

Directions:
1. Preheat the air fryer to 400°F (205°C).
2. Use a vegetable peeler or mandoline to make long strips from the potato(es). You'll need anywhere from 8 to 12 strips per fillet, depending on the shape of the potato and of the salmon fillet.
3. Drape potato strips over a salmon fillet, overlapping the strips to create an even "crust." Tuck the potato strips under the fillet, overlapping the strips underneath to create as smooth a bottom as you can. Wrap the remaining fillet(s) in the same way.
4. Gently turn the fillets over. Generously coat the bottoms with olive oil spray. Turn them back seam side down and generously coat the tops with the oil spray. Sprinkle the salt and pepper over the wrapped fillets.
5. Use a nonstick-safe spatula to gently transfer the fillets seam side down to the basket. It helps to remove the basket from the machine and set it on your work surface (keeping in mind that the basket's hot). Leave as much air space as possible between the fillets. Air-fry undisturbed for 8 minutes, or until golden brown and crisp.
6. Use a nonstick-safe spatula to gently transfer the fillets to serving plates. Cool for a couple of minutes before serving.

Baltimore Crab Cakes
Servings: 4
Cooking Time: 35 Minutes
Ingredients:
- ½ lb lump crabmeat, shells discarded
- 2 tbsp mayonnaise
- ½ tsp yellow mustard
- ½ tsp lemon juice
- ½ tbsp minced shallot
- ¼ cup bread crumbs
- 1 egg
- Salt and pepper to taste
- 4 poached eggs
- ½ cup bechamel sauce
- 2 tsp chopped chives
- 1 lemon, cut into wedges
Directions:
1. Preheat air fryer at 400°F (205°C). Combine all ingredients, except eggs, sauce, and chives, in a bowl. Form mixture into 4 patties. Place crab cakes in the greased frying basket and Air Fry for 10 minutes, flipping once. Transfer them to a serving dish. Top each crab cake with 1 poached egg, drizzle with Bechamel sauce and scatter with chives and lemon wedges. Serve and enjoy!

Crab Cakes On A Budget
Servings: 4
Cooking Time: 12 Minutes

Ingredients:
- 8 ounces imitation crabmeat
- 4 ounces leftover cooked fish (such as cod, pollock, or haddock)
- 2 tablespoons minced green onion
- 2 tablespoons minced celery
- ¾ cup crushed saltine cracker crumbs
- 2 tablespoons light mayonnaise
- 1 teaspoon prepared yellow mustard
- 1 tablespoon Worcestershire sauce, plus 2 teaspoons
- 2 teaspoons dried parsley flakes
- ½ teaspoon dried dill weed, crushed
- ½ teaspoon garlic powder
- ½ teaspoon Old Bay Seasoning
- ½ cup panko breadcrumbs
- oil for misting or cooking spray
Directions:
1. Use knives or a food processor to finely shred crabmeat and fish.
2. In a large bowl, combine all ingredients except panko and oil. Stir well.
3. Shape into 8 small, fat patties.
4. Carefully roll patties in panko crumbs to coat. Spray both sides with oil or cooking spray.
5. Place patties in air fryer basket and cook at 390°F (200°C) for 12 minutes or until golden brown and crispy.

British Fish & Chips
Servings: 4
Cooking Time: 40 Minutes
Ingredients:
- 2 peeled russet potatoes, thinly sliced
- 1 egg white
- 1 tbsp lemon juice
- 1/3 cup ground almonds
- 2 bread slices, crumbled
- ½ tsp dried basil
- 4 haddock fillets
Directions:
1. Preheat air fryer to 390°F (200°C). Lay the potato slices in the frying basket and Air Fry for 11-15 minutes. Turn the fries a couple of times while cooking. While the fries are cooking, whisk the egg white and lemon juice together in a bowl. On a plate, combine the almonds, breadcrumbs, and basil. First, one at a time, dip the fillets into the egg mix and then coat in the almond/breadcrumb mix. Lay the fillets on a wire rack until the fries are done. Preheat the oven to 350°F (175°C). After the fries are done, move them to a pan and place in the oven to keep warm. Put the fish in the frying basket and Air Fry for 10-14 minutes or until cooked through, golden, and crispy. Serve with the fries.

Basil Crab Cakes With Fresh Salad

Servings:2
Cooking Time: 25 Minutes
Ingredients:

- 8 oz lump crabmeat
- 2 tbsp mayonnaise
- ½ tsp Dijon mustard
- ½ tsp lemon juice
- ½ tsp lemon zest
- 2 tsp minced yellow onion
- ¼ tsp prepared horseradish
- ¼ cup flour
- 1 egg white, beaten
- 1 tbsp basil, minced
- 1 tbsp olive oil
- 2 tsp white wine vinegar
- Salt and pepper to taste
- 4 oz arugula
- ½ cup blackberries
- ¼ cup pine nuts
- 2 lemon wedges

Directions:

1. Preheat air fryer to 400ºF（205°C）. Combine the crabmeat, mayonnaise, mustard, lemon juice and zest, onion, horseradish, flour, egg white, and basil in a bowl. Form mixture into 4 patties. Place the patties in the lightly greased frying basket and Air Fry for 10 minutes, flipping once. Combine olive oil, vinegar, salt, and pepper in a bowl. Toss in the arugula and share into 2 medium bowls. Add 2 crab cakes to each bowl and scatter with blackberries, pine nuts, and lemon wedges. Serve warm.

Firecracker Popcorn Shrimp

Servings: 6
Cooking Time: 8 Minutes
Ingredients:

- ½ cup all-purpose flour
- 2 teaspoons ground paprika
- 1 teaspoon garlic powder
- ½ teaspoon black pepper
- ¼ teaspoon salt
- 2 eggs, whisked
- 1½ cups panko breadcrumbs
- 1 pound small shrimp, peeled and deveined

Directions:

1. Preheat the air fryer to 360°F（180°C）.
2. In a medium bowl, place the flour and mix in the paprika, garlic powder, pepper, and salt.
3. In a shallow dish, place the eggs.
4. In a third dish, place the breadcrumbs.

5. Assemble the shrimp by covering them in the flour, then dipping them into the egg, and then coating them with the breadcrumbs. Repeat until all the shrimp are covered in the breading.
6. Liberally spray the metal trivet that fits in the air fryer basket with olive oil mist. Place the shrimp onto the trivet, leaving space between the shrimp to flip. Cook for 4 minutes, flip the shrimp, and cook another 4 minutes. Repeat until all the shrimp are cooked.
7. Serve warm with desired dipping sauce.

King Prawns Al Ajillo

Servings: 4
Cooking Time: 15 Minutes
Ingredients:

- 1 ¼ lb peeled king prawns, deveined
- ½ cup grated Parmesan
- 1 tbsp olive oil
- 1 tbsp lemon juice
- ½ tsp garlic powder
- 2 garlic cloves, minced

Directions:

1. Preheat the air fryer to 350°F（175°C）. In a large bowl, add the prawns and sprinkle with olive oil, lemon juice, and garlic powder. Toss in the minced garlic and Parmesan, then toss to coat. Put the prawns in the frying basket and Air Fry for 10-15 minutes or until the prawns cook through. Shake the basket once while cooking. Serve immediately.

Malaysian Shrimp With Sambal Mayo

Servings: 4
Cooking Time: 30 Minutes
Ingredients:

- 24 jumbo shrimp, peeled and deveined
- 2/3 cup panko bread crumbs
- 3 tbsp mayonnaise
- 1 tbsp sambal oelek paste
- 2/3 cup shredded coconut
- 1 lime, zested
- ½ tsp ground coriander
- Salt to taste
- 2 tbsp flour
- 2 eggs

Directions:

1. Mix together mayonnaise and sambal oelek in a bowl. Set aside. In another bowl, stir together coconut, lime, coriander, panko bread crumbs, and salt. In a shallow bowl, add flour. In another shallow bowl, whisk eggs until blended. Season shrimp with salt. First, dip the shrimp into the flour, shake, and dip into the egg mix. Dip again in the coconut

mix. Gently press the coconut and panko to the shrimp. Preheat air fryer to 360°F（180°C）. Put the shrimp in the greased frying basket and Air Fry for 8 minutes, flipping once until the crust is golden and the shrimp is cooked. Serve alongside the sweet chili mayo.

Hot Calamari Rings

Servings: 4
Cooking Time: 25 Minutes
Ingredients:

- ½ cup all-purpose flour
- 2 tsp hot chili powder
- 2 eggs
- 1 tbsp milk
- 1 cup bread crumbs
- Salt and pepper to taste
- 1 lb calamari rings
- 1 lime, quartered
- ½ cup aioli sauce

Directions:

1. Preheat air fryer at 400ºF（205°C）. In a shallow bowl, add flour and hot chili powder. In another bowl, mix the eggs and milk. In a third bowl, mix the breadcrumbs, salt and pepper. Dip calamari rings in flour mix first, then in eggs mix and shake off excess. Then, roll ring through breadcrumb mixture. Place calamari rings in the greased frying basket and Air Fry for 4 minutes, tossing once. Squeeze lime quarters over calamari. Serve with aioli sauce.

Holiday Shrimp Scampi

Servings: 4
Cooking Time: 25 Minutes
Ingredients:

- 1 ½ lb peeled shrimp, deveined
- ¼ tsp lemon pepper seasoning
- 6 garlic cloves, minced
- 1 tsp salt
- ½ tsp grated lemon zest
- 3 tbsp fresh lemon juice
- 3 tbsp sunflower oil
- 3 tbsp butter
- 2 tsp fresh thyme leaves
- 1 lemon, cut into wedges

Directions:

1. Preheat the air fryer to 400°F（205°C）. Combine the shrimp and garlic in a cake pan, then sprinkle with salt and lemon pepper seasoning. Toss to coat, then add the lemon zest, lemon juice, oil, and butter. Place the cake pan in the frying basket and Bake for 10-13 minutes, stirring once until no longer pink. Sprinkle with thyme leaves. Serve hot with lemon wedges on the side.

Fish Tacos With Jalapeño-lime Sauce

Servings: 4
Cooking Time: 7 Minutes
Ingredients:

- Fish Tacos
- 1 pound fish fillets
- ¼ teaspoon cumin
- ¼ teaspoon coriander
- ⅛ teaspoon ground red pepper
- 1 tablespoon lime zest
- ¼ teaspoon smoked paprika
- 1 teaspoon oil
- cooking spray
- 6–8 corn or flour tortillas (6-inch size)
- Jalapeño-Lime Sauce
- ½ cup sour cream
- 1 tablespoon lime juice
- ¼ teaspoon grated lime zest
- ½ teaspoon minced jalapeño (flesh only)
- ¼ teaspoon cumin
- Napa Cabbage Garnish
- 1 cup shredded Napa cabbage
- ¼ cup slivered red or green bell pepper
- ¼ cup slivered onion

Directions:

1. Slice the fish fillets into strips approximately ½-inch thick.
2. Put the strips into a sealable plastic bag along with the cumin, coriander, red pepper, lime zest, smoked paprika, and oil. Massage seasonings into the fish until evenly distributed.
3. Spray air fryer basket with nonstick cooking spray and place seasoned fish inside.
4. Cook at 390°F（200°C） for approximately 5minutes. Shake basket to distribute fish. Cook an additional 2 minutes, until fish flakes easily.
5. While the fish is cooking, prepare the Jalapeño-Lime Sauce by mixing the sour cream, lime juice, lime zest, jalapeño, and cumin together to make a smooth sauce. Set aside.
6. Mix the cabbage, bell pepper, and onion together and set aside.
7. To warm refrigerated tortillas, wrap in damp paper towels and microwave for 30 to 60 seconds.
8. To serve, spoon some of fish into a warm tortilla. Add one or two tablespoons Napa Cabbage Garnish and drizzle with Jalapeño-Lime Sauce.

Mediterranean Salmon Cakes

Servings: 4
Cooking Time: 30 Minutes
Ingredients:
- ¼ cup heavy cream
- 5 tbsp mayonnaise
- 2 cloves garlic, minced
- ¼ tsp caper juice
- 2 tsp lemon juice
- 1 tbsp capers
- 1 can salmon
- 2 tsp lemon zest
- 1 egg
- ¼ minced red bell peppers
- ½ cup flour
- ⅛ tsp salt
- 2 tbsp sliced green olives

Directions:
1. Combine heavy cream, 2 tbsp of mayonnaise, garlic, caper juices, capers, and lemon juice in a bowl. Place the resulting caper sauce in the fridge until ready to use.
2. Preheat air fryer to 400ºF (205°C). Combine canned salmon, lemon zest, egg, remaining mayo, bell peppers, flour, and salt in a bowl. Form into 8 patties. Place the patties in the greased frying basket and Air Fry for 10 minutes, turning once. Let rest for 5 minutes before drizzling with lemon sauce. Garnish with green olives to serve.

Maple Balsamic Glazed Salmon

Servings: 4
Cooking Time: 10 Minutes
Ingredients:
- 4 (6-ounce) fillets of salmon
- salt and freshly ground black pepper
- vegetable oil
- ¼ cup pure maple syrup
- 3 tablespoons balsamic vinegar
- 1 teaspoon Dijon mustard

Directions:
1. Preheat the air fryer to 400°F (205°C).
2. Season the salmon well with salt and freshly ground black pepper. Spray or brush the bottom of the air fryer basket with vegetable oil and place the salmon fillets inside. Air-fry the salmon for 5 minutes.
3. While the salmon is air-frying, combine the maple syrup, balsamic vinegar and Dijon mustard in a small saucepan over medium heat and stir to blend well. Let the mixture simmer while the fish is cooking. It should start to thicken slightly, but keep your eye on it so it doesn't burn.
4. Brush the glaze on the salmon fillets and air-fry for an additional 5 minutes. The salmon should feel firm to the

touch when finished and the glaze should be nicely browned on top. Brush a little more glaze on top before removing and serving with rice and vegetables, or a nice green salad.

Mojo Sea Bass

Servings: 2
Cooking Time: 15 Minutes
Ingredients:
- 1 tbsp butter, melted
- ¼ tsp chili powder
- 2 cloves garlic, minced
- 1 tbsp lemon juice
- ¼ tsp salt
- 2 sea bass fillets
- 2 tsp chopped cilantro

Directions:
1. Preheat air fryer to 370ºF (185°C). Whisk the butter, chili powder, garlic, lemon juice, and salt in a bowl. Rub mixture over the tops of each fillet. Place the fillets in the frying basket and Air Fry for 7 minutes. Let rest for 5 minutes. Divide between 2 plates and garnish with cilantro to serve.

Popcorn Crawfish

Servings: 4
Cooking Time: 18 Minutes
Ingredients:
- ½ cup flour, plus 2 tablespoons
- ½ teaspoon garlic powder
- 1½ teaspoons Old Bay Seasoning
- ½ teaspoon onion powder
- ½ cup beer, plus 2 tablespoons
- 12-ounce package frozen crawfish tail meat, thawed and drained
- oil for misting or cooking spray
- Coating
- 1½ cups panko crumbs
- 1 teaspoon Old Bay Seasoning
- ½ teaspoon ground black pepper

Directions:
1. In a large bowl, mix together the flour, garlic powder, Old Bay Seasoning, and onion powder. Stir in beer to blend.
2. Add crawfish meat to batter and stir to coat.
3. Combine the coating ingredients in food processor and pulse to finely crush the crumbs. Transfer crumbs to shallow dish.
4. Preheat air fryer to 390°F (200°C).
5. Pour the crawfish and batter into a colander to drain. Stir with a spoon to drain excess batter.
6. Working with a handful of crawfish at a time, roll in crumbs and place on a cookie sheet. It's okay if some of the smaller pieces of crawfish meat stick together.

7. Spray breaded crawfish with oil or cooking spray and place all at once into air fryer basket.

8. Cook at 390°F (20°C) for 5minutes. Shake basket or stir and mist again with olive oil or spray. Cook 5 moreminutes, shake basket again, and mist lightly again. Continue cooking 5 more minutes, until browned and crispy.

Almond Topped Trout

Servings: 4
Cooking Time: 20 Minutes
Ingredients:
- 4 trout fillets
- 2 tbsp olive oil
- Salt and pepper to taste
- 2 garlic cloves, sliced
- 1 lemon, sliced
- 1 tbsp flaked almonds

Directions:
1. Preheat air fryer to 380°F (195°C). Lightly brush each fillet with olive oil on both sides and season with salt and pepper. Put the fillets in a single layer in the frying basket. Put the sliced garlic over the tops of the trout fillets, then top with lemon slices and cook for 12-15 minutes. Serve topped with flaked almonds and enjoy!

Crabmeat-stuffed Flounder

Servings:3
Cooking Time: 12 Minutes
Ingredients:
- 4½ ounces Purchased backfin or claw crabmeat, picked over for bits of shell and cartilage
- 6 Saltine crackers, crushed into fine crumbs
- 2 tablespoons plus 1 teaspoon Regular or low-fat mayonnaise (not fat-free)
- ¾ teaspoon Yellow prepared mustard
- 1½ teaspoons Worcestershire sauce
- ⅛ teaspoon Celery salt
- 3 5- to 6-ounce skinless flounder fillets
- Vegetable oil spray
- Mild paprika

Directions:
1. Preheat the air fryer to 400°F (205°C).
2. Gently mix the crabmeat, crushed saltines, mayonnaise, mustard, Worcestershire sauce, and celery salt in a bowl until well combined.
3. Generously coat the flat side of a fillet with vegetable oil spray. Set the fillet sprayed side down on your work surface. Cut the fillet in half widthwise, then cut one of the halves in half lengthwise. Set a scant ⅓ cup of the crabmeat mixture on top of the undivided half of the fish fillet, mounding the mixture to make an oval that somewhat fits the shape of the fillet with at least a ¼-inch border of fillet beyond the filling all around.

4. Take the two thin divided quarters (that is, the halves of the half) and lay them lengthwise over the filling, overlapping at each end and leaving a little space in the middle where the filling peeks through. Coat the top of the stuffed flounder piece with vegetable oil spray, then sprinkle paprika over the stuffed flounder fillet. Set aside and use the remaining fillet(s) to make more stuffed flounder "packets," repeating steps 3 and

5. Use a nonstick-safe spatula to transfer the stuffed flounder fillets to the basket. Leave as much space between them as possible. Air-fry undisturbed for 12 minutes, or until lightly brown and firm (but not hard).

6. Use that same spatula, plus perhaps another one, to transfer the fillets to a serving platter or plates. Cool for a minute or two, then serve hot.

Holliday Lobster Salad

Servings:2
Cooking Time: 20 Minutes
Ingredients:
- 2 lobster tails
- ¼ cup mayonnaise
- 2 tsp lemon juice
- 1 stalk celery, sliced
- 2 tsp chopped chives
- 2 tsp chopped tarragon
- Salt and pepper to taste
- 2 tomato slices
- 4 cucumber slices
- 1 avocado, diced

Directions:
1. Preheat air fryer to 400ºF (205°C). Using kitchen shears, cut down the middle of each lobster tail on the softer side. Carefully run your finger between the lobster meat and the shell to loosen meat. Place lobster tails, cut sides up, in the frying basket, and Air Fry for 8 minutes. Transfer to a large plate and let cool for 3 minutes until easy to handle, then pull lobster meat from the shell and roughly chop it. Combine chopped lobster, mayonnaise, lemon juice, celery, chives, tarragon, salt, and pepper in a bowl. Divide between 2 medium plates and top with tomato slices, cucumber and avocado cubes. Serve immediately.

Herby Prawn & Zucchini Bake

Servings: 4
Cooking Time: 30 Minutes
Ingredients:
- 1 ¼ lb prawns, peeled and deveined
- 2 zucchini, sliced
- 2 tbsp butter, melted

- ½ tsp garlic salt
- 1 ½ tsp dried oregano
- ⅛ tsp red pepper flakes
- ½ lemon, juiced
- 1 tbsp chopped mint
- 1 tbsp chopped dill

Directions:

1. Preheat air fryer to 350°F (175°C). Combine prawns, zucchini, butter, garlic salt, oregano, and pepper flakes in a large bowl. Toss to coat. Put the prawns and zucchini in the greased frying basket and Air Fry for about 6-8 minutes, shaking the basket once until the zucchini is golden and the shrimp are cooked. Remove the shrimp to a serving plate and cover with foil. Serve hot topped with lemon juice, mint, and dill. Enjoy!

Spiced Shrimp Empanadas

Servings: 5
Cooking Time: 30 Minutes
Ingredients:

- ½ lb peeled and deveined shrimp, chopped
- 2 tbsp diced red bell peppers
- 1 shallot, minced
- 1 scallion, chopped
- 2 garlic cloves, minced
- 2 tbsp chopped cilantro
- ½ tbsp lemon juice
- ¼ tsp sweet paprika
- ⅛ tsp salt
- ⅛ tsp red pepper flakes
- ¼ tsp ground nutmeg
- 1 large egg, beaten
- 10 empanada discs

Directions:

1. Combine all ingredients, except the egg and empanada discs, in a bowl. Toss to coat. Beat the 1 egg with 1 tsp of water in a small bowl until blended. Set aside.

2. On your work board, place one empanada disc. Add 2 tbsp of shrimp mixture in the middle. Brush the edges of the disc with the egg mixture. Fold the disc in half and seal the edges. Crimp with a fork by pressing around the edges. Brush the tops with the egg mixture. Preheat air fryer to 380°F (195°C). Put the empanadas in the greased frying basket and Air Fry for 9 minutes, flipping once until golden and crispy. Serve hot.

Easy Scallops With Lemon Butter

Servings:3
Cooking Time: 4 Minutes
Ingredients:

- 1 tablespoon Olive oil
- 2 teaspoons Minced garlic
- 1 teaspoon Finely grated lemon zest
- ½ teaspoon Red pepper flakes
- ¼ teaspoon Table salt
- 1 pound Sea scallops
- 3 tablespoons Butter, melted
- 1½ tablespoons Lemon juice

Directions:

1. Preheat the air fryer to 400°F (205°C).

2. Gently stir the olive oil, garlic, lemon zest, red pepper flakes, and salt in a bowl. Add the scallops and stir very gently until they are evenly and well coated.

3. When the machine is at temperature, arrange the scallops in a single layer in the basket. Some may touch. Air-fry undisturbed for 4 minutes, or until the scallops are opaque and firm.

4. While the scallops cook, stir the melted butter and lemon juice in a serving bowl. When the scallops are ready, pour them from the basket into this bowl. Toss well before serving.

Yummy Salmon Burgers With Salsa Rosa

Servings: 4
Cooking Time: 35 Minutes + Chilling Time
Ingredients:

- ¼ cup minced red onion
- ¼ cup slivered onions
- ½ cup mayonnaise
- 2 tsp ketchup
- 1 tsp brandy
- 2 tsp orange juice
- 1 lb salmon fillets
- 5 tbsp panko bread crumbs
- 1 garlic clove, minced
- 1 large egg, lightly beaten
- 1 tbsp Dijon mustard
- 1 tsp fresh lemon juice
- 1 tbsp chopped parsley
- Salt to taste
- 4 buns
- 8 Boston lettuce leaves

Directions:

1. Mix the mayonnaise, ketchup, brandy, and orange juice in a bowl until blended. Set aside the resulting salsa rosa until ready to serve. Cut a 4-oz section of salmon and place in a food processor. Pulse until it turns into a paste. Chop the remaining salmon into cubes and transfer to a bowl along with the salmon paste. Add the panko, minced onion, garlic, egg, mustard, lemon juice, parsley, and salt. Toss to

combine. Divide into 5 patties about ¾-inch thick. Refrigerate for 30 minutes.

2. Preheat air fryer to 400°F (200°C). Place the patties in the greased frying basket. Air Fry for 12-14 minutes, flipping once until golden. Serve each patty on a bun, 2 lettuce leaves, 2 tbsp of salsa rosa, and slivered onions. Enjoy!

Coconut-shrimp Po' Boys

Servings: 4
Cooking Time: 5 Minutes
Ingredients:
- ½ cup cornstarch
- 2 eggs
- 2 tablespoons milk
- ¾ cup shredded coconut
- ½ cup panko breadcrumbs
- 1 pound (31–35 count) shrimp, peeled and deveined
- Old Bay Seasoning
- oil for misting or cooking spray
- 2 large hoagie rolls
- honey mustard or light mayonnaise
- 1½ cups shredded lettuce
- 1 large tomato, thinly sliced

Directions:
1. Place cornstarch in a shallow dish or plate.
2. In another shallow dish, beat together eggs and milk.
3. In a third dish mix the coconut and panko crumbs.
4. Sprinkle shrimp with Old Bay Seasoning to taste.
5. Dip shrimp in cornstarch to coat lightly, dip in egg mixture, shake off excess, and roll in coconut mixture to coat well.
6. Spray both sides of coated shrimp with oil or cooking spray.
7. Cook half the shrimp in a single layer at 390°F (200°C) for 5minutes.
8. Repeat to cook remaining shrimp.
9. To Assemble
10. Split each hoagie lengthwise, leaving one long edge intact.
11. Place in air fryer basket and cook at 390°F (200°C) for 1 to 2minutes or until heated through.
12. Remove buns, break apart, and place on 4 plates, cut side up.
13. Spread with honey mustard and/or mayonnaise.
14. Top with shredded lettuce, tomato slices, and coconut shrimp.

Flounder Fillets

Servings: 4
Cooking Time: 8 Minutes
Ingredients:

- 1 egg white
- 1 tablespoon water
- 1 cup panko breadcrumbs
- 2 tablespoons extra-light virgin olive oil
- 4 4-ounce flounder fillets
- salt and pepper
- oil for misting or cooking spray

Directions:
1. Preheat air fryer to 390°F (200°C).
2. Beat together egg white and water in shallow dish.
3. In another shallow dish, mix panko crumbs and oil until well combined and crumbly (best done by hand).
4. Season flounder fillets with salt and pepper to taste. Dip each fillet into egg mixture and then roll in panko crumbs, pressing in crumbs so that fish is nicely coated.
5. Spray air fryer basket with nonstick cooking spray and add fillets. Cook at 390°F (200°C) for 3minutes.
6. Spray fish fillets but do not turn. Cook 5 minutes longer or until golden brown and crispy. Using a spatula, carefully remove fish from basket and serve.

Stuffed Shrimp Wrapped In Bacon

Servings:4
Cooking Time: 30 Minutes
Ingredients:
- 1 lb shrimp, deveined and shelled
- 3 tbsp crumbled goat cheese
- 2 tbsp panko bread crumbs
- ¼ tsp soy sauce
- ½ tsp prepared horseradish
- ¼ tsp garlic powder
- ½ tsp chili powder
- 2 tsp mayonnaise
- Black pepper to taste
- 5 slices bacon, quartered
- ¼ cup chopped parsley

Directions:
1. Preheat air fryer to 400°F (205°C). Butterfly shrimp by cutting down the spine of each shrimp without going all the way through. Combine the goat cheese, bread crumbs, soy sauce, horseradish, garlic powder, chili powder, mayonnaise, and black pepper in a bowl. Evenly press goat cheese mixture into shrimp. Wrap a piece of bacon around each piece of shrimp to hold in the cheese mixture. Place them in the frying basket and Air Fry for 8-10 minutes, flipping once. Top with parsley to serve.

Fish Tacos With Hot Coleslaw

Servings: 4
Cooking Time: 25 Minutes
Ingredients:

- 2 cups shredded green cabbage
- ½ red onion, thinly sliced
- 1 jalapeño, thinly sliced
- 1 tsp lemon juice
- 1 tbsp chives, chopped
- 3 tbsp mayonnaise
- 1 tbsp hot sauce
- 2 tbsp chopped cilantro
- 1 tbsp apple cider vinegar
- Salt to taste
- 1 large egg, beaten
- 1 cup crushed tortilla chips
- 1 lb cod fillets, cubed
- 8 corn tortillas

Directions:

1. Mix the lemon juice, chives, mayonnaise, and hot sauce in a bowl until blended. Add the cabbage to a large bowl. Then add onion, jalapeño, cilantro, vinegar and salt. Toss until well mixed. Put in the fridge until ready to serve.
2. Preheat air fryer to 360°F（180°C）. In one shallow bowl, add the beaten egg. In another shallow bowl, add the crushed tortilla chips. Salt the cod, then dip into the egg mixture. Allow excess to drip off. Next, dip into the crumbs, gently pressing into the crumbs. Place the fish in the greased frying basket and Air Fry for 6 minutes, flipping once until crispy and completely cooked. Place 2 warm tortillas on each plate. Top with cod cubes, ¼ cup of slaw, and drizzle with spicy mayo. Serve and enjoy!

Catalan-style Crab Samfaina

Servings: 4
Cooking Time: 30 Minutes
Ingredients:

- 1 peeled eggplant, cubed
- 1 zucchini, cubed
- 1 onion, chopped
- 1 red bell pepper, chopped
- 2 large tomatoes, chopped
- 1 tbsp olive oil
- ½ tsp dried thyme
- ½ tsp dried basil
- Salt and pepper to taste
- 1 ½ cups cooked crab meat

Directions:

1. Preheat air fryer to 400°F（205°C）. In a pan, mix together all ingredients, except the crabmeat. Place the pan

in the air fryer and Bake for 9 minutes. Remove the bowl and stir in the crabmeat. Return to the air fryer and roast for another 2-5 minutes until the vegetables are tender and ratatouille bubbling. Serve hot.

Shrimp "scampi"

Servings:4
Cooking Time: 5 Minutes
Ingredients:

- 1½ pounds Large shrimp (20–25 per pound), peeled and deveined
- ¼ cup Olive oil
- 2 tablespoons Minced garlic
- 1 teaspoon Dried oregano
- Up to 1 teaspoon Red pepper flakes
- ½ teaspoon Table salt
- 2 tablespoons White balsamic vinegar (see here)

Directions:

1. Preheat the air fryer to 400°F（205°C）.
2. Stir the shrimp, olive oil, garlic, oregano, red pepper flakes, and salt in a large bowl until the shrimp are well coated.
3. When the machine is at temperature, transfer the shrimp to the basket. They will overlap and even sit on top of each other. Air-fry for 5 minutes, tossing and rearranging the shrimp twice to make sure the covered surfaces are exposed, until pink and firm.
4. Pour the contents of the basket into a serving bowl. Pour the vinegar over the shrimp while hot and toss to coat.

Beer-breaded Halibut Fish Tacos

Servings: 4
Cooking Time: 10 Minutes
Ingredients:

- 1 pound halibut, cut into 1-inch strips
- 1 cup light beer
- 1 jalapeño, minced and divided
- 1 clove garlic, minced
- ¼ teaspoon ground cumin
- ½ cup cornmeal
- ¼ cup all-purpose flour
- 1¼ teaspoons sea salt, divided
- 2 cups shredded cabbage
- 1 lime, juiced and divided
- ¼ cup Greek yogurt
- ¼ cup mayonnaise
- 1 cup grape tomatoes, quartered
- ½ cup chopped cilantro
- ¼ cup chopped onion
- 1 egg, whisked

- 8 corn tortillas

Directions:

1. In a shallow baking dish, place the fish, the beer, 1 teaspoon of the minced jalapeño, the garlic, and the cumin. Cover and refrigerate for 30 minutes.

2. Meanwhile, in a medium bowl, mix together the cornmeal, flour, and ½ teaspoon of the salt.

3. In large bowl, mix together the shredded cabbage, 1 tablespoon of the lime juice, the Greek yogurt, the mayonnaise, and ½ teaspoon of the salt.

4. In a small bowl, make the pico de gallo by mixing together the tomatoes, cilantro, onion, ¼ teaspoon of the salt, the remaining jalapeño, and the remaining lime juice.

5. Remove the fish from the refrigerator and discard the marinade. Dredge the fish in the whisked egg; then dredge the fish in the cornmeal flour mixture, until all pieces of fish have been breaded.

6. Preheat the air fryer to 350°F (175°C).

7. Place the fish in the air fryer basket and spray liberally with cooking spray. Cook for 6 minutes, flip and shake the fish, and cook another 4 minutes.

8. While the fish is cooking, heat the tortillas in a heavy skillet for 1 to 2 minutes over high heat.

9. To assemble the tacos, place the battered fish on the heated tortillas, and top with slaw and pico de gallo. Serve immediately.

Southeast Asian-style Tuna Steaks

Servings: 4
Cooking Time: 20 Minutes
Ingredients:

- 1 stalk lemongrass, bent in half
- 4 tuna steaks
- 2 tbsp soy sauce
- 2 tsp sesame oil
- 2 tsp rice wine vinegar
- 1 tsp grated fresh ginger
- ⅛ tsp pepper
- 3 tbsp lemon juice
- 2 tbsp chopped cilantro
- 1 sliced red chili

Directions:

1. Preheat air fryer to 390°F (200°C). Place the tuna steak on a shallow plate. Mix together soy sauce, sesame oil, rice wine vinegar, and ginger in a small bowl. Pour over the tuna, rubbing the marinade gently into both sides of the fish. Marinate for about 10 minutes. Then sprinkle with pepper. Place the lemongrass in the frying basket and top with tuna steaks. Add the remaining lemon juice and 1 tablespoon of water in the pan below the basket. Bake until the tuna is

cooked through, 8-10 minutes. Discard the lemongrass before topping with cilantro and red chili. Serve and enjoy!

Basil Mushroom & Shrimp Spaghetti

Servings: 6
Cooking Time: 20 Minutes
Ingredients:

- 8 oz baby Bella mushrooms, sliced
- ½ cup grated Parmesan
- 1 lb peeled shrimp, deveined
- 3 tbsp olive oil
- ¼ tsp garlic powder
- ¼ tsp shallot powder
- ¼ tsp cayenne
- 1 lb cooked pasta spaghetti
- 5 garlic cloves, minced
- Salt and pepper to taste
- ½ cup dill

Directions:

1. Preheat air fryer to 380°F (195°C). Toss the shrimp, 1 tbsp of olive oil, garlic powder, shallot powder and cayenne in a bowl. Put the shrimp into the frying basket and Roast for 5 minutes. Remove and set aside.

2. Warm the remaining olive oil in a large skillet over medium heat. Add the garlic and mushrooms and cook for 5 minutes. Pour in the pasta, ½ cup of water, Parmesan, salt, pepper, and dill and stir to coat the pasta. Stir in the shrimp. Remove from heat, then let the mixture rest for 5 minutes. Serve and enjoy!

Summer Sea Scallops

Servings: 4
Cooking Time: 30 Minutes
Ingredients:

- 1 cup asparagus
- 1 cup peas
- 1 cup chopped broccoli
- 2 tsp olive oil
- ½ tsp dried oregano
- 12 oz sea scallops

Directions:

1. Preheat air fryer to 400°F (205°C). Add the asparagus, peas, and broccoli to a bowl and mix with olive oil. Put the bowl in the fryer and Air Fry for 4-6 minutes until crispy and soft. Take the veggies out and add the herbs; let sit. Add the scallops to the fryer and Air Fry for 4-5 minutes until the scallops are springy to the touch. Serve immediately with the vegetables. Enjoy!

Salmon Patties With Lemon-dill Sauce

Servings: 4
Cooking Time: 40 Minutes
Ingredients:
* 2 tbsp diced red bell peppers
* ¼ cup sour cream
* 6 tbsp mayonnaise
* 2 cloves garlic, minced
* 2 tbsp cup onion
* 2 tbsp chopped dill
* 2 tsp lime juice
* 1 tsp honey
* 1 can salmon
* 1 egg
* ½ cup bread crumbs
* Salt and pepper to taste

Directions:
1. Mix the sour cream, 2 tbsp of mayonnaise, honey, onion, garlic, dill, lime juice, salt and pepper in a bowl. Let chill the resulting dill sauce in the fridge until ready to use.
2. Preheat air fryer at 400ºF (205°C) . Combine the salmon, remaining mayonnaise, egg, bell peppers, breadcrumbs, and salt in a bowl. Form mixture into patties. Place salmon cakes in the greased frying basket and Air Fry for 10 minutes, flipping once. Let rest for 5 minutes before serving with dill sauce on the side.

Garlic-lemon Steamer Clams

Servings:2
Cooking Time: 30 Minutes
Ingredients:
* 25 Manila clams, scrubbed
* 2 tbsp butter, melted
* 1 garlic clove, minced
* 2 lemon wedges

Directions:
1. Add the clams to a large bowl filled with water and let sit for 10 minutes. Drain. Pour more water and let sit for 10 more minutes. Drain. Preheat air fryer to 350ºF (175°C) . Place clams in the basket and Air Fry for 7 minutes. Discard any clams that don´t open. Remove clams from shells and place them into a large serving dish. Drizzle with melted butter and garlic and squeeze lemon on top. Serve.

French Grouper Nicoise

Servings: 4
Cooking Time: 20 Minutes
Ingredients:
* 4 grouper fillets
* Salt to taste

* ½ tsp ground cumin
* 3 garlic cloves, minced
* 1 tomato, sliced
* ¼ cup sliced Nicoise olives
* ¼ cup dill, chopped
* 1 lemon, juiced
* ¼ cup olive oil

Directions:
1. Preheat air fryer to 380°F (195°C) . Sprinkle the grouper fillets with salt and cumin. Arrange them on the greased frying basket and top with garlic, tomato slices, olives, and fresh dill. Drizzle with lemon juice and olive oil. Bake for 10-12 minutes. Serve and enjoy!

Curried Sweet-and-spicy Scallops

Servings:3
Cooking Time: 5 Minutes
Ingredients:
* 6 tablespoons Thai sweet chili sauce
* 2 cups (from about 5 cups cereal) Crushed Rice Krispies or other rice-puff cereal
* 2 teaspoons Yellow curry powder, purchased or homemade (see here)
* 1 pound Sea scallops
* Vegetable oil spray

Directions:
1. Preheat the air fryer to 400°F (205°C) .
2. Set up and fill two shallow soup plates or small pie plates on your counter: one for the chili sauce and one for crumbs, mixed with the curry powder.
3. Dip a scallop into the chili sauce, coating it on all sides. Set it in the cereal mixture and turn several times to coat evenly. Gently shake off any excess and set the scallop on a cutting board. Continue dipping and coating the remaining scallops. Coat them all on all sides with the vegetable oil spray.
4. Set the scallops in the basket with as much air space between them as possible. Air-fry undisturbed for 5 minutes, or until lightly browned and crunchy.
5. Remove the basket. Set aside for 2 minutes to let the coating set up. Then gently pour the contents of the basket onto a platter and serve at once.

Almond-crusted Fish

Servings: 4
Cooking Time: 10 Minutes
Ingredients:
* 4 4-ounce fish fillets
* ¾ cup breadcrumbs
* ¼ cup sliced almonds, crushed
* 2 tablespoons lemon juice

- ⅛ teaspoon cayenne
- salt and pepper
- ¾ cup flour
- 1 egg, beaten with 1 tablespoon water
- oil for misting or cooking spray

Directions:
1. Split fish fillets lengthwise down the center to create 8 pieces.
2. Mix breadcrumbs and almonds together and set aside.
3. Mix the lemon juice and cayenne together. Brush on all sides of fish.
4. Season fish to taste with salt and pepper.
5. Place the flour on a sheet of wax paper.
6. Roll fillets in flour, dip in egg wash, and roll in the crumb mixture.
7. Mist both sides of fish with oil or cooking spray.
8. Spray air fryer basket and lay fillets inside.
9. Cook at 390°F (200°C) for 5minutes, turn fish over, and cook for an additional 5minutes or until fish is done and flakes easily.

Catalan Sardines With Romesco Sauce

Servings:2
Cooking Time: 15 Minutes
Ingredients:
- 2 cans skinless, boneless sardines in oil, drained
- ½ cup warmed romesco sauce
- ½ cup bread crumbs

Directions:
1. Preheat air fryer to 350ºF (175°C). In a shallow dish, add bread crumbs. Roll in sardines to coat. Place sardines in the greased frying basket and Air Fry for 6 minutes, turning once. Serve with romesco sauce.

Tilapia Teriyaki

Servings: 3
Cooking Time: 10 Minutes
Ingredients:
- 4 tablespoons teriyaki sauce
- 1 tablespoon pineapple juice
- 1 pound tilapia fillets
- cooking spray
- 6 ounces frozen mixed peppers with onions, thawed and drained
- 2 cups cooked rice

Directions:
1. Mix the teriyaki sauce and pineapple juice together in a small bowl.
2. Split tilapia fillets down the center lengthwise.

3. Brush all sides of fish with the sauce, spray air fryer basket with nonstick cooking spray, and place fish in the basket.
4. Stir the peppers and onions into the remaining sauce and spoon over the fish. Save any leftover sauce for drizzling over the fish when serving.
5. Cook at 360°F (180°C) for 10 minutes, until fish flakes easily with a fork and is done in center.
6. Divide into 3 or 4 servings and serve each with approximately ½ cup cooked rice.

Caribbean Jerk Cod Fillets

Servings:2
Cooking Time: 20 Minutes
Ingredients:
- ¼ cup chopped cooked shrimp
- ¼ cup diced mango
- 1 tomato, diced
- 2 tbsp diced red onion
- 1 tbsp chopped parsley
- ¼ tsp ginger powder
- 2 tsp lime juice
- Salt and pepper to taste
- 2 cod fillets
- 2 tsp Jerk seasoning

Directions:
1. In a bowl, combine the shrimp, mango, tomato, red onion, parsley, ginger powder, lime juice, salt, and black pepper. Let chill the salsa in the fridge until ready to use.
2. Preheat air fryer to 350ºF (175°C). Sprinkle cod fillets with Jerk seasoning. Place them in the greased frying basket and Air Fry for 10 minutes or until the cod is opaque and flakes easily with a fork. Divide between 2 medium plates. Serve topped with the Caribbean salsa.

Italian Tuna Roast

Servings: 8
Cooking Time: 21 Minutes
Ingredients:
- cooking spray
- 1 tablespoon Italian seasoning
- ⅛ teaspoon ground black pepper
- 1 tablespoon extra-light olive oil
- 1 teaspoon lemon juice
- 1 tuna loin (approximately 2 pounds, 3 to 4 inches thick, large enough to fill a 6 x 6-inch baking dish)

Directions:
1. Spray baking dish with cooking spray and place in air fryer basket. Preheat air fryer to 390°F (200°C).
2. Mix together the Italian seasoning, pepper, oil, and lemon juice.

3. Using a dull table knife or butter knife, pierce top of tuna about every half inch: Insert knife into top of tuna roast and pierce almost all the way to the bottom.

4. Spoon oil mixture into each of the holes and use the knife to push seasonings into the tuna as deeply as possible.

5. Spread any remaining oil mixture on all outer surfaces of tuna.

6. Place tuna roast in baking dish and cook at 390°F (200°C) for 20 minutes. Check temperature with a meat thermometer. Cook for an additional 1 minutes or until temperature reaches 145°F (60°C).

7. Remove basket from fryer and let tuna sit in basket for 10minutes.

Halibut Quesadillas

Servings: 2
Cooking Time: 30 Minutes
Ingredients:
- ¼ cup shredded cheddar
- ¼ cup shredded mozzarella
- 1 tsp olive oil
- 2 tortilla shells
- 1 halibut fillet
- ½ peeled avocado, sliced
- 1 garlic clove, minced
- Salt and pepper to taste
- ½ tsp lemon juice

Directions:
1. Preheat air fryer to 350°F (175°C). Brush the halibut fillet with olive oil and sprinkle with salt and pepper. Bake in the air fryer for 12-14 minutes, flipping once until cooked through. Combine the avocado, garlic, salt, pepper, and lemon juice in a bowl and, using a fork, mash lightly until the avocado is slightly chunky. Add and spread the resulting guacamole on one tortilla. Top with the cooked fish and cheeses, and cover with the second tortilla. Bake in the air fryer 6-8, flipping once until the cheese is melted. Serve immediately.

Autenthic Greek Fish Pitas

Servings: 4
Cooking Time: 25 Minutes
Ingredients:
- 1 lb pollock, cut into 1-inch pieces
- ¼ cup olive oil
- 1 tsp salt
- ½ tsp dried oregano
- ½ tsp dried thyme
- ½ tsp garlic powder
- ¼ tsp chili powder
- 4 pitas
- 1 cup grated lettuce
- 4 Kalamata olives, chopped
- 2 tomatoes, diced
- 1 cup Greek yogurt

Directions:
1. Preheat air fryer to 380°F (195°C). Coat the pollock with olive oil, salt, oregano, thyme, garlic powder, and chili powder in a bowl. Put the pollock into the frying basket and Air Fry for 15 minutes. Serve inside pitas with lettuce, tomato, olives and Greek yogurt. Enjoy!

Shrimp, Chorizo And Fingerling Potatoes

Servings: 4
Cooking Time: 16 Minutes
Ingredients:
- ½ red onion, chopped into 1-inch chunks
- 8 fingerling potatoes, sliced into 1-inch slices or halved lengthwise
- 1 teaspoon olive oil
- salt and freshly ground black pepper
- 8 ounces raw chorizo sausage, sliced into 1-inch chunks
- 16 raw large shrimp, peeled, deveined and tails removed
- 1 lime
- ¼ cup chopped fresh cilantro
- chopped orange zest (optional)

Directions:
1. Preheat the air fryer to 380°F (195°C).

2. Combine the red onion and potato chunks in a bowl and toss with the olive oil, salt and freshly ground black pepper.

3. Transfer the vegetables to the air fryer basket and air-fry for 6 minutes, shaking the basket a few times during the cooking process.

4. Add the chorizo chunks and continue to air-fry for another 5 minutes.

5. Add the shrimp, season with salt and continue to air-fry, shaking the basket every once in a while, for another 5 minutes.

6. Transfer the tossed shrimp, chorizo and potato to a bowl and squeeze some lime juice over the top to taste. Toss in the fresh cilantro, orange zest and a drizzle of olive oil, and season again to taste.

7. Serve with a fresh green salad.

Crab Stuffed Salmon Roast

Servings: 4
Cooking Time: 20 Minutes
Ingredients:
- 1 (1½-pound) salmon fillet
- salt and freshly ground black pepper
- 6 ounces crabmeat
- 1 teaspoon finely chopped lemon zest
- 1 teaspoon Dijon mustard

- 1 tablespoon chopped fresh parsley, plus more for garnish
- 1 scallion, chopped
- ¼ teaspoon salt
- olive oil

Directions:

1. Prepare the salmon fillet by butterflying it. Slice into the thickest side of the salmon, parallel to the countertop and along the length of the fillet. Don't slice all the way through to the other side – stop about an inch from the edge. Open the salmon up like a book. Season the salmon with salt and freshly ground black pepper.

2. Make the crab filling by combining the crabmeat, lemon zest, mustard, parsley, scallion, salt and freshly ground black pepper in a bowl. Spread this filling in the center of the salmon. Fold one side of the salmon over the filling. Then fold the other side over on top.

3. Transfer the rolled salmon to the center of a piece of parchment paper that is roughly 6- to 7-inches wide and about 12-inches long. The parchment paper will act as a sling, making it easier to put the salmon into the air fryer. Preheat the air fryer to 370°F (185°C). Use the parchment paper to transfer the salmon roast to the air fryer basket and tuck the ends of the paper down beside the salmon. Drizzle a little olive oil on top and season with salt and pepper.

4. Air-fry the salmon at 370°F (185°C) for 20 minutes.

5. Remove the roast from the air fryer and let it rest for a few minutes. Then, slice it, sprinkle some more lemon zest and parsley (or fresh chives) on top and serve.

Shrimp-jalapeño Poppers In Prosciutto

Servings: 4
Cooking Time: 30 Minutes
Ingredients:
- 1 lb shelled tail on shrimp, deveined, sliced down the spine
- 2 jalapeños, diced
- 2 tbsp grated cheddar
- 3 tbsp mascarpone cheese
- ¼ tsp garlic powder
- 1 tbsp mayonnaise
- ¼ tsp ground black pepper
- 20 prosciutto slices
- ¼ cup chopped parsley
- 1 lemon

Directions:

1. Preheat air fryer at 400ºF (205°C). Combine the mascarpone and cheddar cheeses, jalapeños, garlic, mayonnaise, and black pepper in a bowl. Press cheese mixture into shrimp. Wrap 1 piece of prosciutto around each shrimp to hold in the cheese mixture. Place wrapped shrimp

in the frying basket and Air Fry for 8-10 minutes, flipping once. To serve, scatter with parsley and squeeze lemon.

Salty German-style Shrimp Pancakes

Servings: 4
Cooking Time: 15 Minutes
Ingredients:
- 1 tbsp butter
- 3 eggs, beaten
- ½ cup flour
- ½ cup milk
- ⅛ tsp salt
- 1 cup salsa
- 1 cup cooked shrimp, minced
- 2 tbsp cilantro, chopped

Directions:

1. Preheat air fryer to 390°F (200°C). Mix the eggs, flour, milk, and salt in a bowl until frothy. Pour the batter into a greased baking pan and place in the air fryer. Bake for 15 minutes or until the pancake is puffed and golden. Flip the pancake onto a plate. Mix salsa, shrimp, and cilantro. Top the pancake and serve.

Shrimp Po' boy With Remoulade Sauce

Servings: 6
Cooking Time: 8 Minutes
Ingredients:
- ½ cup all-purpose flour
- ½ teaspoon paprika
- 1 teaspoon garlic powder
- ½ teaspoon black pepper
- ¼ teaspoon salt
- 2 eggs, whisked
- 1½ cups panko breadcrumbs
- 1 pound small shrimp, peeled and deveined
- Six 6-inch French rolls
- 2 cups shredded lettuce
- 12 ⅛-inch tomato slices
- ¾ cup Remoulade Sauce (see the following recipe)

Directions:

1. Preheat the air fryer to 360°F (180°C).

2. In a medium bowl, mix the flour, paprika, garlic powder, pepper, and salt.

3. In a shallow dish, place the eggs.

4. In a third dish, place the panko breadcrumbs.

5. Covering the shrimp in the flour, dip them into the egg, and coat them with the breadcrumbs. Repeat until all shrimp are covered in the breading.

6.   Liberally spray the metal trivet that fits inside the air fryer basket with olive oil spray. Place the shrimp onto the trivet, leaving space between the shrimp to flip. Cook for 4 minutes, flip the shrimp, and cook another 4 minutes. Repeat until all the shrimp are cooked.

7.   Slice the rolls in half. Stuff each roll with shredded lettuce, tomato slices, breaded shrimp, and remoulade sauce. Serve immediately.

Catfish Nuggets

Servings: 4
Cooking Time: 7 Minutes Per Batch
Ingredients:
- 2 medium catfish fillets, cut in chunks (approximately 1 x 2 inch)
- salt and pepper
- 2 eggs
- 2 tablespoons skim milk
- ½ cup cornstarch
- 1 cup panko breadcrumbs, crushed
- oil for misting or cooking spray

Directions:
1.   Season catfish chunks with salt and pepper to your liking.
2.   Beat together eggs and milk in a small bowl.
3.   Place cornstarch in a second small bowl.
4.   Place breadcrumbs in a third small bowl.
5.   Dip catfish chunks in cornstarch, dip in egg wash, shake off excess, then roll in breadcrumbs.
6.   Spray all sides of catfish chunks with oil or cooking spray.
7.   Place chunks in air fryer basket in a single layer, leaving space between for air circulation.
8.   Cook at 390°F（200°C）for 4minutes, turn, and cook an additional 3 minutes, until fish flakes easily and outside is crispy brown.
9.   Repeat steps 7 and 8 to cook remaining catfish nuggets.

Lime Flaming Halibut

Servings:2
Cooking Time: 20 Minutes
Ingredients:
- 2 tbsp butter, melted
- ½ tsp chili powder
- ½ cup bread crumbs
- 2 halibut fillets

Directions:
1.   Preheat air fryer to 350ºF（175°C）. In a bowl, mix the butter, chili powder and bread crumbs. Press mixture onto tops of halibut fillets. Place halibut in the greased frying basket and Air Fry for 10 minutes or until the fish is opaque and flake easily with a fork. Serve right away.

Fish Goujons With Tartar Sauce

Servings: 4
Cooking Time: 20 Minutes
Ingredients:
- ¼ cup flour
- Salt and pepper to taste
- ¼ tsp smoked paprika
- ¼ tsp dried oregano
- 1 tsp dried thyme
- 1 egg
- 4 haddock fillets
- 1 lemon, thinly sliced
- ½ cup tartar sauce

Directions:
1.   Preheat air fryer to 400°F（205°C）. Combine flour, salt, pepper, paprika, thyme, and oregano in a wide bowl. Whisk egg and 1 teaspoon water in another wide bowl. Slice each fillet into 4 strips. Dip the strips in the egg mixture. Then roll them in the flour mixture and coat completely. Arrange the fish strips on the greased frying basket. Air Fry for 4 minutes. Flip the fish and Air Fry for another 4 to 5 minutes until crisp. Serve warm with lemon slices and tartar sauce on the side and enjoy.

Crunchy And Buttery Cod With Ritz® Cracker Crust

Servings: 2
Cooking Time: 10 Minutes
Ingredients:
- 4 tablespoons butter, melted
- 8 to 10 RITZ® crackers, crushed into crumbs
- 2 (6-ounce) cod fillets
- salt and freshly ground black pepper
- 1 lemon

Directions:
1.   Preheat the air fryer to 380°F（195°C）.
2.   Melt the butter in a small saucepan on the stovetop or in a microwavable dish in the microwave, and then transfer the butter to a shallow dish. Place the crushed RITZ® crackers into a second shallow dish.
3.   Season the fish fillets with salt and freshly ground black pepper. Dip them into the butter and then coat both sides with the RITZ® crackers.
4.   Place the fish into the air fryer basket and air-fry at 380°F（195°C）for 10 minutes, flipping the fish over halfway through the cooking time.
5.   Serve with a wedge of lemon to squeeze over the top.

Salmon

Servings: 4
Cooking Time: 8 Minutes

Ingredients:

- Marinade
- 3 tablespoons low-sodium soy sauce
- 3 tablespoons rice vinegar
- 3 tablespoons ketchup
- 3 tablespoons olive oil
- 3 tablespoons brown sugar
- 1 teaspoon garlic powder
- ½ teaspoon ground ginger
- 4 salmon fillets (½-inch thick, 3 to 4 ounces each)
- cooking spray

Directions:

1. Mix all marinade ingredients until well blended.
2. Place salmon in sealable plastic bag or shallow container with lid. Pour marinade over fish and turn to coat well. Refrigerate for 30minutes.
3. Drain marinade, and spray air fryer basket with cooking spray.
4. Place salmon in basket, skin-side down.
5. Cook at 360°F（180°C）for 10 minutes, watching closely to avoid overcooking. Salmon is done when just beginning to flake and still very moist.

Parmesan Crusted Chicken Cordon Bleu

Servings: 2
Cooking Time: 14 Minutes
Ingredients:

- 2 (6-ounce) boneless, skinless chicken breasts
- salt and freshly ground black pepper
- 1 tablespoon Dijon mustard
- 4 slices Swiss cheese
- 4 slices deli-sliced ham
- ¼ cup all-purpose flour*
- 1 egg, beaten
- ¾ cup panko breadcrumbs*
- ⅓ cup grated Parmesan cheese
- olive oil, in a spray bottle

Directions:
1. Butterfly the chicken breasts. Place the chicken breast on a cutting board and press down on the breast with the palm of your hand. Slice into the long side of the chicken breast, parallel to the cutting board, but not all the way through to the other side. Open the chicken breast like a "book". Place a piece of plastic wrap over the chicken breast and gently pound it with a meat mallet to make it evenly thick.
2. Season the chicken with salt and pepper. Spread the Dijon mustard on the inside of each chicken breast. Layer one slice of cheese on top of the mustard, then top with the 2 slices of ham and the other slice of cheese.
3. Starting with the long edge of the chicken breast, roll the chicken up to the other side. Secure it shut with 1 or 2 toothpicks.
4. Preheat the air fryer to 350°F（175°C）.
5. Set up a dredging station with three shallow dishes. Place the flour in the first dish. Place the beaten egg in the second shallow dish. Combine the panko breadcrumbs and Parmesan cheese together in the third shallow dish. Dip the stuffed and rolled chicken breasts in the flour, then the beaten egg and then roll in the breadcrumb-cheese mixture to cover on all sides. Press the crumbs onto the chicken breasts with your hands to make sure they are well adhered. Spray the chicken breasts with olive oil and transfer to the air fryer basket.
6. Air-fry at 350°F（175°C）for 14 minutes, flipping the breasts over halfway through the cooking time. Let the chicken rest for a few minutes before removing the toothpicks, slicing and serving.

Fiesta Chicken Plate

Servings: 4
Cooking Time: 15 Minutes
Ingredients:

- 1 pound boneless, skinless chicken breasts (2 large breasts)
- 2 tablespoons lime juice
- 1 teaspoon cumin
- ½ teaspoon salt
- ½ cup grated Pepper Jack cheese
- 1 16-ounce can refried beans
- ½ cup salsa
- 2 cups shredded lettuce
- 1 medium tomato, chopped
- 2 avocados, peeled and sliced
- 1 small onion, sliced into thin rings
- sour cream
- tortilla chips (optional)

Directions:
1. Split each chicken breast in half lengthwise.
2. Mix lime juice, cumin, and salt together and brush on all surfaces of chicken breasts.
3. Place in air fryer basket and cook at 390°F（200°C）for 15 minutes, until well done.
4. Divide the cheese evenly over chicken breasts and cook for an additional minute to melt cheese.
5. While chicken is cooking, heat refried beans on stovetop or in microwave.
6. When ready to serve, divide beans among 4 plates. Place chicken breasts on top of beans and spoon salsa over. Arrange the lettuce, tomatoes, and avocados artfully on each plate and scatter with the onion rings.
7. Pass sour cream at the table and serve with tortilla chips if desired.

Spicy Black Bean Turkey Burgers With Cumin-avocado Spread

Servings: 2
Cooking Time: 20 Minutes
Ingredients:

- 1 cup canned black beans, drained and rinsed
- ¾ pound lean ground turkey
- 2 tablespoons minced red onion
- 1 Jalapeño pepper, seeded and minced
- 2 tablespoons plain breadcrumbs
- ½ teaspoon chili powder
- ¼ teaspoon cayenne pepper
- salt, to taste
- olive or vegetable oil

- 2 slices pepper jack cheese
- toasted burger rolls, sliced tomatoes, lettuce leaves
- Cumin-Avocado Spread:
- 1 ripe avocado
- juice of 1 lime
- 1 teaspoon ground cumin
- ½ teaspoon salt
- 1 tablespoon chopped fresh cilantro
- freshly ground black pepper

Directions:

1.   Place the black beans in a large bowl and smash them slightly with the back of a fork. Add the ground turkey, red onion, Jalapeño pepper, breadcrumbs, chili powder and cayenne pepper. Season with salt. Mix with your hands to combine all the ingredients and then shape them into 2 patties. Brush both sides of the burger patties with a little olive or vegetable oil.

2.   Preheat the air fryer to 380°F (195°C) .

3.   Transfer the burgers to the air fryer basket and air-fry for 20 minutes, flipping them over halfway through the cooking process. Top the burgers with the pepper jack cheese (securing the slices to the burgers with a toothpick) for the last 2 minutes of the cooking process.

4.   While the burgers are cooking, make the cumin avocado spread. Place the avocado, lime juice, cumin and salt in food processor and process until smooth. (For a chunkier spread, you can mash this by hand in a bowl.) Stir in the cilantro and season with freshly ground black pepper. Chill the spread until you are ready to serve.

5.   When the burgers have finished cooking, remove them from the air fryer and let them rest on a plate, covered gently with aluminum foil. Brush a little olive oil on the insides of the burger rolls. Place the rolls, cut side up, into the air fryer basket and air-fry at 400°F (205°C) for 1 minute to toast and warm them.

6.   Spread the cumin-avocado spread on the rolls and build your burgers with lettuce and sliced tomatoes and any other ingredient you like. Serve warm with a side of sweet potato fries.

Party Buffalo Chicken Drumettes

Servings: 6
Cooking Time: 30 Minutes
Ingredients:

- 16 chicken drumettes
- 1 tsp garlic powder
- 1 tbsp chicken seasoning
- Black pepper to taste
- ¼ cup Buffalo wings sauce
- 2 spring onions, sliced

Directions:

1.   Preheat air fryer to 400°F (205°C) . Sprinkle garlic, chicken seasoning, and black pepper on the drumettes. Place them in the fryer and spray with cooking oil. Air Fry for 10 minutes, shaking the basket once. Transfer the drumettes to a large bowl. Drizzle with Buffalo wing sauce and toss to coat. Place in the fryer and Fry for 7-8 minutes, until crispy. Allow to cool slightly. Top with spring onions and serve warm.

Southwest Gluten-free Turkey Meatloaf

Servings: 8
Cooking Time: 35 Minutes
Ingredients:

- 1 pound lean ground turkey
- ¼ cup corn grits
- ¼ cup diced onion
- 1 teaspoon minced garlic
- ½ teaspoon black pepper
- ½ teaspoon salt
- 1 large egg
- ½ cup ketchup
- 4 teaspoons chipotle hot sauce
- ⅓ cup shredded cheddar cheese

Directions:

1.   Preheat the air fryer to 350°F (175°C) .

2.   In a large bowl, mix together the ground turkey, corn grits, onion, garlic, black pepper, and salt.

3.   In a small bowl, whisk the egg. Add the egg to the turkey mixture and combine.

4.   In a small bowl, mix the ketchup and hot sauce. Set aside.

5.   Liberally spray a 9-x-4-inch loaf pan with olive oil spray. Depending on the size of your air fryer, you may need to use 2 or 3 mini loaf pans.

6.   Spoon the ground turkey mixture into the loaf pan and evenly top with half of the ketchup mixture. Cover with foil and place the meatloaf into the air fryer. Cook for 30 minutes; remove the foil and discard. Check the internal temperature (it should be nearing 165°F (75°C)).

7.   Coat the top of the meatloaf with the remaining ketchup mixture, and sprinkle the cheese over the top. Place the meatloaf back in the air fryer for the remaining 5 minutes (or until the internal temperature reaches 165°F (75°C)).

8.   Remove from the oven and let cool 5 minutes before serving. Serve warm with desired sides.

Chicken Nuggets

Servings: 20
Cooking Time: 14 Minutes Per Batch
Ingredients:

* 1 pound boneless, skinless chicken thighs, cut into 1-inch chunks
* ¾ teaspoon salt
* ½ teaspoon black pepper
* ½ teaspoon garlic powder
* ½ teaspoon onion powder
* ½ cup flour
* 2 eggs, beaten
* ½ cup panko breadcrumbs
* 3 tablespoons plain breadcrumbs
* oil for misting or cooking spray

Directions:
1. In the bowl of a food processor, combine chicken, ½ teaspoon salt, pepper, garlic powder, and onion powder. Process in short pulses until chicken is very finely chopped and well blended.
2. Place flour in one shallow dish and beaten eggs in another. In a third dish or plastic bag, mix together the panko crumbs, plain breadcrumbs, and ¼ teaspoon salt.
3. Shape chicken mixture into small nuggets. Dip nuggets in flour, then eggs, then panko crumb mixture.
4. Spray nuggets on both sides with oil or cooking spray and place in air fryer basket in a single layer, close but not overlapping.
5. Cook at 360°F (180°C) for 10minutes. Spray with oil and cook 4 minutes, until chicken is done and coating is golden brown.
6. Repeat step 5 to cook remaining nuggets.

Quick Chicken For Filling

Servings: 2
Cooking Time: 8 Minutes
Ingredients:

* 1 pound chicken tenders, skinless and boneless
* ½ teaspoon ground cumin
* ½ teaspoon garlic powder
* cooking spray

Directions:
1. Sprinkle raw chicken tenders with seasonings.
2. Spray air fryer basket lightly with cooking spray to prevent sticking.
3. Place chicken in air fryer basket in single layer.
4. Cook at 390°F (200°C) for 4minutes, turn chicken strips over, and cook for an additional 4minutes.
5. Test for doneness. Thick tenders may require an additional minute or two.

Pesto Chicken Cheeseburgers

Servings:4
Cooking Time: 40 Minutes
Ingredients:

* ¼ cup shredded Pepper Jack cheese
* 1 lb ground chicken
* 2 tbsp onion
* ¼ cup chopped parsley
* 1 egg white, beaten
* 1 tbsp pesto
* Salt and pepper to taste

Directions:
1. Preheat air fryer to 350°F (175°C). Combine ground chicken, onion, cheese, parsley, egg white, salt, and pepper in a bowl. Make 4 patties out of the mixture. Place them in the greased frying basket and Air Fry for 12-14 minutes until golden, flipping once. Serve topped with pesto.

Crispy Chicken Parmesan

Servings: 4
Cooking Time: 12 Minutes
Ingredients:

* 4 skinless, boneless chicken breasts, pounded thin to ¼-inch thickness
* 1 teaspoon salt, divided
* ½ teaspoon black pepper, divided
* 1 cup flour
* 2 eggs
* 1 cup panko breadcrumbs
* ½ teaspoon dried oregano
* ½ cup grated Parmesan cheese

Directions:
1. Pat the chicken breasts with a paper towel. Season the chicken with ½ teaspoon of the salt and ¼ teaspoon of the pepper.
2. In a medium bowl, place the flour.
3. In a second bowl, whisk the eggs.
4. In a third bowl, place the breadcrumbs, oregano, cheese, and the remaining ½ teaspoon of salt and ¼ teaspoon of pepper.
5. Dredge the chicken in the flour and shake off the excess. Dip the chicken into the eggs and then into the breadcrumbs. Set the chicken on a plate and repeat with the remaining chicken pieces.
6. Preheat the air fryer to 360°F (180°C).
7. Place the chicken in the air fryer basket and spray liberally with cooking spray. Cook for 8 minutes, turn the chicken breasts over, and cook another 4 minutes. When golden brown, check for an internal temperature of 165°F (70°C).

Christmas Chicken & Roasted Grape Salad

Servings: 4
Cooking Time: 40 Minutes

Ingredients:

- 3 chicken breasts, pat-dried
- 1 tsp paprika
- Salt and pepper to taste
- 2 cups seedless red grapes
- ½ cup mayonnaise
- ½ cup plain yogurt
- 2 tbsp honey mustard
- 2 tbsp fresh lemon juice
- 1 cup chopped celery
- 2 scallions, chopped
- 2 tbsp walnuts, chopped

Directions:

1. Preheat the air fryer to 370°F (185°C). Sprinkle the chicken breasts with paprika, salt, and pepper. Transfer to the greased frying basket and Air Fry for 16-19 minutes, flipping once. Remove and set on a cutting board. Put the grapes in the fryer and spray with cooking oil. Fry for 4 minutes or until the grapes are hot and tender.Mix the mayonnaise, yogurt, honey mustard, and lemon juice in a bowl and whisk. Cube the chicken and add to the dressing along with the grapes, walnuts, celery, and scallions. Toss gently and serve.

Coconut Chicken With Apricot-ginger Sauce

Servings: 4
Cooking Time: 8 Minutes Per Batch

Ingredients:

- 1½ pounds boneless, skinless chicken tenders, cut in large chunks (about 1¼ inches)
- salt and pepper
- ½ cup cornstarch
- 2 eggs
- 1 tablespoon milk
- 3 cups shredded coconut (see below)
- oil for misting or cooking spray
- Apricot-Ginger Sauce
- ½ cup apricot preserves
- 2 tablespoons white vinegar
- ¼ teaspoon ground ginger
- ¼ teaspoon low-sodium soy sauce
- 2 teaspoons white or yellow onion, grated or finely minced

Directions:

1. Mix all ingredients for the Apricot-Ginger Sauce well and let sit for flavors to blend while you cook the chicken.

2. Season chicken chunks with salt and pepper to taste.
3. Place cornstarch in a shallow dish.
4. In another shallow dish, beat together eggs and milk.
5. Place coconut in a third shallow dish. (If also using panko breadcrumbs, as suggested below, stir them to mix well.)
6. Spray air fryer basket with oil or cooking spray.
7. Dip each chicken chunk into cornstarch, shake off excess, and dip in egg mixture.
8. Shake off excess egg mixture and roll lightly in coconut or coconut mixture. Spray with oil.
9. Place coated chicken chunks in air fryer basket in a single layer, close together but without sides touching.
10. Cook at 360°F (180°C) for 4minutes, stop, and turn chunks over.
11. Cook an additional 4 minutes or until chicken is done inside and coating is crispy brown.
12. Repeat steps 9 through 11 to cook remaining chicken chunks.

Chicken Adobo

Servings: 6
Cooking Time: 12 Minutes

Ingredients:

- 6 boneless chicken thighs
- ¼ cup soy sauce or tamari
- ½ cup rice wine vinegar
- 4 cloves garlic, minced
- ⅛ teaspoon crushed red pepper flakes
- ½ teaspoon black pepper

Directions:

1. Place the chicken thighs into a resealable plastic bag with the soy sauce or tamari, the rice wine vinegar, the garlic, and the crushed red pepper flakes. Seal the bag and let the chicken marinate at least 1 hour in the refrigerator.
2. Preheat the air fryer to 400°F (205°C).
3. Drain the chicken and pat dry with a paper towel. Season the chicken with black pepper and liberally spray with cooking spray.
4. Place the chicken in the air fryer basket and cook for 9 minutes, turn over at 9 minutes and check for an internal temperature of 165°F (75°C), and cook another 3 minutes.

Classic Chicken Cobb Salad

Servings:4
Cooking Time: 30 Minutes

Ingredients:

- 4 oz cooked bacon, crumbled
- 2 chicken breasts, cubed
- 1 tbsp sesame oil
- Salt and pepper to taste
- 4 cups torn romaine lettuce

- 2 tbsp olive oil
- 1 tbsp white wine vinegar
- 2 hard-boiled eggs, sliced
- 2 tomatoes, diced
- 6 radishes, finely sliced
- ¼ cup blue cheese crumbles
- ¼ cup diced red onions
- 1 avocado, diced

Directions:

1. Preheat air fryer to 350ºF (175°C). Combine chicken cubes, sesame oil, salt, and black pepper in a bowl. Place chicken cubes in the frying basket and Air Fry for 9 minutes, flipping once. Reserve. In a bowl, combine the lettuce, olive oil, and vinegar. Divide between 4 bowls. Add in the cooked chicken, hard-boiled egg slices, bacon, tomato cubes, radishes, blue cheese, onion, and avocado cubes. Serve.

Yummy Maple-mustard Chicken Kabobs

Servings:4

Cooking Time: 35 Minutes+ Chilling Time

Ingredients:

- 1 lb boneless, skinless chicken thighs, cubed
- 1 green bell pepper, chopped
- ½ cup honey mustard
- ½ yellow onion, chopped
- 8 cherry tomatoes
- 2 tbsp chopped scallions

Directions:

1. Toss chicken cubes and honey mustard in a bowl and let chill covered in the fridge for 30 minutes. Preheat air fryer to 350ºF (175°C). Thread chicken cubes, onion, cherry tomatoes, and bell peppers, alternating, onto 8 skewers. Place them on a kebab rack. Place rack in the frying basket and Air Fry for 12 minutes. Top with scallions to serve.

Japanese-style Turkey Meatballs

Servings: 4

Cooking Time: 25 Minutes

Ingredients:

- 1 1/3 lb ground turkey
- ¼ cup panko bread crumbs
- 4 chopped scallions
- ¼ cup chopped cilantro
- 1 egg
- 1 tbsp grated ginger
- 1 garlic clove, minced
- 3 tbsp shoyu
- 2 tsp toasted sesame oil
- ¾ tsp salt

- 2 tbsp oyster sauce sauce
- 2 tbsp fresh orange juice

Directions:

1. Add ground turkey, panko, 3 scallions, cilantro, egg, ginger, garlic, 1 tbsp of shoyu sauce, sesame oil, and salt in a bowl. Mix with hands until combined. Divide the mixture into 12 equal parts and roll into balls. Preheat air fryer to 380ºF (195°C). Place the meatballs in the greased frying basket. Bake for about 9-11 minutes, flipping once until browned and cooked through. Repeat for all meatballs.

2. In a small saucepan over medium heat, add oyster sauce, orange juice and remaining shoyu sauce. Bring to a boil, then reduce the heat to low. Cook until the sauce is slightly reduced, 3 minutes. Serve the meatballs with the oyster sauce drizzled over them and topped with the remaining scallions.

Chicken Parmigiana

Servings: 2

Cooking Time: 35 Minutes

Ingredients:

- 2 chicken breasts
- 1 cup breadcrumbs
- 2 eggs, beaten
- Salt and pepper to taste
- 1 tbsp dried basil
- 1 cup passata
- 2 provolone cheese slices
- 1 tbsp Parmesan cheese

Directions:

1. Preheat air fryer to 350°F (175°C). Mix the breadcrumbs, basil, salt, and pepper in a mixing bowl. Coat the chicken breasts with the crumb mixture, then dip in the beaten eggs. Finally, coat again with the dry ingredients. Arrange the coated chicken breasts on the greased frying basket and Air Fry for 20 minutes. At the 10-minutes mark, turn the breasts over and cook for the remaining 10 minutes.

2. Pour half of the passata into a baking pan. When the chicken is ready, remove it to the passata-covered pan. Pour the remaining passata over the fried chicken and arrange the provolone cheese slices on top and sprinkle with Parmesan cheese. Bake for 5 minutes until the chicken is crisped and the cheese melted and lightly toasted. Serve.

Herb-marinated Chicken

Servings: 4

Cooking Time: 25 Minutes

Ingredients:

- 4 chicken breasts
- 2 tsp rosemary, minced
- 2 tsp thyme, minced
- Salt and pepper to taste

- ½ cup chopped cilantro
- 1 lime, juiced

Directions:

1. Place chicken in a resealable bag. Add rosemary, thyme, salt, pepper, cilantro, and lime juice. Seal the bag and toss to coat, then place in the refrigerator for 2 hours.
2. Preheat air fryer to 400°F (205°C). Arrange the chicken in a single layer in the greased frying basket. Spray the chicken with cooking oil. Air Fry for 6-7 minutes, then flip the chicken. Cook for another 3 minutes. Serve and enjoy!

Honey Lemon Thyme Glazed Cornish Hen

Servings: 2
Cooking Time: 20 Minutes

Ingredients:

- 1 (2-pound) Cornish game hen, split in half
- olive oil
- salt and freshly ground black pepper
- ¼ teaspoon dried thyme
- ¼ cup honey
- 1 tablespoon lemon zest
- juice of 1 lemon
- 1½ teaspoons chopped fresh thyme leaves
- ½ teaspoon soy sauce
- freshly ground black pepper

Directions:

1. Split the game hen in half by cutting down each side of the backbone and then cutting through the breast. Brush or spray both halves of the game hen with the olive oil and then season with the salt, pepper and dried thyme.
2. Preheat the air fryer to 390°F (200°C).
3. Place the game hen, skin side down, into the air fryer and air-fry for 5 minutes. Turn the hen halves over and air-fry for 10 minutes.
4. While the hen is cooking, combine the honey, lemon zest and juice, fresh thyme, soy sauce and pepper in a small bowl.
5. When the air fryer timer rings, brush the honey glaze onto the game hen and continue to air-fry for another 3 to 5 minutes, just until the hen is nicely glazed, browned and has an internal temperature of 165°F (75°C).
6. Let the hen rest for 5 minutes and serve warm.

Buffalo Egg Rolls

Servings: 8
Cooking Time: 9 Minutes Per Batch

Ingredients:

- 1 teaspoon water
- 1 tablespoon cornstarch
- 1 egg

- 2½ cups cooked chicken, diced or shredded (see opposite page)
- ⅓ cup chopped green onion
- ⅓ cup diced celery
- ⅓ cup buffalo wing sauce
- 8 egg roll wraps
- oil for misting or cooking spray
- Blue Cheese Dip
- 3 ounces cream cheese, softened
- ⅓ cup blue cheese, crumbled
- 1 teaspoon Worcestershire sauce
- ¼ teaspoon garlic powder
- ¼ cup buttermilk (or sour cream)

Directions:

1. Mix water and cornstarch in a small bowl until dissolved. Add egg, beat well, and set aside.
2. In a medium size bowl, mix together chicken, green onion, celery, and buffalo wing sauce.
3. Divide chicken mixture evenly among 8 egg roll wraps, spooning ½ inch from one edge.
4. Moisten all edges of each wrap with beaten egg wash.
5. Fold the short ends over filling, then roll up tightly and press to seal edges.
6. Brush outside of wraps with egg wash, then spritz with oil or cooking spray.
7. Place 4 egg rolls in air fryer basket.
8. Cook at 390°F (200°C) for 9minutes or until outside is brown and crispy.
9. While the rolls are cooking, prepare the Blue Cheese Dip. With a fork, mash together cream cheese and blue cheese.
10. Stir in remaining ingredients.
11. Dip should be just thick enough to slightly cling to egg rolls. If too thick, stir in buttermilk or milk 1 tablespoon at a time until you reach the desired consistency.
12. Cook remaining 4 egg rolls as in steps 7 and 8.
13. Serve while hot with Blue Cheese Dip, more buffalo wing sauce, or both.

Jerk Chicken Drumsticks

Servings: 2
Cooking Time: 20 Minutes

Ingredients:

- 1 or 2 cloves garlic
- 1 inch of fresh ginger
- 2 serrano peppers, (with seeds if you like it spicy, seeds removed for less heat)
- 1 teaspoon ground allspice
- 1 teaspoon ground nutmeg
- 1 teaspoon chili powder
- ½ teaspoon dried thyme
- ½ teaspoon ground cinnamon

- ½ teaspoon paprika
- 1 tablespoon brown sugar
- 1 teaspoon soy sauce
- 2 tablespoons vegetable oil
- 6 skinless chicken drumsticks

Directions:

1. Combine all the ingredients except the chicken in a small chopper or blender and blend to a paste. Make slashes into the meat of the chicken drumsticks and rub the spice blend all over the chicken (a pair of plastic gloves makes this really easy). Transfer the rubbed chicken to a non-reactive covered container and let the chicken marinate for at least 30 minutes or overnight in the refrigerator.

2. Preheat the air fryer to 400°F（205°C）.

3. Transfer the drumsticks to the air fryer basket. Air-fry for 10 minutes. Turn the drumsticks over and air-fry for another 10 minutes. Serve warm with some rice and vegetables or a green salad.

Chicken Cordon Bleu Patties

Servings: 4
Cooking Time: 30 Minutes
Ingredients:

- 1/3 cup grated Fontina cheese
- 3 tbsp milk
- 1/3 cup bread crumbs
- 1 egg, beaten
- ½ tsp dried parsley
- Salt and pepper to taste
- 1 ¼ lb ground chicken
- ¼ cup finely chopped ham

Directions:

1. Preheat air fryer to 350°F（175°C）. Mix milk, breadcrumbs, egg, parsley, salt and pepper in a bowl. Using your hands, add the chicken and gently mix until just combined. Divide into 8 portions and shape into thin patties. Place on waxed paper. On 4 of the patties, top with ham and Fontina cheese, then place another patty on top of that. Gently pinch the edges together so that none of the ham or cheese is peeking out. Arrange the burgers in the greased frying basket and Air Fry until cooked through, for 14-16 minutes. Serve and enjoy!

Chicken & Rice Sautée

Servings: 4
Cooking Time: 25 Minutes
Ingredients:

- 1 can pineapple chunks, drained, ¼ cup juice reserved
- 1 cup cooked long-grain rice
- 1 lb chicken breasts, cubed
- 1 red onion, chopped
- 1 tbsp peanut oil

- 1 peeled peach, cubed
- 1 tbsp cornstarch
- ½ tsp ground ginger
- ¼ tsp chicken seasoning

Directions:

1. Preheat air fryer to 400°F（205°C）. Combine the chicken, red onion, pineapple, and peanut oil in a metal bowl, then put the bowl in the fryer. Air Fry for 9 minutes, remove and stir. Toss the peach in and put the bowl back into the fryer for 3 minutes. Slide out and stir again. Mix the reserved pineapple juice, corn starch, ginger, and chicken seasoning in a bowl, then pour over the chicken mixture and stir well. Put the bowl back into the fryer and cook for 3 more minutes or until the chicken is cooked through and the sauce is thick. Serve over cooked rice.

Teriyaki Chicken Bites

Servings:4
Cooking Time: 30 Minutes
Ingredients:

- 1 lb boneless, skinless chicken thighs, cubed
- 1 green onion, sliced diagonally
- 1 large egg
- 1 tbsp teriyaki sauce
- 4 tbsp flour
- 1 tsp sesame oil
- 2 tsp balsamic vinegar
- 2 tbsp tamari
- 3 cloves garlic, minced
- 2 tsp grated fresh ginger
- 2 tsp chili garlic sauce
- 2 tsp granular honey
- Salt and pepper to taste

Directions:

1. Preheat air fryer to 400°F（205°C）. Beat the egg, teriyaki sauce, and flour in a bowl. Stir in chicken pieces until fully coated. In another bowl, combine the remaining ingredients, except for the green onion. Reserve. Place chicken pieces in the frying basket lightly greased with olive oil and Air Fry for 15 minutes, tossing every 5 minutes. Remove them to the bowl with the sauce and toss to coat. Scatter with green onions to serve. Enjoy!

Basic Chicken Breasts[2]

Servings:4
Cooking Time: 15 Minutes
Ingredients:

- 2 tsp olive oil
- 2 chicken breasts
- Salt and pepper to taste
- ½ tsp garlic powder
- ½ tsp rosemary

Directions:

1. Preheat air fryer to 350°F (175°C). Rub the chicken breasts with olive oil over tops and bottom and sprinkle with garlic powder, rosemary, salt, and pepper. Place the chicken in the frying basket and Air Fry for 9 minutes, flipping once. Let rest onto a serving plate for 5 minutes before cutting into cubes. Serve and enjoy!

Turkey Scotch Eggs

Servings: 4
Cooking Time: 30 Minutes
Ingredients:

- 1 ½ lb ground turkey
- 1 tbsp ground cumin
- 1 tsp ground coriander
- 2 garlic cloves, minced
- 3 raw eggs
- 1 ½ cups bread crumbs
- 6 hard-cooked eggs, peeled
- ½ cup flour

Directions:

1. Preheat air fryer to 370°F (185°C). Place the ground turkey, cumin, coriander, garlic, one egg, and ½ cup of bread crumbs in a large bowl and mix until well incorporated.
2. Divide into 6 equal portions, then flatten each into long ovals. Set aside. In a shallow bowl, beat the remaining raw eggs. In another shallow bowl, add flour. Do the same with another plate for bread crumbs. Roll each cooked egg in flour, then wrap with one oval of chicken sausage until completely covered.
3. Roll again in flour, then coat in the beaten egg before rolling in bread crumbs. Arrange the eggs in the greased frying basket. Air Fry for 12-14 minutes, flipping once until the sausage is cooked and the eggs are brown. Serve.

Sage & Paprika Turkey Cutlets

Servings: 4
Cooking Time: 15 Minutes
Ingredients:

- ½ cup bread crumbs
- ¼ tsp paprika
- Salt and pepper to taste
- ⅛ tsp dried sage
- ⅛ tsp garlic powder
- ¼ tsp ground cumin
- 1 egg
- 4 turkey breast cutlets
- 2 tbsp chopped chervil

Directions:

1. Preheat air fryer to 380°F (195°C). Combine the bread crumbs, paprika, salt, black pepper, sage, cumin, and garlic powder in a bowl and mix well. Beat the egg in another bowl until frothy. Dip the turkey cutlets into the egg mixture, then coat them in the bread crumb mixture. Put the breaded turkey cutlets in the frying basket. Bake for 4 minutes. Turn the cutlets over, then Bake for 4 more minutes. Decorate with chervil and serve.

Peachy Chicken Chunks With Cherries

Servings: 4
Cooking Time: 16 Minutes
Ingredients:

- ⅓ cup peach preserves
- 1 teaspoon ground rosemary
- ½ teaspoon black pepper
- ½ teaspoon salt
- ½ teaspoon marjoram
- 1 teaspoon light olive oil
- 1 pound boneless chicken breasts, cut in 1½-inch chunks
- oil for misting or cooking spray
- 10-ounce package frozen unsweetened dark cherries, thawed and drained

Directions:

1. In a medium bowl, mix together peach preserves, rosemary, pepper, salt, marjoram, and olive oil.
2. Stir in chicken chunks and toss to coat well with the preserve mixture.
3. Spray air fryer basket with oil or cooking spray and lay chicken chunks in basket.
4. Cook at 390°F (20°C) for 7minutes. Stir. Cook for 8 more minutes or until chicken juices run clear.
5. When chicken has cooked through, scatter the cherries over and cook for additional minute to heat cherries.

Chicken Chimichangas

Servings: 4
Cooking Time: 10 Minutes
Ingredients:

- 2 cups cooked chicken, shredded
- 2 tablespoons chopped green chiles
- ½ teaspoon oregano
- ½ teaspoon cumin
- ½ teaspoon onion powder
- ¼ teaspoon garlic powder
- salt and pepper
- 8 flour tortillas (6- or 7-inch diameter)
- oil for misting or cooking spray
- Chimichanga Sauce

Directions:

- 2 tablespoons butter
- 2 tablespoons flour
- 1 cup chicken broth
- ¼ cup light sour cream
- ¼ teaspoon salt
- 2 ounces Pepper Jack or Monterey Jack cheese, shredded

Directions:

1. Make the sauce by melting butter in a saucepan over medium-low heat. Stir in flour until smooth and slightly bubbly. Gradually add broth, stirring constantly until smooth. Cook and stir 1 minute, until the mixture slightly thickens. Remove from heat and stir in sour cream and salt. Set aside.
2. In a medium bowl, mix together the chicken, chiles, oregano, cumin, onion powder, garlic, salt, and pepper. Stir in 3 to 4 tablespoons of the sauce, using just enough to make the filling moist but not soupy.
3. Divide filling among the 8 tortillas. Place filling down the center of tortilla, stopping about 1 inch from edges. Fold one side of tortilla over filling, fold the two sides in, and then roll up. Mist all sides with oil or cooking spray.
4. Place chimichangas in air fryer basket seam side down. To fit more into the basket, you can stand them on their sides with the seams against the sides of the basket.
5. Cook at 360°F（180°C）for 10 minutes or until heated through and crispy brown outside.
6. Add the shredded cheese to the remaining sauce. Stir over low heat, warming just until the cheese melts. Don't boil or sour cream may curdle.
7. Drizzle the sauce over the chimichangas.

Chicago-style Turkey Meatballs

Servings: 6
Cooking Time: 15 Minutes

Ingredients:

- 1 lb ground turkey
- 1 tbsp orange juice
- Salt and pepper to taste
- ½ tsp smoked paprika
- ½ tsp chili powder
- 1 tsp cumin powder
- ¼ red bell pepper, diced
- 1 diced jalapeño pepper
- 2 garlic cloves, minced

Directions:

1. Preheat air fryer to 400°F（205°C）. Combine all of the ingredients in a large bowl. Shape into meatballs. Transfer the meatballs into the greased frying basket. Air Fry for 4 minutes, then flip the meatballs. Air Fry for another 3 minutes until cooked through. Serve immediately.

Asian Meatball Tacos

Servings: 4
Cooking Time: 10 Minutes

Ingredients:

- 1 pound lean ground turkey
- 3 tablespoons soy sauce
- 1 tablespoon brown sugar
- ½ teaspoon onion powder
- ½ teaspoon garlic powder
- 1 tablespoon sesame seeds
- 1 English cucumber
- 4 radishes
- 2 tablespoons white wine vinegar
- 1 lime, juiced and divided
- 1 tablespoon avocado oil
- Salt, to taste
- ½ cup Greek yogurt
- 1 to 3 teaspoons Sriracha, based on desired spiciness
- 1 cup shredded cabbage
- ¼ cup chopped cilantro
- Eight 6-inch flour tortillas

Directions:

1. Preheat the air fryer to 360°F（180°C）.
2. In a large bowl, mix the ground turkey, soy sauce, brown sugar, onion powder, garlic powder, and sesame seeds. Form the meat into 1-inch meatballs and place in the air fryer basket. Cook for 5 minutes, shake the basket, and cook another 5 minutes. Using a food thermometer, make sure the internal temperature of the meatballs is 165°F（75°C）.
3. Meanwhile, dice the cucumber and radishes and place in a medium bowl. Add the white wine vinegar, 1 teaspoon of the lime juice, and the avocado oil, and stir to coat. Season with salt to desired taste.
4. In a large bowl, mix the Greek yogurt, Sriracha, and the remaining lime juice, and stir. Add in the cabbage and cilantro; toss well to create a slaw.
5. In a heavy skillet, heat the tortillas over medium heat for 1 to 2 minutes on each side, or until warmed.
6. To serve, place a tortilla on a plate, top with 5 meatballs, then with cucumber and radish salad, and finish with 2 tablespoons of cabbage slaw.

Southern-fried Chicken Livers

Servings: 4
Cooking Time: 12 Minutes

Ingredients:

- 2 eggs
- 2 tablespoons water
- ¾ cup flour
- 1½ cups panko breadcrumbs
- ½ cup plain breadcrumbs

- 1 teaspoon salt
- ½ teaspoon black pepper
- 20 ounces chicken livers, salted to taste
- oil for misting or cooking spray

Directions:

1. Beat together eggs and water in a shallow dish. Place the flour in a separate shallow dish.

2. In the bowl of a food processor, combine the panko, plain breadcrumbs, salt, and pepper. Process until well mixed and panko crumbs are finely crushed. Place crumbs in a third shallow dish.

3. Dip livers in flour, then egg wash, and then roll in panko mixture to coat well with crumbs.

4. Spray both sides of livers with oil or cooking spray. Cooking in two batches, place livers in air fryer basket in single layer.

5. Cook at 390°F（200°C）for 7minutes. Spray livers, turn over, and spray again. Cook for 5 more minutes, until done inside and coating is golden brown.

6. Repeat to cook remaining livers.

Farmer's Fried Chicken

Servings: 4
Cooking Time: 55 Minutes
Ingredients:

- 3 lb whole chicken, cut into breasts, drumsticks, and thighs
- 2 cups flour
- 4 tsp salt
- 4 tsp dried basil
- 4 tsp dried thyme
- 2 tsp dried shallot powder
- 2 tsp smoked paprika
- 1 tsp mustard powder
- 1 tsp celery salt
- 1 cup kefir
- ¼ cup honey

Directions:

1. Preheat the air fryer to 370°F（185°C）. Combine the flour, salt, basil, thyme, shallot, paprika, mustard powder, and celery salt in a bowl. Pour into a glass jar. Mix the kefir and honey in a large bowl and add the chicken, stir to coat. Marinate for 15 minutes at room temperature. Remove the chicken from the kefir mixture; discard the rest. Put 2/3 cup of the flour mix onto a plate and dip the chicken. Shake gently and put on a wire rack for 10 minutes. Line the frying basket with round parchment paper with holes punched in it. Place the chicken in a single layer and spray with cooking oil. Air Fry for 18-25 minutes, flipping once around minute 10. Serve hot.

Goat Cheese Stuffed Turkey Roulade

Servings: 4
Cooking Time: 55 Minutes
Ingredients:

- 1 boneless turkey breast, skinless
- Salt and pepper to taste
- 4 oz goat cheese
- 1 tbsp marjoram
- 1 tbsp sage
- 2 garlic cloves, minced
- 2 tbsp olive oil
- 2 tbsp chopped cilantro

Directions:

1. Preheat air fryer to 380°F（195°C）. Butterfly the turkey breast with a sharp knife and season with salt and pepper. Mix together the goat cheese, marjoram, sage, and garlic in a bowl. Spread the cheese mixture over the turkey breast, then roll it up tightly, tucking the ends underneath.

2. Put the turkey breast roulade onto a piece of aluminum foil, wrap it up, and place it into the air fryer. Bake for 30 minutes. Turn the turkey breast, brush the top with oil, and then continue to cook for another 10-15 minutes. Slice and serve sprinkled with cilantro.

Chicken Pigs In Blankets

Servings: 4
Cooking Time: 40 Minutes
Ingredients:

- 8 chicken drumsticks, boneless, skinless
- 2 tbsp light brown sugar
- 2 tbsp ketchup
- 1 tbsp grainy mustard
- 8 smoked bacon slices
- 1 tsp chopped fresh sage

Directions:

1. Preheat the air fryer to 350°F（175°C）. Mix brown sugar, sage, ketchup, and mustard in a bowl and brush the chicken with it. Wrap slices of bacon around the drumsticks and brush with the remaining mix. Line the frying basket with round parchment paper with holes. Set 4 drumsticks on the paper, add a raised rack and set the other drumsticks on it. Bake for 25-35 minutes, moving the bottom drumsticks to the top, top to the bottom, and flipping at about 14-16 minutes. Sprinkle with sage and serve.

Irresistible Cheesy Chicken Sticks

Servings: 2
Cooking Time: 30 Minutes
Ingredients:

- 6 mozzarella sticks
- 1 cup flour
- 2 eggs, beaten
- 1 lb ground chicken
- 1 ½ cups breadcrumbs
- ¼ tsp crushed chilis
- ¼ tsp cayenne pepper
- ½ tsp garlic powder
- ¼ tsp shallot powder
- ½ tsp oregano

Directions:

1. Preheat air fryer to 390°F (200°C). Combine crushed chilis, cayenne pepper, garlic powder, shallot powder, and oregano in a bowl. Add the ground chicken and mix well with your hands until evenly combined. In another mixing bowl, beat the eggs until fluffy and until the yolks and whites are fully combined, and set aside.

2. Pour the beaten eggs, flour, and bread crumbs into 3 separate bowls. Roll the mozzarella sticks in the flour, then dip them in the beaten eggs. With hands, wrap the stick in a thin layer of the chicken mixture. Finally, coat the sticks in the crumbs. Place the sticks in the greased frying basket fryer and Air Fry for 18-20 minutes, turning once until crispy. Serve hot.

Cheesy Chicken-avocado Paninis

Servings: 2
Cooking Time: 25 Minutes
Ingredients:

- 2 tbsp mayonnaise
- 4 tsp yellow mustard
- 4 sandwich bread slices
- 4 oz sliced deli chicken ham
- 2 oz sliced provolone cheese
- 2 oz sliced mozzarella
- 1 avocado, sliced
- 1 tomato, sliced
- Salt and pepper to taste
- 1 tsp sesame seeds
- 2 tbsp butter, melted

Directions:

1. Preheat air fryer at 350ºF (175°C). Rub mayonnaise and mustard on the inside of each bread slice. Top 2 bread slices with chicken ham, provolone and mozzarella cheese, avocado, sesame seeds, and tomato slices. Season with salt

and pepper. Then, close sandwiches with the remaining bread slices. Brush the top and bottom of each sandwich lightly with melted butter. Place sandwiches in the frying basket and Bake for 6 minutes, flipping once. Serve.

Granny Pesto Chicken Caprese

Servings: 4
Cooking Time: 30 Minutes
Ingredients:

- 2 tbsp grated Parmesan cheese
- 4 oz fresh mozzarella cheese, thinly sliced
- 16 grape tomatoes, halved
- 4 garlic cloves, minced
- 1 tsp olive oil
- Salt and pepper to taste
- 4 chicken cutlets
- 1 tbsp prepared pesto
- 1 large egg, beaten
- ½ cup bread crumbs
- 2 tbsp Italian seasoning
- 1 tsp balsamic vinegar
- 2 tbsp chopped fresh basil

Directions:

1. Preheat air fryer to 400°F (205°C). In a bowl, coat the tomatoes with garlic, olive oil, salt and pepper. Air Fry for 5 minutes, shaking them twice. Set aside when soft.

2. Place the cutlets between two sheets of parchment paper. Pound the chicken to ¼-inch thickness using a meat mallet. Season on both sides with salt and pepper. Spread an even coat of pesto. Put the beaten egg in a shallow bowl. Mix the crumbs, Italian seasoning, and Parmesan in a second shallow bowl. Dip the chicken in the egg bowl, and then in the crumb mix. Press the crumbs so that they stick to the chicken.

3. Place the chicken in the greased frying basket. Air Fry the chicken for 6-8 minutes, flipping once until golden and cooked through. Put 1 oz of mozzarella and ¼ of the tomatoes on top of each cutlet. When all of the cutlets are cooked, return them to the frying basket and melt the cheese for 2 minutes. Remove from the fryer, drizzle with balsamic vinegar and basil on top.

Chicken Pasta Pie

Servings: 4
Cooking Time: 40 Minutes
Ingredients:

- 1/3 cup green bell peppers, diced
- ¼ cup yellow bell peppers, diced
- ½ cup mozzarella cheese, grated
- 3/4 cup grated Parmesan cheese
- 2/3 cup ricotta cheese

- 2 tbsp butter, melted
- 1 egg
- ¼ tsp salt
- 6 oz cooked spaghetti
- 2 tsp olive oil
- 1/3 cup diced onions
- 2 cloves minced garlic
- ¼ lb ground chicken
- 1 cup marinara sauce
- ½ tsp dried oregano

Directions:

1. Combine the ricotta cheese, 1 tbsp of Parmesan cheese, minced garlic, and salt in a bowl. Whisk the melted butter and egg in another bowl. Add the remaining Parmesan cheese and cooked spaghetti and mix well. Set aside. Warm the olive oil in a skillet over medium heat. Add in onions, green bell peppers, yellow bell peppers and cook for 3 minutes until the onions tender. Stir in ground chicken and cook for 5 minutes until no longer pink.

2. Preheat air fryer at 350ºF（175°C）. Press spaghetti mixture into a greased baking pan, then spread ricotta mixture on top, and finally top with the topping mixture, followed by the marinara sauce. Place baking pan in the frying basket and Bake for 10 minutes. Scatter with mozzarella cheese on top and cook for 4 more minutes. Let rest for 20 minutes before releasing the sides of the baking pan. Cut into slices and serve sprinkled with oregano.

Asian Sweet Chili Chicken

Servings: 4
Cooking Time: 30 Minutes
Ingredients:
- 2 chicken breasts, cut into 1-inch pieces
- 1 cup cornstarch
- 1 tsp chicken seasoning
- Salt and pepper to taste
- 2 eggs
- 1 ½ cups sweet chili sauce

Directions:

1. Preheat air fryer to 360°F（180°C）. Mix cornstarch, chicken seasoning, salt and pepper in a large bowl. In another bowl, beat the eggs. Dip the chicken in the cornstarch mixture to coat. Next, dip the chicken into the egg, then return to the cornstarch. Transfer chicken to the air fryer.

2. Lightly spray all of the chicken with cooking oil. Air Fry for 15-16 minutes, shaking the basket once or until golden. Transfer chicken to a serving dish and drizzle with sweet-and-sour sauce. Serve immediately.

Buttered Chicken Thighs

Servings: 4

Cooking Time: 30 Minutes
Ingredients:
- 4 bone-in chicken thighs, skinless
- 2 tbsp butter, melted
- 1 tsp garlic powder
- 1 tsp lemon zest
- Salt and pepper to taste
- 1 lemon, sliced

Directions:

1. Preheat air fryer to 380°F（195°C）.Stir the chicken thighs in the butter, lemon zest, garlic powder, and salt. Divide the chicken thighs between 4 pieces of foil and sprinkle with black pepper, and then top with slices of lemon. Bake in the air fryer for 20-22 minutes until golden. Serve.

Pulled Turkey Quesadillas

Servings: 4
Cooking Time: 15 Minutes
Ingredients:
- ¾ cup pulled cooked turkey breast
- 6 tortilla wraps
- 1/3 cup grated Swiss cheese
- 1 small red onion, sliced
- 2 tbsp Mexican chili sauce

Directions:

1. Preheat air fryer to 400°F（205°C）. Lay 3 tortilla wraps on a clean workspace, then spoon equal amounts of Swiss cheese, turkey, Mexican chili sauce, and red onion on the tortillas. Spritz the exterior of the tortillas with cooking spray. Air Fry the quesadillas, one at a time, for 5-8 minutes. The cheese should be melted and the outsides crispy. Serve.

Masala Chicken With Charred Vegetables

Servings: 4
Cooking Time: 35 Minutes
Ingredients:
- 8 boneless, skinless chicken thighs
- ¼ cup yogurt
- 3 garlic cloves, minced
- 1 tbsp lime juice
- 1 tsp ginger-garlic paste
- 1 tsp garam masala
- ¼ tsp ground turmeric
- ¼ tsp red pepper flakes
- 1 ¼ tsp salt
- 7 oz shishito peppers
- 2 vine tomatoes, quartered
- 1 tbsp chopped cilantro
- 1 lime, cut into wedges

Directions:

1. Mix yogurt, garlic, lime juice, ginger paste, garam masala, turmeric, flakes, and salt in a bowl. Place the thighs in a zipper bag and pour in the marinade. Massage the chicken to coat and refrigerate for 2 hours.

2. Preheat air fryer to 400°F (205°C). Remove the chicken from the bag and discard the marinade. Put the chicken in the greased frying basket and Arr Fry for 13-15 minutes, flipping once until browned and thoroughly cooked. Set chicken aside and cover with foil. Lightly spray shishitos and tomatoes with cooking oil. Place in the frying basket and Bake for 8 minutes, shaking the basket once until soft and slightly charred. Sprinkle with salt. Top the chicken and veggies with cilantro and lemon wedges.

Chicken Breasts Wrapped In Bacon

Servings: 4
Cooking Time: 35 Minutes
Ingredients:
- ¼ cup mayonnaise
- ¼ cup sour cream
- 3 tbsp ketchup
- 1 tbsp yellow mustard
- 1 tbsp light brown sugar
- 1 lb chicken tenders
- 1 tsp dried parsley
- 8 bacon slices

Directions:
1. Preheat the air fryer to 370°F (185°C). Combine the mayonnaise, sour cream, ketchup, mustard, and brown sugar in a bowl and mix well, then set aside. Sprinkle the chicken with the parsley and wrap each one in a slice of bacon. Put the wrapped chicken in the frying basket in a single layer and Air Fry for 18-20 minutes, flipping once until the bacon is crisp. Serve with sauce.

Greek Chicken Wings

Servings: 4
Cooking Time: 30 Minutes
Ingredients:
- 8 whole chicken wings
- ½ lemon, juiced
- ½ tsp garlic powder
- 1 tsp shallot powder
- ½ tsp Greek seasoning
- Salt and pepper to taste
- ¼ cup buttermilk
- ½ cup all-purpose flour

Directions:
1. Preheat air fryer to 400°F (205°C). Put the wings in a resealable bag along with lemon juice, garlic, shallot, Greek seasoning, salt and pepper. Seal the bag and shake to coat. Set up bowls large enough to fit the wings.

2. In one bowl, pour the buttermilk. In the other, add flour. Using tongs, dip the wings into the buttermilk, then dredge in flour. Transfer the wings in the greased frying basket, spraying lightly with cooking oil. Air Fry for 25 minutes, shaking twice, until golden and cooked through. Allow to cool slightly, and serve.

Greek Gyros With Chicken & Rice

Servings: 4
Cooking Time: 25 Minutes
Ingredients:
- 1 lb chicken breasts, cubed
- ¼ cup cream cheese
- 2 tbsp olive oil
- 1 tsp dried oregano
- 1 tsp ground cumin
- 1 tsp ground cinnamon
- ¼ tsp ground nutmeg
- Salt and pepper to taste
- ¼ tsp ground turmeric
- 2 cups cooked rice
- 1 cup Tzatziki sauce

Directions:
1. Preheat air fryer to 380°F (195°C). Put all ingredients in a bowl and mix together until the chicken is coated well. Spread the chicken mixture in the frying basket, then Bake for 10 minutes. Stir the chicken mixture and Bake for an additional 5 minutes. Serve with rice and tzatziki sauce.

Country Chicken Hoagies

Servings: 2
Cooking Time: 30 Minutes
Ingredients:
- ¼ cup button mushrooms, sliced
- 1 hoagie bun, halved
- 1 chicken breast, cubed
- ½ white onion, sliced
- 1 cup bell pepper strips
- 2 cheddar cheese slices

Directions:
1. Preheat air fryer to 320°F (160°C). Place the chicken pieces, onions, bell pepper strips, and mushroom slices on one side of the frying basket. Lay the hoagie bun halves, crusty side up and soft side down, on the other half of the air fryer. Bake for 10 minutes. Flip the hoagie buns and cover with cheddar cheese. Stir the chicken and vegetables. Cook for another 6 minutes until the cheese is melted and the chicken is juicy on the inside and crispy on the outside. Place the cheesy hoagie halves on a serving plate and cover one half with the chicken and veggies. Close with the other cheesy hoagie half. Serve.

Coconut Curry Chicken With Coconut Rice

Servings: 4
Cooking Time: 56 Minutes
Ingredients:

- 1 (14-ounce) can coconut milk
- 2 tablespoons green or red curry paste
- zest and juice of one lime
- 1 clove garlic, minced
- 1 tablespoon grated fresh ginger
- 1 teaspoon ground cumin
- 1 (3- to 4-pound) chicken, cut into 8 pieces
- vegetable or olive oil
- salt and freshly ground black pepper
- fresh cilantro leaves
- For the rice:
- 1 cup basmati or jasmine rice
- 1 cup water
- 1 cup coconut milk
- ½ teaspoon salt
- freshly ground black pepper

Directions:

1. Make the marinade by combining the coconut milk, curry paste, lime zest and juice, garlic, ginger and cumin. Coat the chicken on all sides with the marinade and marinate the chicken for 1 hour to overnight in the refrigerator.

2. Preheat the air fryer to 380°F (195°C).

3. Brush the bottom of the air fryer basket with oil. Transfer the chicken thighs and drumsticks from the marinade to the air fryer basket, letting most of the marinade drip off. Season to taste with salt and freshly ground black pepper.

4. Air-fry the chicken drumsticks and thighs at 380°F (195°C) for 12 minutes. Flip the chicken over and continue to air-fry for another 12 minutes. Set aside and air-fry the chicken breast pieces at 380°F (195°C) for 15 minutes. Turn the chicken breast pieces over and air-fry for another 12 minutes. Return the chicken thighs and drumsticks to the air fryer and air-fry for an additional 5 minutes.

5. While the chicken is cooking, make the coconut rice. Rinse the rice kernels with water and drain well. Place the rice in a medium saucepan with a tight fitting lid, along with the water, coconut milk, salt and freshly ground black pepper. Bring the mixture to a boil and then cover, reduce the heat and let it cook gently for 20 minutes without lifting the lid. When the time is up, lift the lid, fluff with a fork and set aside.

6. Remove the chicken from the air fryer and serve warm with the coconut rice and fresh cilantro scattered around.

Spiced Chicken Breasts

Servings: 4
Cooking Time: 20 Minutes
Ingredients:

- ½ tsp dried oregano
- ½ tsp granulated garlic
- ½ tsp granulated onion
- ½ tsp chili powder
- ¼ tsp sweet paprika
- Salt and pepper to taste
- 1 lb chicken breasts, sliced
- 2 tbsp yellow mustard

Directions:

1. Preheat air fryer to 375°F (190°C). Mix together oregano, salt, garlic, onion, chili powder, paprika, and black pepper in a small bowl. Coat the chicken with mustard in a bowl. Sprinkle the seasoning mix over the chicken. Place the chicken in the greased frying basket and Air Fry for 7-8, flipping once until cooked through. Serve immediately.

Sesame Orange Chicken

Servings: 2
Cooking Time: 9 Minutes
Ingredients:

- 1 pound boneless, skinless chicken breasts, cut into cubes
- salt and freshly ground black pepper
- ¼ cup cornstarch
- 2 eggs, beaten
- 1½ cups panko breadcrumbs
- vegetable or peanut oil, in a spray bottle
- 12 ounces orange marmalade
- 1 tablespoon soy sauce
- 1 teaspoon minced ginger
- 2 tablespoons hoisin sauce
- 1 tablespoon sesame oil
- sesame seeds, toasted

Directions:

1. Season the chicken pieces with salt and pepper. Set up a dredging station. Put the cornstarch in a zipper-sealable plastic bag. Place the beaten eggs in a bowl and put the panko breadcrumbs in a shallow dish. Transfer the seasoned chicken to the bag with the cornstarch and shake well to completely coat the chicken on all sides. Remove the chicken from the bag, shaking off any excess cornstarch and dip the pieces into the egg. Let any excess egg drip from the chicken and transfer into the breadcrumbs, pressing the crumbs onto the chicken pieces with your hands. Spray the chicken pieces with vegetable or peanut oil.

2. Preheat the air fryer to 400°F (205°C).

3. Combine the orange marmalade, soy sauce, ginger, hoisin sauce and sesame oil in a saucepan. Bring the mixture

to a boil on the stovetop, lower the heat and simmer for 10 minutes, until the sauce has thickened. Set aside and keep warm.

4.   Transfer the coated chicken to the air fryer basket and air-fry at 400°F（205°C） for 9 minutes, shaking the basket a few times during the cooking process to help the chicken cook evenly.

5.   Right before serving, toss the browned chicken pieces with the sesame orange sauce. Serve over white rice with steamed broccoli. Sprinkle the sesame seeds on top.

Pickle Brined Fried Chicken

Servings: 4
Cooking Time: 47 Minutes
Ingredients:

- 4 bone-in, skin-on chicken legs, cut into drumsticks and thighs (about 3½ pounds)
- pickle juice from a 24-ounce jar of kosher dill pickles
- ½ cup flour
- salt and freshly ground black pepper
- 2 eggs
- 1 cup fine breadcrumbs
- 1 teaspoon salt
- 1 teaspoon freshly ground black pepper
- ½ teaspoon ground paprika
- ⅛ teaspoon ground cayenne pepper
- vegetable or canola oil in a spray bottle

Directions:

1.   Place the chicken in a shallow dish and pour the pickle juice over the top. Cover and transfer the chicken to the refrigerator to brine in the pickle juice for 3 to 8 hours.

2.   When you are ready to cook, remove the chicken from the refrigerator to let it come to room temperature while you set up a dredging station. Place the flour in a shallow dish and season well with salt and freshly ground black pepper. Whisk the eggs in a second shallow dish. In a third shallow dish, combine the breadcrumbs, salt, pepper, paprika and cayenne pepper.

3.   Preheat the air fryer to 370°F（185°C）.

4.   Remove the chicken from the pickle brine and gently dry it with a clean kitchen towel. Dredge each piece of chicken in the flour, then dip it into the egg mixture, and finally press it into the breadcrumb mixture to coat all sides of the chicken. Place the breaded chicken on a plate or baking sheet and spray each piece all over with vegetable oil.

5.   Air-fry the chicken in two batches. Place two chicken thighs and two drumsticks into the air fryer basket. Air-fry for 10 minutes. Then, gently turn the chicken pieces over and air-fry for another 10 minutes. Remove the chicken pieces and let them rest on plate – do not cover. Repeat with the second batch of chicken, air-frying for 20 minutes, turning the chicken over halfway through.

6.   Lower the temperature of the air fryer to 340°F（170°C）. Place the first batch of chicken on top of the second batch already in the basket and air-fry for an additional 7 minutes. Serve warm and enjoy.

Vegetarians Recipes

Vegetable Hand Pies

Servings: 8
Cooking Time: 10 Minutes Per Batch
Ingredients:
- ¾ cup vegetable broth
- 8 ounces potatoes
- ¾ cup frozen chopped broccoli, thawed
- ¼ cup chopped mushrooms
- 1 tablespoon cornstarch
- 1 tablespoon milk
- 1 can organic flaky biscuits (8 large biscuits)
- oil for misting or cooking spray

Directions:
1. Place broth in medium saucepan over low heat.
2. While broth is heating, grate raw potato into a bowl of water to prevent browning. You will need ¾ cup grated potato.
3. Roughly chop the broccoli.
4. Drain potatoes and put them in the broth along with the broccoli and mushrooms. Cook on low for 5 minutes.
5. Dissolve cornstarch in milk, then stir the mixture into the broth. Cook about a minute, until mixture thickens a little. Remove from heat and cool slightly.
6. Separate each biscuit into 2 rounds. Divide vegetable mixture evenly over half the biscuit rounds, mounding filling in the center of each.
7. Top the four rounds with filling, then the other four rounds and crimp the edges together with a fork.
8. Spray both sides with oil or cooking spray and place 4 pies in a single layer in the air fryer basket.
9. Cook at 330°F (165°C) for approximately 10 minutes.
10. Repeat with the remaining biscuits. The second batch may cook more quickly because the fryer will be hot.

Pineapple & Veggie Souvlaki

Servings: 4
Cooking Time: 35 Minutes
Ingredients:
- 1 can pineapple rings in pineapple juice
- 1 red bell pepper, stemmed and seeded
- 1/3 cup butter
- 2 tbsp apple cider vinegar
- 2 tbsp hot sauce
- 1 tbsp allspice
- 1 tsp ground nutmeg
- 16 oz feta cheese
- 1 red onion, peeled
- 8 mushrooms, quartered

Directions:

1. Preheat air fryer to 400°F (205°C). Whisk the butter, pineapple juice, apple vinegar, hot sauce, allspice, and nutmeg until smooth. Set aside. Slice feta cheese into 16 cubes, then the bell pepper into 16 chunks, and finally red onion into 8 wedges, separating each wedge into 2 pieces.
2. Cut pineapple ring into quarters. Place veggie cubes and feta into the butter bowl and toss to coat. Thread the veggies, tofu, and pineapple onto 8 skewers, alternating 16 pieces on each skewer. Grill for 15 minutes until golden brown and cooked. Serve warm.

Sweet Corn Bread

Servings: 6
Cooking Time: 35 Minutes
Ingredients:
- 2 eggs, beaten
- ½ cup cornmeal
- ½ cup pastry flour
- 1/3 cup sugar
- 1 tsp lemon zest
- ½ tbsp baking powder
- ¼ tsp salt
- ¼ tsp baking soda
- ½ tbsp lemon juice
- ½ cup milk
- ¼ cup sunflower oil

Directions:
1. Preheat air fryer to 350°F (175°C). Add the cornmeal, flour, sugar, lemon zest, baking powder, salt, and baking soda in a bowl. Stir with a whisk until combined. Add the eggs, lemon juice, milk, and oil to another bowl and stir well. Add the wet mixture to the dry mixture and stir gently until combined. Spray a baking pan with oil. Pour the batter in and Bake in the fryer for 25 minutes or until golden and a knife inserted in the center comes out clean. Cut into wedges and serve.

Pinto Bean Casserole

Servings: 2
Cooking Time: 15 Minutes
Ingredients:
- 1 can pinto beans
- ¼ cup tomato sauce
- 2 tbsp cornstarch
- 2 garlic cloves, minced
- ½ tsp dried oregano
- ½ tsp cumin
- 1 tsp smoked paprika
- Salt and pepper to taste

Directions:

1. Preheat air fryer to 390°F（200°C）. Stir the beans, tomato sauce, cornstarch, garlic, oregano, cumin, smoked paprika, salt, and pepper in a bowl until combined. Pour the bean mix into a greased baking pan. Bake in the fryer for 4 minutes. Remove, stir, and Bake for 4 minutes or until the mix is thick and heated through. Serve hot.

Harissa Veggie Fries

Servings: 4
Cooking Time: 55 Minutes
Ingredients:

*   1 pound red potatoes, cut into rounds
*   1 onion, diced
*   1 green bell pepper, diced
*   1 red bell pepper, diced
*   2 tbsp olive oil
*   Salt and pepper to taste
*   ¾ tsp garlic powder
*   ¾ tsp harissa seasoning

Directions:

1. Combine all ingredients in a large bowl and mix until potatoes are well coated and seasoned. Preheat air fryer to 350°F（175°C）. Pour all of the contents in the bowl into the frying basket. Bake for 35 minutes, shaking every 10 minutes, until golden brown and soft. Serve hot.

Party Giant Nachos

Servings: 2
Cooking Time: 20 Minutes
Ingredients:

*   2 tbsp sour cream
*   ½ tsp chili powder
*   Salt to taste
*   2 soft corn tortillas
*   2 tsp avocado oil
*   ½ cup refried beans
*   ¼ cup cheddar cheese shreds
*   2 tbsp Parmesan cheese
*   2 tbsp sliced black olives
*   ¼ cup torn iceberg lettuce
*   ¼ cup baby spinach
*   ½ sliced avocado
*   1 tomato, diced
*   2 lime wedges

Directions:

1. Preheat air fryer at 400°F（205°C）. Whisk the sour cream, chili powder, and salt in a small bowl. Brush tortillas with avocado oil and season one side with salt. Place tortillas in the frying basket and Bake for 3 minutes. Set aside.

2. Layer the refried beans, Parmesan and cheddar cheeses in the tortillas. Place them back into the basket and Bake for 2 minutes. Divide tortillas into 2 serving plates. Top each tortilla with black olives, baby spinach, lettuce, and tomatoes. Dollop sour cream mixture on each. Serve with lime and avocado wedges on the side.

Veggie Burgers

Servings: 4
Cooking Time: 15 Minutes
Ingredients:

*   2 cans black beans, rinsed and drained
*   ½ cup cooked quinoa
*   ½ cup shredded raw sweet potato
*   ¼ cup diced red onion
*   2 teaspoons ground cumin
*   1 teaspoon coriander powder
*   ½ teaspoon salt
*   oil for misting or cooking spray
*   8 slices bread
*   suggested toppings: lettuce, tomato, red onion, Pepper Jack cheese, guacamole

Directions:

1. In a medium bowl, mash the beans with a fork.
2. Add the quinoa, sweet potato, onion, cumin, coriander, and salt and mix well with the fork.
3. Shape into 4 patties, each ¾-inch thick.
4. Mist both sides with oil or cooking spray and also mist the basket.
5. Cook at 390°F（200°C）for 15minutes.
6. Follow the recipe for Toast, Plain & Simple.
7. Pop the veggie burgers back in the air fryer for a minute or two to reheat if necessary.
8. Serve on the toast with your favorite burger toppings.

Fennel Tofu Bites

Servings: 4
Cooking Time: 35 Minutes
Ingredients:

*   1/3 cup vegetable broth
*   2 tbsp tomato sauce
*   2 tsp soy sauce
*   1 tbsp nutritional yeast
*   1 tsp Italian seasoning
*   1 tsp granulated sugar
*   1 tsp ginger grated
*   ½ tsp fennel seeds
*   ½ tsp garlic powder
*   Salt and pepper to taste
*   14 oz firm tofu, cubed
*   2/3 cup bread crumbs
*   1 tsp Italian seasoning

- 2 tsp toasted sesame seeds
- 1 cup marinara sauce, warm

Directions:

1. In a large bowl, whisk the vegetable broth, soy sauce, ginger, tomato sauce, nutritional yeast, Italian seasoning, sugar, fennel seeds, garlic powder, salt and black pepper. Toss in tofu to coat. Let marinate covered in the fridge for 30 minutes, tossing once.

2. Preheat air fryer at 350ºF（175°C）. Mix the breadcrumbs, Italian seasoning, and salt in a bowl. Strain marinade from tofu cubes and dredge them in the breadcrumb mixture. Place tofu cubes in the greased frying basket and Air Fry for 10 minutes, turning once. Serve sprinkled with sesame seeds and marinara sauce on the side.

Corn And Pepper Jack Chile Rellenos With Roasted Tomato Sauce

Servings: 3
Cooking Time: 30 Minutes
Ingredients:

- 3 Poblano peppers
- 1 cup all-purpose flour*
- salt and freshly ground black pepper
- 2 eggs, lightly beaten
- 1 cup plain breadcrumbs*
- olive oil, in a spray bottle
- Sauce
- 2 cups cherry tomatoes
- 1 Jalapeño pepper, halved and seeded
- 1 clove garlic
- ¼ red onion, broken into large pieces
- 1 tablespoon olive oil
- salt, to taste
- 2 tablespoons chopped fresh cilantro
- Filling
- olive oil
- ¼ red onion, finely chopped
- 1 teaspoon minced garlic
- 1 cup corn kernels, fresh or frozen
- 2 cups grated pepper jack cheese

Directions:

1. Start by roasting the peppers. Preheat the air fryer to 400°F（205°C）. Place the peppers into the air fryer basket and air-fry at 400°F（205°C）for 10 minutes, turning them over halfway through the cooking time. Remove the peppers from the basket and cover loosely with foil.

2. While the peppers are cooling, make the roasted tomato sauce. Place all sauce Ingredients except for the cilantro into the air fryer basket and air-fry at 400°F（205°C）for 10

minutes, shaking the basket once or twice. When the sauce Ingredients have finished air-frying, transfer everything to a blender or food processor and blend or process to a smooth sauce, adding a little warm water to get the desired consistency. Season to taste with salt, add the cilantro and set aside.

3. While the sauce Ingredients are cooking in the air fryer, make the filling. Heat a skillet on the stovetop over medium heat. Add the olive oil and sauté the red onion and garlic for 4 to 5 minutes. Transfer the onion and garlic to a bowl, stir in the corn and cheese, and set aside.

4. Set up a dredging station with three shallow dishes. Place the flour, seasoned with salt and pepper, in the first shallow dish. Place the eggs in the second dish, and fill the third shallow dish with the breadcrumbs. When the peppers have cooled, carefully slice into one side of the pepper to create an opening. Pull the seeds out of the peppers and peel away the skins, trying not to tear the pepper. Fill each pepper with some of the corn and cheese filling and close the pepper up again by folding one side of the opening over the other. Carefully roll each pepper in the seasoned flour, then into the egg and finally into the breadcrumbs to coat on all sides, trying not to let the pepper fall open. Spray the peppers on all sides with a little olive oil.

5. Air-fry two peppers at a time at 350°F（175°C）for 6 minutes. Turn the peppers over and air-fry for another 4 minutes. Serve the peppers warm on a bed of the roasted tomato sauce.

Gorgeous Jalapeño Poppers

Servings: 6
Cooking Time: 25 Minutes
Ingredients:

- 6 center-cut bacon slices, halved
- 6 jalapeños, halved lengthwise
- 4 oz cream cheese
- ¼ cup grated Gruyere cheese
- 2 tbsp chives, chopped

Directions:

1. Scoop out seeds and membranes of the jalapeño halves, discard. Combine cream cheese, Gruyere cheese, and chives in a bowl. Fill the jalapeño halves with the cream cheese filling using a small spoon. Wrap each pepper with a slice of bacon and secure with a toothpick.

2. Preheat air fryer to 325°F（160°C）. Put the stuffed peppers in a single layer on the greased frying basket and Bake until the peppers are tender, cheese is melted, and the bacon is brown, 11-13minutes. Serve warm and enjoy!

Spinach And Cheese Calzone

Servings: 2
Cooking Time: 10 Minutes
Ingredients:
- ⅔ cup frozen chopped spinach, thawed
- 1 cup grated mozzarella cheese
- 1 cup ricotta cheese
- ½ teaspoon Italian seasoning
- ½ teaspoon salt
- freshly ground black pepper
- 1 store-bought or homemade pizza dough* (about 12 to 16 ounces)
- 2 tablespoons olive oil
- pizza or marinara sauce (optional)

Directions:
1. Drain and squeeze all the water out of the thawed spinach and set it aside. Mix the mozzarella cheese, ricotta cheese, Italian seasoning, salt and freshly ground black pepper together in a bowl. Stir in the chopped spinach.
2. Divide the dough in half. With floured hands or on a floured surface, stretch or roll one half of the dough into a 10-inch circle. Spread half of the cheese and spinach mixture on half of the dough, leaving about one inch of dough empty around the edge.
3. Fold the other half of the dough over the cheese mixture, almost to the edge of the bottom dough to form a half moon. Fold the bottom edge of dough up over the top edge and crimp the dough around the edges in order to make the crust and seal the calzone. Brush the dough with olive oil. Repeat with the second half of dough to make the second calzone.
4. Preheat the air fryer to 360°F (180°C).
5. Brush or spray the air fryer basket with olive oil. Air-fry the calzones one at a time for 10 minutes, flipping the calzone over half way through. Serve with warm pizza or marinara sauce if desired.

Fried Potatoes With Bell Peppers

Servings: 4
Cooking Time: 30 Minutes
Ingredients:
- 3 russet potatoes, cubed
- 1 tbsp canola oil
- 1 tbsp olive oil
- 1 tsp paprika
- Salt and pepper to taste
- 1 chopped shallot
- ½ chopped red bell peppers
- ½ diced yellow bell peppers

Directions:
1. Preheat air fryer to 370°F (185°C). Whisk the canola oil, olive oil, paprika, salt, and pepper in a bowl. Toss in the

potatoes to coat. Place the potatoes in the air fryer and Bake for 20 minutes, shaking the basket periodically. Top the potatoes with shallot and bell peppers and cook for an additional 3-4 minutes or until the potatoes are cooked through and the peppers are soft. Serve warm.

Quinoa & Black Bean Stuffed Peppers

Servings: 4
Cooking Time: 30 Minutes
Ingredients:
- ½ cup vegetable broth
- ½ cup quinoa
- 1 can black beans
- ½ cup diced red onion
- 1 garlic clove, minced
- ½ tsp salt
- ½ tsp ground cumin
- ¼ tsp paprika
- ¼ tsp ancho chili powder
- 4 bell peppers, any color
- ½ cup grated cheddar
- ¼ cup chopped cilantro
- ½ cup red enchilada sauce

Directions:
1. Add vegetable broth and quinoa to a small saucepan over medium heat. Bring to a boil, then cover and let it simmer for 5 minutes. Turn off the heat.
2. Preheat air fryer to 350°F (175°C). Transfer quinoa to a medium bowl and stir in black beans, onion, red enchilada sauce, ancho chili powder, garlic, salt, cumin, and paprika. Cut the top ¼-inch off the bell peppers. Remove seeds and membranes. Scoop quinoa filling into each pepper and top with cheddar cheese. Transfer peppers to the frying basket and bake for 10 minutes until peppers are soft and filling is heated through. Garnish with cilantro. Serve warm along with salsa. Enjoy!

Hellenic Zucchini Bites

Servings:4
Cooking Time: 20 Minutes
Ingredients:
- 8 pitted Kalamata olives, halved
- 2 tsp olive oil
- 1 zucchini, sliced
- ½ tsp salt
- ½ tsp Greek oregano
- ½ cup marinara sauce
- ½ cup feta cheese crumbles
- 2 tbsp chopped dill

Directions:

1. Preheat air fryer to 350ºF (175°C). Brush olive oil over both sides of the zucchini circles. Lay out slices on a large plate and sprinkle with salt. Then, top with marinara sauce, feta crumbles, Greek oregano and olives. Place the topped circles in the frying basket and Air Fry for 5 minutes. Garnish with chopped dill to serve.

Vegan French Toast

Servings: 4
Cooking Time: 15 Minutes
Ingredients:
- 1 ripe banana, mashed
- ¼ cup protein powder
- ½ cup milk
- 2 tbsp ground flaxseed
- 4 bread slices
- 2 tbsp agave syrup

Directions:
1. Preheat air fryer to 370ºF (185°C). Combine the banana, protein powder, milk, and flaxseed in a shallow bowl and mix well Dip bread slices into the mixture. Place the slices on a lightly greased pan in a single layer and pour any of the remaining mixture evenly over the bread. Air Fry for 10 minutes, or until golden brown and crispy, flipping once. Serve warm topped with agave syrup.

Mexican Twice Air-fried Sweet Potatoes

Servings: 2
Cooking Time: 42 Minutes
Ingredients:
- 2 large sweet potatoes
- olive oil
- salt and freshly ground black pepper
- ⅓ cup diced red onion
- ⅓ cup diced red bell pepper
- ½ cup canned black beans, drained and rinsed
- ½ cup corn kernels, fresh or frozen
- ½ teaspoon chili powder
- 1½ cups grated pepper jack cheese, divided
- Jalapeño peppers, sliced

Directions:
1. Preheat the air fryer to 400ºF (205°C).
2. Rub the outside of the sweet potatoes with olive oil and season with salt and freshly ground black pepper. Transfer the potatoes into the air fryer basket and air-fry at 400ºF (205°C) for 30 minutes, rotating the potatoes a few times during the cooking process.
3. While the potatoes are air-frying, start the potato filling. Preheat a large sauté pan over medium heat on the stovetop. Add the onion and pepper and sauté for a few minutes, until the vegetables start to soften. Add the black beans, corn, and chili powder and sauté for another 3 minutes. Set the mixture aside.
4. Remove the sweet potatoes from the air fryer and let them rest for 5 minutes. Slice off one inch of the flattest side of both potatoes. Scrape the potato flesh out of the potatoes, leaving half an inch of potato flesh around the edge of the potato. Place all the potato flesh into a large bowl and mash it with a fork. Add the black bean mixture and 1 cup of the pepper jack cheese to the mashed sweet potatoes. Season with salt and freshly ground black pepper and mix well. Stuff the hollowed out potato shells with the black bean and sweet potato mixture, mounding the filling high in the potatoes.
5. Transfer the stuffed potatoes back into the air fryer basket and air-fry at 370ºF (185°C) for 10 minutes. Sprinkle the remaining cheese on top of each stuffed potato, lower the heat to 340ºF (170°C) and air-fry for an additional 2 minutes to melt the cheese. Top with a couple slices of Jalapeño pepper and serve warm with a green salad.

Breaded Avocado Tacos

Servings: 3
Cooking Time: 20 Minutes
Ingredients:
- 2 tomatoes, diced
- ¼ cup diced red onion
- 1 jalapeño, finely diced
- 1 tbsp lime juice
- 1 tsp lime zest
- ¼ cup chopped cilantro
- 1 tsp salt
- 1 egg
- 2 tbsp milk
- 1 cup crumbs
- ¼ cup of almond flour
- 1 avocado, sliced into fries
- 6 flour tortillas
- 1 cup coleslaw mix

Directions:
1. In a bowl, combine the tomatoes, jalapeño, red onion, lime juice, lime zest, cilantro, and salt. Let chill the pico de gallo covered in the fridge until ready to use.
2. Preheat air fryer at 375ºF (190°C). In a small bowl, beat egg and milk. In another bowl, add breadcrumbs. Dip avocado slices in the egg mixture, then dredge them in the mixed almond flour and breadcrumbs. Place avocado slices in the greased frying basket and Air Fry for 5 minutes. Add 2 avocado fries to each tortilla. Top each with coleslaw mix. Serve immediately.

Curried Cauliflower

Servings: 2
Cooking Time: 30 Minutes
Ingredients:
- 1 cup canned diced tomatoes
- 2 cups milk
- 2 tbsp lime juice
- 1 tbsp allspice
- 1 tbsp curry powder
- 1 tsp ground ginger
- ½ tsp ground cumin
- 12 oz frozen cauliflower
- 16 oz cheddar cheese, cubed
- ¼ cup chopped cilantro

Directions:
1. Preheat air fryer to 375°F (190°C). Combine the tomatoes and their juices, milk, lime juice, allspice, curry powder, ginger, and cumin in a baking pan. Toss in cauliflower and cheddar cheese until coated. Roast for 15 minutes, stir and Roast for another 10 minutes until bubbly. Scatter with cilantro before serving.

Roasted Vegetable, Brown Rice And Black Bean Burrito

Servings: 2
Cooking Time: 20 Minutes
Ingredients:
- ½ zucchini, sliced ¼-inch thick
- ½ red onion, sliced
- 1 yellow bell pepper, sliced
- 2 teaspoons olive oil
- salt and freshly ground black pepper
- 2 burrito size flour tortillas
- 1 cup grated pepper jack cheese
- ½ cup cooked brown rice
- ½ cup canned black beans, drained and rinsed
- ¼ teaspoon ground cumin
- 1 tablespoon chopped fresh cilantro
- fresh salsa, guacamole and sour cream, for serving

Directions:
1. Preheat the air fryer to 400°F (205°C).
2. Toss the vegetables in a bowl with the olive oil, salt and freshly ground black pepper. Air-fry at 400°F (205°C) for 12 to 15 minutes, shaking the basket a few times during the cooking process. The vegetables are done when they are cooked to your liking.
3. In the meantime, start building the burritos. Lay the tortillas out on the counter. Sprinkle half of the cheese in the center of the tortillas. Combine the rice, beans, cumin and cilantro in a bowl, season to taste with salt and freshly ground black pepper and then divide the mixture between the two tortillas. When the vegetables have finished cooking, transfer them to the two tortillas, placing the vegetables on top of the rice and beans. Sprinkle the remaining cheese on top and then roll the burritos up, tucking in the sides of the tortillas as you roll. Brush or spray the outside of the burritos with olive oil and transfer them to the air fryer.
4. Air-fry at 360°F (180°C) for 8 minutes, turning them over when there are about 2 minutes left. The burritos will have slightly brown spots, but will still be pliable.
5. Serve with some fresh salsa, guacamole and sour cream.

Tomato & Squash Stuffed Mushrooms

Servings:2
Cooking Time: 15 Minutes
Ingredients:
- 12 whole white button mushrooms
- 3 tsp olive oil
- 2 tbsp diced zucchini
- 1 tsp soy sauce
- ¼ tsp salt
- 2 tbsp tomato paste
- 1 tbsp chopped parsley

Directions:
1. Preheat air fryer to 350ºF (175°C). Remove the stems from the mushrooms. Chop the stems finely and set in a bowl. Brush 1 tsp of olive oil around the top ridge of mushroom caps. To the bowl of the stem, add all ingredients, except for parsley, and mix. Divide and press mixture into tops of mushroom caps. Place the mushrooms in the frying basket and Air Fry for 5 minutes. Top with parsley. Serve.

Meatless Kimchi Bowls

Servings:4
Cooking Time: 20 Minutes
Ingredients:
- 2 cups canned chickpeas
- 1 carrot, julienned
- 6 scallions, sliced
- 1 zucchini, diced
- 2 tbsp coconut aminos
- 2 tsp sesame oil
- 1 tsp rice vinegar
- 2 tsp granulated sugar
- 1 tbsp gochujang
- ¼ tsp salt
- ½ cup kimchi
- 2 tsp roasted sesame seeds

Directions:
1. Preheat air fryer to 350ºF (175°C). Combine all ingredients, except for the kimchi, 2 scallions, and sesame seeds, in a baking pan. Place the pan in the frying basket and Air Fry for 6 minutes. Toss in kimchi and cook for 2 more minutes. Divide between 2 bowls and garnish with the remaining scallions and sesame seeds. Serve immediately.

Roasted Vegetable Stromboli

Servings: 2
Cooking Time: 29 Minutes
Ingredients:
- ½ onion, thinly sliced
- ½ red pepper, julienned
- ½ yellow pepper, julienned
- olive oil
- 1 small zucchini, thinly sliced
- 1 cup thinly sliced mushrooms
- 1½ cups chopped broccoli
- 1 teaspoon Italian seasoning
- salt and freshly ground black pepper
- ½ recipe of Blue Jean Chef Pizza dough (page 231) OR 1 (14-ounce) tube refrigerated pizza dough
- 2 cups grated mozzarella cheese
- ¼ cup grated Parmesan cheese
- ½ cup sliced black olives, optional
- dried oregano
- pizza or marinara sauce

Directions:
1. Preheat the air fryer to 400°F (205°C).
2. Toss the onions and peppers with a little olive oil and air-fry the vegetables for 7 minutes, shaking the basket once or twice while the vegetables cook. Add the zucchini, mushrooms, broccoli and Italian seasoning to the basket. Add a little more olive oil and season with salt and freshly ground black pepper. Air-fry for an additional 7 minutes, shaking the basket halfway through. Let the vegetables cool slightly while you roll out the pizza dough.
3. On a lightly floured surface, roll or press the pizza dough out into a 13-inch by 11-inch rectangle, with the long side closest to you. Sprinkle half of the mozzarella and Parmesan cheeses over the dough leaving an empty 1-inch border from the edge farthest away from you. Spoon the roasted vegetables over the cheese, sprinkle the olives over everything and top with the remaining cheese.
4. Start rolling the stromboli away from you and toward the empty border. Make sure the filling stays tightly tucked inside the roll. Finally, tuck the ends of the dough in and pinch the seam shut. Place the seam side down and shape the stromboli into a U-shape to fit into the air fryer basket. Cut 4 small slits with the tip of a sharp knife evenly in the top of the dough, lightly brush the stromboli with a little oil and sprinkle with some dried oregano.
5. Preheat the air fryer to 360°F (180°C).
6. Spray or brush the air fryer basket with oil and transfer the U-shaped stromboli to the air fryer basket. Air-fry for 15 minutes, flipping the stromboli over after the first 10 minutes. (Use a plate to invert the Stromboli out of the air fryer basket and then slide it back into the basket off the plate.)
7. To remove, carefully flip the stromboli over onto a cutting board. Let it rest for a couple of minutes before serving. Cut it into 2-inch slices and serve with pizza or marinara sauce.

Rainbow Quinoa Patties

Servings: 4
Cooking Time: 20 Minutes
Ingredients:
- 1 cup canned tri-bean blend, drained and rinsed
- 2 tbsp olive oil
- ½ tsp ground cumin
- ½ tsp garlic salt
- 1 tbsp paprika
- 1/3 cup uncooked quinoa
- 2 tbsp chopped onion
- ¼ cup shredded carrot
- 2 tbsp chopped cilantro
- 1 tsp chili powder
- ½ tsp salt
- 2 tbsp mascarpone cheese

Directions:
1. Place 1/3 cup of water, 1 tbsp of olive oil, cumin, and salt in a saucepan over medium heat and bring it to a boil. Remove from the heat and stir in quinoa. Let rest covered for 5 minutes.
2. Preheat air fryer at 350ºF (175°C). Using the back of a fork, mash beans until smooth. Toss in cooked quinoa and the remaining ingredients. Form mixture into 4 patties. Place patties in the greased frying basket and Air Fry for 6 minutes, turning once, and brush with the remaining olive oil. Serve immediately.

Vegetarian Paella

Servings: 3
Cooking Time: 50 Minutes
Ingredients:
- ½ cup chopped artichoke hearts
- ½ sliced red bell peppers
- 4 mushrooms, thinly sliced
- ½ cup canned diced tomatoes
- ½ cup canned chickpeas
- 3 tbsp hot sauce
- 2 tbsp lemon juice
- 1 tbsp allspice
- 1 cup rice

Directions:
1. Preheat air fryer to 400°F (205°C). Combine the artichokes, peppers, mushrooms, tomatoes and their juices, chickpeas, hot sauce, lemon juice, and allspice in a baking pan. Roast for 10 minutes. Pour in rice and 2 cups of boiling water, cover with aluminum foil, and Roast for 22 minutes. Discard the foil and Roast for 3 minutes until the top is crisp. Let cool slightly before stirring. Serve.

Colorful Vegetable Medley

Servings: 4
Cooking Time: 20 Minutes
Ingredients:
- 1 lb green beans, chopped
- 2 carrots, cubed
- Salt and pepper to taste
- 1 zucchini, cut into chunks
- 1 red bell pepper, sliced

Directions:
1. Preheat air fryer to 390°F (200°C). Combine green beans, carrots, salt and pepper in a large bowl. Spray with cooking oil and transfer to the frying basket. Roast for 6 minutes.
2. Combine zucchini and red pepper in a bowl. Season to taste and spray with cooking oil; set aside. When the cooking time is up, add the zucchini and red pepper to the basket. Cook for another 6 minutes. Serve and enjoy.

Cheesy Eggplant Rounds

Servings: 4
Cooking Time: 35 Minutes
Ingredients:
- 1 eggplant, peeled
- 2 eggs
- ½ cup all-purpose flour
- ¾ cup bread crumbs
- 2 tbsp grated Swiss cheese
- Salt and pepper to taste
- ¾ cup tomato passata
- ½ cup shredded Parmesan
- ½ cup shredded mozzarella

Directions:
1. Preheat air fryer to 400°F (205°C). Slice the eggplant into ½-inch rounds. Set aside. Set out three small bowls. In the first bowl, add flour. In the second bowl, beat the eggs. In the third bowl, mix the crumbs, 2 tbsp of grated Swiss cheese, salt, and pepper. Dip each eggplant in the flour, then dredge in egg, then coat with bread crumb mixture. Arrange the eggplant rounds on the greased frying basket and spray with cooking oil. Bake for 7 minutes. Top each eggplant round with 1 tsp passata and ½ tbsp each of shredded Parmesan and mozzarella. Cook until the cheese melts, 2-3 minutes. Serve warm and enjoy!

Stuffed Portobellos

Servings: 4
Cooking Time: 45 Minutes
Ingredients:
- 1 cup cherry tomatoes
- 2 ¼ tsp olive oil
- 3 tbsp grated mozzarella
- 1 cup chopped baby spinach
- 1 garlic clove, minced
- ¼ tsp dried oregano
- ¼ tsp dried thyme
- Salt and pepper to taste
- ¼ cup bread crumbs
- 4 portobello mushrooms, stemmed and gills removed
- 1 tbsp chopped parsley

Directions:
1. Preheat air fryer to 360°F (180°C). Combine tomatoes, ¼ teaspoon olive oil, and salt in a small bowl. Arrange in a single layer in the parchment-lined frying basket and Air Fry for 10 minutes. Stir and flatten the tomatoes with the back of a spoon, then Air Fry for another 6-8 minutes. Transfer the tomatoes to a medium bowl and combine with spinach, garlic, oregano, thyme, pepper, bread crumbs, and the rest of the olive oil.
2. Place the mushrooms on a work surface with the gills facing up. Spoon tomato mixture and mozzarella cheese equally into the mushroom caps and transfer the mushrooms to the frying basket. Air Fry for 8-10 minutes until the mushrooms have softened and the tops are golden. Garnish with chopped parsley and serve.

Creamy Broccoli & Mushroom Casserole

Servings:4
Cooking Time: 30 Minutes
Ingredients:
- 4 cups broccoli florets, chopped
- 1 cup crushed cheddar cheese crisps
- ¼ cup diced onion
- ¼ tsp dried thyme
- ¼ tsp dried marjoram
- ¼ tsp dried oregano
- ½ cup diced mushrooms
- 1 egg
- 2 tbsp sour cream
- ¼ cup mayonnaise
- Salt and pepper to taste

Directions:
1. Preheat air fryer to 350ºF (175°C). Combine all ingredients, except for the cheese crisps, in a bowl. Spoon mixture into a round cake pan. Place cake pan in the frying basket and Bake for 14 minutes. Let sit for 10 minutes. Distribute crushed cheddar cheese crisps over the top and serve.

Fake Shepherd's Pie

Servings:6
Cooking Time: 40 Minutes
Ingredients:

- ½ head cauliflower, cut into florets
- 1 sweet potato, diced
- 1 tbsp olive oil
- ¼ cup cheddar shreds
- 2 tbsp milk
- Salt and pepper to taste
- 2 tsp avocado oil
- 1 cup beefless grounds
- ½ onion, diced
- 2 cloves garlic, minced
- 1 carrot, diced
- ½ cup green peas
- 1 stalk celery, diced
- 2/3 cup tomato sauce
- 1 tsp chopped rosemary
- 1 tsp thyme leaves

Directions:

1. Place cauliflower and sweet potato in a pot of salted boiling water over medium heat and simmer for 7 minutes until fork tender. Strain and transfer to a bowl. Put in avocado oil, cheddar, milk, salt and pepper. Mash until smooth.
2. Warm olive oil in a skillet over medium-high heat and stir in beefless grounds and vegetables and stir-fry for 4 minutes until veggies are tender. Stir in tomato sauce, rosemary, thyme, salt, and black pepper. Set aside.
3. Preheat air fryer to 350ºF (175°C). Spoon filling into a round cake pan lightly greased with olive oil and cover with the topping. Using the tines of a fork, run shallow lines in the top of cauliflower for a decorative touch. Place cake pan in the frying basket and Air Fry for 12 minutes. Let sit for 10 minutes before serving.

Tacos

Servings: 24
Cooking Time: 8 Minutes Per Batch
Ingredients:

- 1 24-count package 4-inch corn tortillas
- 1½ cups refried beans (about ¾ of a 15-ounce can)
- 4 ounces sharp Cheddar cheese, grated
- ½ cup salsa
- oil for misting or cooking spray

Directions:

1. Preheat air fryer to 390°F (200°C).
2. Wrap refrigerated tortillas in damp paper towels and microwave for 30 to 60 seconds to warm. If necessary, rewarm tortillas as you go to keep them soft enough to fold without breaking.
3. Working with one tortilla at a time, top with 1 tablespoon of beans, 1 tablespoon of grated cheese, and 1 teaspoon of salsa. Fold over and press down very gently on the center. Press edges firmly all around to seal. Spray both sides with oil or cooking spray.
4. Cooking in two batches, place half the tacos in the air fryer basket. To cook 12 at a time, you may need to stand them upright and lean some against the sides of basket. It's okay if they're crowded as long as you leave a little room for air to circulate around them.
5. Cook for 8 minutes or until golden brown and crispy.
6. Repeat steps 4 and 5 to cook remaining tacos.

Mushroom-rice Stuffed Bell Peppers

Servings: 4
Cooking Time: 30 Minutes
Ingredients:

- 4 red bell peppers, tops sliced
- 1 ½ cups cooked rice
- ¼ cup chopped leeks
- ¼ cup sliced mushrooms
- ¾ cup tomato sauce
- Salt and pepper to taste
- ¾ cup shredded mozzarella
- 2 tbsp parsley, chopped

Directions:

1. Fill a large pot of water and heat on high until it boils. Remove seeds and membranes from the peppers. Carefully place peppers into the boiling water for 5 minutes. Remove and set aside to cool. Mix together rice, leeks, mushrooms, tomato sauce, parsley, salt, and pepper in a large bowl. Stuff each pepper with the rice mixture. Top with mozzarella.
2. Preheat air fryer to 350°F (175°C). Arrange the peppers on the greased frying basket and Bake for 10 minutes. Serve.

Charred Cauliflower Tacos

Servings: 4
Cooking Time: 10 Minutes
Ingredients:

- 1 head cauliflower, washed and cut into florets
- 2 tablespoons avocado oil
- 2 teaspoons taco seasoning
- 1 medium avocado
- ½ teaspoon garlic powder
- ¼ teaspoon black pepper
- ¼ teaspoon salt
- 2 tablespoons chopped red onion
- 2 teaspoons fresh squeezed lime juice
- ¼ cup chopped cilantro
- Eight 6-inch corn tortillas
- ½ cup cooked corn
- ½ cup shredded purple cabbage

Directions:

1. Preheat the air fryer to 390°F (200°C).

2. In a large bowl, toss the cauliflower with the avocado oil and taco seasoning. Set the metal trivet inside the air fryer basket and liberally spray with olive oil.
3. Place the cauliflower onto the trivet and cook for 10 minutes, shaking every 3 minutes to allow for an even char.
4. While the cauliflower is cooking, prepare the avocado sauce. In a medium bowl, mash the avocado; then mix in the garlic powder, pepper, salt, and onion. Stir in the lime juice and cilantro; set aside.
5. Remove the cauliflower from the air fryer basket.
6. Place 1 tablespoon of avocado sauce in the middle of a tortilla, and top with corn, cabbage, and charred cauliflower. Repeat with the remaining tortillas. Serve immediately.

Tandoori Paneer Naan Pizza

Servings: 4
Cooking Time: 10 Minutes
Ingredients:

- 6 tablespoons plain Greek yogurt, divided
- 1¼ teaspoons garam marsala, divided
- ½ teaspoon turmeric, divided
- ¼ teaspoon garlic powder
- ½ teaspoon paprika, divided
- ½ teaspoon black pepper, divided
- 3 ounces paneer, cut into small cubes
- 1 tablespoon extra-virgin olive oil
- 2 teaspoons minced garlic
- 4 cups baby spinach
- 2 tablespoons marinara sauce
- ¼ teaspoon salt
- 2 plain naan breads (approximately 6 inches in diameter)
- ½ cup shredded part-skim mozzarella cheese

Directions:
1. Preheat the air fryer to 350°F (175°C).
2. In a small bowl, mix 2 tablespoons of the yogurt, ½ teaspoon of the garam marsala, ¼ teaspoon of the turmeric, the garlic powder, ¼ teaspoon of the paprika, and ¼ teaspoon of the black pepper. Toss the paneer cubes in the mixture and let marinate for at least an hour.
3. Meanwhile, in a pan, heat the olive oil over medium heat. Add in the minced garlic and sauté for 1 minute. Stir in the spinach and begin to cook until it wilts. Add in the remaining 4 tablespoons of yogurt and the marinara sauce. Stir in the remaining ¾ teaspoon of garam marsala, the remaining ¼ teaspoon of turmeric, the remaining ¼ teaspoon of paprika, the remaining ¼ teaspoon of black pepper, and the salt. Let simmer a minute or two, and then remove from the heat.
4. Equally divide the spinach mixture amongst the two naan breads. Place 1½ ounces of the marinated paneer on each naan.
5. Liberally spray the air fryer basket with olive oil mist.
6. Use a spatula to pick up one naan and place it in the air fryer basket.

7. Cook for 4 minutes, open the basket and sprinkle ¼ cup of mozzarella cheese on top, and cook another 4 minutes.
8. Remove from the air fryer and repeat with the remaining naan.
9. Serve warm.

Fried Rice With Curried Tofu

Servings: 4
Cooking Time: 25 Minutes
Ingredients:

- 8 oz extra-firm tofu, cubed
- ½ cup canned coconut milk
- 2 tsp red curry paste
- 2 cloves garlic, minced
- 1 tbsp avocado oil
- 1 tbsp coconut oil
- 2 cups cooked rice
- 1 tbsp turmeric powder
- Salt and pepper to taste
- 4 lime wedges
- ¼ cup chopped cilantro

Directions:
1. Preheat air fryer to 350°F (175°C). Combine tofu, coconut milk, curry paste, garlic, and avocado oil in a bowl. Pour the mixture into a baking pan. Place the pan in the frying basket and Air Fry for 10 minutes, stirring once.
2. Melt the coconut oil in a skillet over medium heat. Add in rice, turmeric powder, salt, and black pepper, and cook for 2 minutes or until heated through. Divide the cooked rice between 4 medium bowls and top with tofu mixture and sauce. Top with cilantro and lime wedges to serve.

Grilled Cheese Sandwich

Servings: 1
Cooking Time: 15 Minutes
Ingredients:

- 2 sprouted bread slices
- 1 tsp sunflower oil
- 2 Halloumi cheese slices
- 1 tsp mellow white miso
- 1 garlic clove, minced
- 2 tbsp kimchi
- 1 cup Iceberg lettuce, torn

Directions:
1. Preheat air fryer to 390°F (200°C). Brush the outside of the bread with sunflower oil. Put the sliced cheese, buttered sides facing out inside and close the sandwich. Put the sandwich in the frying basket and Air Fry for 12 minutes, flipping once until golden and crispy on the outside.
2. On a plate, open the sandwich and spread the miso and garlic clove over the inside of one slice. Top with kimchi and lettuce, close the sandwich, cut in half, and serve.

Desserts And Sweets

Cherry Hand Pies

Servings: 8
Cooking Time: 8 Minutes
Ingredients:

- 4 cups frozen or canned pitted tart cherries (if using canned, drain and pat dry)
- 2 teaspoons lemon juice
- ½ cup sugar
- ¼ cup cornstarch
- 1 teaspoon vanilla extract
- 1 Basic Pie Dough (see the preceding recipe) or store-bought pie dough

Directions:
1. In a medium saucepan, place the cherries and lemon juice and cook over medium heat for 10 minutes, or until the cherries begin to break down.
2. In a small bowl, stir together the sugar and cornstarch. Pour the sugar mixture into the cherries, stirring constantly. Cook the cherry mixture over low heat for 2 to 3 minutes, or until thickened. Remove from the heat and stir in the vanilla extract. Allow the cherry mixture to cool to room temperature, about 30 minutes.
3. Meanwhile, bring the pie dough to room temperature. Divide the dough into 8 equal pieces. Roll out the dough to ¼-inch thickness in circles. Place ¼ cup filling in the center of each rolled dough. Fold the dough to create a half-circle. Using a fork, press around the edges to seal the hand pies. Pierce the top of the pie with a fork for steam release while cooking. Continue until 8 hand pies are formed.
4. Preheat the air fryer to 350°F (175°C).
5. Place a single layer of hand pies in the air fryer basket and spray with cooking spray. Cook for 8 to 10 minutes or until golden brown and cooked through.

Easy Bread Pudding

Servings: 4
Cooking Time: 25 Minutes
Ingredients:

- 2 cups sandwich bread cubes
- ½ cup pecan pieces
- ½ cup raisins
- 3 eggs
- ¼ cup half-and-half
- ¼ cup dark corn syrup
- 1 tsp vanilla extract
- 2 tbsp bourbon
- 2 tbsp dark brown sugar
- ¼ tsp ground cinnamon
- ½ tsp nutmeg

- ¼ tsp salt

Directions:
1. Preheat air fryer at 325ºF (160°C). Spread the bread pieces in a cake pan and layer pecan pieces and raisins over the top. Whisk the eggs, half-and-half, corn syrup, bourbon, vanilla extract, sugar, cinnamon, nutmeg, and salt in a bowl. Pour egg mixture over pecan pieces. Let sit for 10 minutes. Place the cake pan in the frying basket and Bake for 15 minutes. Let cool onto a cooling rack for 10 minutes before slicing. Serve immediately.

Almond-roasted Pears

Servings: 4
Cooking Time: 15 Minutes
Ingredients:

- Yogurt Topping
- 1 container vanilla Greek yogurt (5–6 ounces)
- ¼ teaspoon almond flavoring
- 2 whole pears
- ¼ cup crushed Biscoff cookies (approx. 4 cookies)
- 1 tablespoon sliced almonds
- 1 tablespoon butter

Directions:
1. Stir almond flavoring into yogurt and set aside while preparing pears.
2. Halve each pear and spoon out the core.
3. Place pear halves in air fryer basket.
4. Stir together the cookie crumbs and almonds. Place a quarter of this mixture into the hollow of each pear half.
5. Cut butter into 4 pieces and place one piece on top of crumb mixture in each pear.
6. Cook at 360°F (180°C) for 15 minutes or until pears have cooked through but are still slightly firm.
7. Serve pears warm with a dollop of yogurt topping.

Nutty Banana Bread

Servings: 6
Cooking Time: 30 Minutes
Ingredients:

- 2 bananas
- 2 tbsp ground flaxseed
- ¼ cup milk
- 1 tbsp apple cider vinegar
- 1 tbsp vanilla extract
- ½ tsp ground cinnamon
- 2 tbsp honey
- ½ cup oat flour
- ½ tsp baking soda
- 3 tbsp butter

Directions:

1. Preheat air fryer to 320°F (160°C). Using a fork, mash the bananas until chunky. Mix in flaxseed, milk, apple vinegar, vanilla extract, cinnamon, and honey. Finally, toss in oat flour and baking soda until smooth but still chunky. Divide the batter between 6 cupcake molds. Top with one and a half teaspoons of butter each and swirl it a little. Bake for 18 minutes until golden brown and puffy. Let cool completely before serving.

Giant Buttery Chocolate Chip Cookie

Servings: 4
Cooking Time: 16 Minutes
Ingredients:

* ⅔ cup plus 1 tablespoon All-purpose flour
* ¼ teaspoon Baking soda
* ¼ teaspoon Table salt
* Baking spray (see the headnote)
* 4 tablespoons (¼ cup/½ stick) plus 1 teaspoon Butter, at room temperature
* ¼ cup plus 1 teaspoon Packed dark brown sugar
* 3 tablespoons plus 1 teaspoon Granulated white sugar
* 2½ tablespoons Pasteurized egg substitute, such as Egg Beaters
* ½ teaspoon Vanilla extract
* ¾ cup plus 1 tablespoon Semisweet or bittersweet chocolate chips

Directions:

1. Preheat the air fryer to 350°F (175°C).
2. Whisk the flour, baking soda, and salt in a bowl until well combined.
3. For a small air fryer, coat the inside of a 6-inch round cake pan with baking spray. For a medium air fryer, coat the inside of a 7-inch round cake pan with baking spray. And for a large air fryer, coat the inside of an 8-inch round cake pan with baking spray.
4. Using a hand electric mixer at medium speed, beat the butter, brown sugar, and granulated white sugar in a bowl until smooth and thick, about 3 minutes, scraping down the inside of the bowl several times.
5. Beat in the pasteurized egg substitute or egg (as applicable) and vanilla until uniform. Scrape down and remove the beaters. Fold in the flour mixture and chocolate chips with a rubber spatula, just until combined. Scrape and gently press this dough into the prepared pan, getting it even across the pan to the perimeter.
6. Set the pan in the basket and air-fry undisturbed for 16 minutes, or until the cookie is puffed, browned, and feels set to the touch.
7. Transfer the pan to a wire rack and cool for 10 minutes. Loosen the cookie from the perimeter with a spatula, then

invert the pan onto a cutting board and let the cookie come free. Remove the pan and reinvert the cookie onto the wire rack. Cool for 5 minutes more before slicing into wedges to serve.

Baked Apple

Servings: 6
Cooking Time: 20 Minutes
Ingredients:

* 3 small Honey Crisp or other baking apples
* 3 tablespoons maple syrup
* 3 tablespoons chopped pecans
* 1 tablespoon firm butter, cut into 6 pieces

Directions:

1. Put ½ cup water in the drawer of the air fryer.
2. Wash apples well and dry them.
3. Split apples in half. Remove core and a little of the flesh to make a cavity for the pecans.
4. Place apple halves in air fryer basket, cut side up.
5. Spoon 1½ teaspoons pecans into each cavity.
6. Spoon ½ tablespoon maple syrup over pecans in each apple.
7. Top each apple with ½ teaspoon butter.
8. Cook at 360°F (180°C) for 20 minutes, until apples are tender.

Banana Bread Cake

Servings: 6
Cooking Time: 18-22 Minutes
Ingredients:

* ¾ cup plus 2 tablespoons All-purpose flour
* ½ teaspoon Baking powder
* ¼ teaspoon Baking soda
* ¼ teaspoon Table salt
* 4 tablespoons (¼ cup/½ stick) Butter, at room temperature
* ½ cup Granulated white sugar
* 2 Small ripe bananas, peeled
* 5 tablespoons Pasteurized egg substitute, such as Egg Beaters
* ¼ cup Buttermilk
* ¾ teaspoon Vanilla extract
* Baking spray (see here)

Directions:

1. Preheat the air fryer to 325°F (160°C) (or 330°F (165°C), if that's the closest setting).
2. Mix the flour, baking powder, baking soda, and salt in a small bowl until well combined.
3. Using an electric hand mixer at medium speed, beat the butter and sugar in a medium bowl until creamy and smooth, about 3 minutes, occasionally scraping down the inside of the bowl.

4. Beat in the bananas until smooth. Then beat in egg substitute or egg, buttermilk, and vanilla until uniform. (The batter may look curdled at this stage. The flour mixture will smooth it out.) Add the flour mixture and beat at low speed until smooth and creamy.

5. Use the baking spray to generously coat the inside of a 6-inch round cake pan for a small batch, a 7-inch round cake pan for a medium batch, or an 8-inch round cake pan for a large batch. Scrape and spread the batter into the pan, smoothing the batter out to an even layer.

6. Set the pan in the basket and air-fry for 18 minutes for a 6-inch layer, 20 minutes for a 7-inch layer, or 22 minutes for an 8-inch layer, or until the cake is well browned and set even if there's a little soft give right at the center. Start checking it at the 16-minute mark to know where you are.

7. Use hot pads or silicone baking mitts to transfer the cake pan to a wire rack. To unmold, set a cutting board over the baking pan and invert both the board and the pan. Lift the still-warm pan off the cake layer. Set the wire rack on top of that layer and invert all of it with the cutting board so that the cake layer is now right side up on the wire rack. Remove the cutting board and continue cooling the cake for at least 10 minutes or to room temperature, about 40 minutes, before slicing into wedges.

Bananas Foster Bread Pudding

Servings: 4
Cooking Time: 25 Minutes
Ingredients:
- ½ cup brown sugar
- 3 eggs
- ¾ cup half and half
- 1 teaspoon pure vanilla extract
- 6 cups cubed Kings Hawaiian bread (½-inch cubes), ½ pound
- 2 bananas, sliced
- 1 cup caramel sauce, plus more for serving

Directions:
1. Preheat the air fryer to 350°F (175°C) .
2. Combine the brown sugar, eggs, half and half and vanilla extract in a large bowl, whisking until the sugar has dissolved and the mixture is smooth. Stir in the cubed bread and toss to coat all the cubes evenly. Let the bread sit for 10 minutes to absorb the liquid.
3. Mix the sliced bananas and caramel sauce together in a separate bowl.
4. Fill the bottom of 4 (8-ounce) greased ramekins with half the bread cubes. Divide the caramel and bananas between the ramekins, spooning them on top of the bread cubes. Top with the remaining bread cubes and wrap each ramekin with aluminum foil, tenting the foil at the top to

leave some room for the bread to puff up during the cooking process.
5. Air-fry two bread puddings at a time for 25 minutes. Let the puddings cool a little and serve warm with additional caramel sauce drizzled on top. A scoop of vanilla ice cream would be nice too and in keeping with our Bananas Foster theme!

Magic Giant Chocolate Cookies

Servings: 2
Cooking Time: 30 Minutes
Ingredients:
- 2 tbsp white chocolate chips
- ½ cup flour
- 1/8 tsp baking soda
- ¼ cup butter, melted
- ¼ cup light brown sugar
- 2 tbsp granulated sugar
- 2 eggs
- 2 tbsp milk chocolate chips
- ¼ cup chopped pecans
- ¼ cup chopped hazelnuts
- ½ tsp vanilla extract
- Salt to taste

Directions:
1. Preheat air fryer at 350ºF (175°C) . In a bowl, combine the flour, baking soda, butter, brown sugar, granulated sugar, eggs, milk chocolate chips, white chocolate chips, pecans, hazelnuts, vanilla extract, and salt. Press cookie mixture onto a greased pizza pan. Place pizza pan in the frying basket and Bake for 10 minutes. Let cool completely for 10 minutes. Turn over on a plate and serve.

Mixed Berry Pie

Servings: 4
Cooking Time: 25 Minutes
Ingredients:
- 2/3 cup blackberries, cut into thirds
- ¼ cup sugar
- 2 tbsp cornstarch
- ¼ tsp vanilla extract
- ¼ tsp peppermint extract
- ½ tsp lemon zest
- 1 cup sliced strawberries
- 1 cup raspberries
- 1 refrigerated piecrust
- 1 large egg

Directions:
1. Mix the sugar, cornstarch, vanilla, peppermint extract, and lemon zest in a bowl. Toss in all berries gently until combined. Pour into a greased dish. On a clean workspace,

lay out the dough and cut into a 7-inch diameter round. Cover the baking dish with the round and crimp the edges. With a knife, cut 4 slits in the top to vent.

2.   Beat 1 egg and 1 tbsp of water to make an egg wash. Brush the egg wash over the crust. Preheat air fryer to 350°F (175°C). Put the baking dish into the frying basket. Bake for 15 minutes or until the crust is golden and the berries are bubbling through the vents. Remove from the air fryer and let cool for 15 minutes. Serve warm.

Baked Stuffed Pears

Servings: 4
Cooking Time: 15 Minutes + Cooling Time
Ingredients:
- 4 cored pears, halved
- ½ cup chopped cashews
- ½ cup dried cranberries
- ¼ cup agave nectar
- ½ stick butter, softened
- ½ tsp ground cinnamon
- ½ cup apple juice

Directions:
1.   Preheat the air fryer to 350°F (175°C). Combine the cashews, cranberries, agave nectar, butter, and cinnamon and mix well. Stuff this mixture into the pears, heaping it up on top. Set the pears in a baking pan and pour the apple juice into the bottom of the pan. Put the pan in the fryer and Bake for 10-12 minutes or until the pears are tender. Let cool before serving.

Fried Oreos

Servings: 12
Cooking Time: 6 Minutes Per Batch
Ingredients:
- oil for misting or nonstick spray
- 1 cup complete pancake and waffle mix
- 1 teaspoon vanilla extract
- ½ cup water, plus 2 tablespoons
- 12 Oreos or other chocolate sandwich cookies
- 1 tablespoon confectioners' sugar

Directions:
1.   Spray baking pan with oil or nonstick spray and place in basket.
2.   Preheat air fryer to 390°F (200°C).
3.   In a medium bowl, mix together the pancake mix, vanilla, and water.
4.   Dip 4 cookies in batter and place in baking pan.
5.   Cook for 6minutes, until browned.
6.   Repeat steps 4 and 5 for the remaining cookies.
7.   Sift sugar over warm cookies.

Coconut Macaroons

Servings: 12
Cooking Time: 8 Minutes

Ingredients:
- 1⅓ cups shredded, sweetened coconut
- 4½ teaspoons flour
- 2 tablespoons sugar
- 1 egg white
- ½ teaspoon almond extract

Directions:
1.   Preheat air fryer to 330°F (165°C).
2.   Mix all ingredients together.
3.   Shape coconut mixture into 12 balls.
4.   Place all 12 macaroons in air fryer basket. They won't expand, so you can place them close together, but they shouldn't touch.
5.   Cook at 330°F (165°C) for 8 minutes, until golden.

Chocolate Soufflés

Servings: 2
Cooking Time: 14 Minutes
Ingredients:
- butter and sugar for greasing the ramekins
- 3 ounces semi-sweet chocolate, chopped
- ¼ cup unsalted butter
- 2 eggs, yolks and white separated
- 3 tablespoons sugar
- ½ teaspoon pure vanilla extract
- 2 tablespoons all-purpose flour
- powdered sugar, for dusting the finished soufflés
- heavy cream, for serving

Directions:
1.   Butter and sugar two 6-ounce ramekins. (Butter the ramekins and then coat the butter with sugar by shaking it around in the ramekin and dumping out any excess.)
2.   Melt the chocolate and butter together, either in the microwave or in a double boiler. In a separate bowl, beat the egg yolks vigorously. Add the sugar and the vanilla extract and beat well again. Drizzle in the chocolate and butter, mixing well. Stir in the flour, combining until there are no lumps.
3.   Preheat the air fryer to 330°F (165°C).
4.   In a separate bowl, whisk the egg whites to soft peak stage (the point at which the whites can almost stand up on the end of your whisk). Fold the whipped egg whites into the chocolate mixture gently and in stages.
5.   Transfer the batter carefully to the buttered ramekins, leaving about ½-inch at the top. (You may have a little extra batter, depending on how airy the batter is, so you might be able to squeeze out a third soufflé if you want to.) Place the ramekins into the air fryer basket and air-fry for 14 minutes. The soufflés should have risen nicely and be brown on top. (Don't worry if the top gets a little dark – you'll be covering it with powdered sugar in the next step.)
6.   Dust with powdered sugar and serve immediately with heavy cream to pour over the top at the table.

Mango-chocolate Custard

Servings: 4
Cooking Time: 40 Minutes
Ingredients:
- 4 egg yolks
- 2 tbsp granulated sugar
- 1/8 tsp almond extract
- 1 ½ cups half-and-half
- 3/4 cup chocolate chips
- 1 mango, pureed
- 1 mango, chopped
- 1 tsp fresh mint, chopped

Directions:
1. Beat the egg yolks, sugar, and almond extract in a bowl. Set aside. Place half-and-half in a saucepan over low heat and bring it to a low simmer. Whisk a spoonful of heated half-and-half into egg mixture, then slowly whisk egg mixture into saucepan. Stir in chocolate chips and mango purée for 10 minutes until chocolate melts. Divide between 4 ramekins.
2. Preheat air fryer at 350ºF（175°C）. Place ramekins in the frying basket and Bake for 6-8 minutes. Let cool onto a cooling rack for 15 minutes, then let chill covered in the fridge for at least 2 hours or up to 2 days. Serve with chopped mangoes and mint on top.

Fruit Turnovers

Servings: 6
Cooking Time: 25 Minutes
Ingredients:
- 1 sheet puff pastry dough
- 6 tsp peach preserves
- 3 kiwi, sliced
- 1 large egg, beaten
- 1 tbsp icing sugar

Directions:
1. Prepare puff pastry by cutting it into 6 rectangles. Roll out the pastry with a rolling pin into 5-inch squares. On your workspace, position one square so that it looks like a diamond with points to the top and bottom. Spoon 1 tsp of the preserves on the bottom half and spread it, leaving a ½-inch border from the edge. Place half of one kiwi on top of the preserves. Brush the clean edges with the egg, then fold the top corner over the filling to make a triangle. Crimp with a fork to seal the pastry. Brush the top of the pastry with egg. Preheat air fryer to 350°F（175°C）. Put the pastries in the greased frying basket. Air Fry for 10 minutes, flipping once until golden and puffy. Remove from the fryer, let cool and dush with icing sugar. Serve.

Cherry Cheesecake Rolls

Servings: 6

Cooking Time: 30 Minutes
Ingredients:
- 1 can crescent rolls
- 4 oz cream cheese
- 1 tbsp cherry preserves
- 1/3 cup sliced fresh cherries

Directions:
1. Roll out the dough into a large rectangle on a flat work surface. Cut the dough into 12 rectangles by cutting 3 cuts across and 2 cuts down. In a microwave-safe bowl, soften cream cheese for 15 seconds. Stir together with cherry preserves. Mound 2 tsp of the cherries-cheese mix on each piece of dough. Carefully spread the mixture but not on the edges. Top with 2 tsp of cherries each. Roll each triangle to make a cylinder.
2. Preheat air fryer to 350°F（175°C）. Place the first batch of the rolls in the greased air fryer. Spray the rolls with cooking oil and Bake for 8 minutes. Let cool in the air fryer for 2-3 minutes before removing. Serve.

Fried Snickers Bars

Servings:8
Cooking Time: 4 Minutes
Ingredients:
- ⅓ cup All-purpose flour
- 1 Large egg white(s), beaten until foamy
- 1½ cups (6 ounces) Vanilla wafer cookie crumbs
- 8 Fun-size (0.6-ounce/17-gram) Snickers bars, frozen
- Vegetable oil spray

Directions:
1. Preheat the air fryer to 400°F（205°C）.
2. Set up and fill three shallow soup plates or small pie plates on your counter: one for the flour, one for the beaten egg white(s), and one for the cookie crumbs.
3. Unwrap the frozen candy bars. Dip one in the flour, turning it to coat on all sides. Gently shake off any excess, then set it in the beaten egg white(s). Turn it to coat all sides, even the ends, then let any excess egg white slip back into the rest. Set the candy bar in the cookie crumbs. Turn to coat on all sides, even the ends. Dip the candy bar back in the egg white(s) a second time, then into the cookie crumbs a second time, making sure you have an even coating all around. Coat the covered candy bar all over with vegetable oil spray. Set aside so you can dip and coat the remaining candy bars.
4. Set the coated candy bars in the basket with as much air space between them as possible. Air-fry undisturbed for 4 minutes, or until golden brown.
5. Remove the basket from the machine and let the candy bars cool in the basket for 10 minutes. Use a nonstick-safe spatula to transfer them to a wire rack and cool for 5 minutes more before chowing down.

Giant Oatmeal - peanut Butter Cookie

Servings: 4
Cooking Time: 18 Minutes
Ingredients:
- 1 cup Rolled oats (not quick-cooking or steel-cut oats)
- ½ cup All-purpose flour
- ½ teaspoon Ground cinnamon
- ½ teaspoon Baking soda
- ⅓ cup Packed light brown sugar
- ¼ cup Solid vegetable shortening
- 2 tablespoons Natural-style creamy peanut butter
- 3 tablespoons Granulated white sugar
- 2 tablespoons (or 1 small egg, well beaten) Pasteurized egg substitute, such as Egg Beaters
- ⅓ cup Roasted, salted peanuts, chopped
- Baking spray

Directions:
1. Preheat the air fryer to 350°F (175°C).
2. Stir the oats, flour, cinnamon, and baking soda in a bowl until well combined.
3. Using an electric hand mixer at medium speed, beat the brown sugar, shortening, peanut butter, granulated white sugar, and egg substitute or egg (as applicable) until smooth and creamy, about 3 minutes, scraping down the inside of the bowl occasionally.
4. Scrape down and remove the beaters. Fold in the flour mixture and peanuts with a rubber spatula just until all the flour is moistened and the peanut bits are evenly distributed in the dough.
5. For a small air fryer, coat the inside of a 6-inch round cake pan with baking spray. For a medium air fryer, coat the inside of a 7-inch round cake pan with baking spray. And for a large air fryer, coat the inside of an 8-inch round cake pan with baking spray. Scrape and gently press the dough into the prepared pan, spreading it into an even layer to the perimeter.
6. Set the pan in the basket and air-fry undisturbed for 18 minutes, or until well browned.
7. Transfer the pan to a wire rack and cool for 15 minutes. Loosen the cookie from the perimeter with a spatula, then invert the pan onto a cutting board and let the cookie come free. Remove the pan and reinvert the cookie onto the wire rack. Cool for 5 minutes more before slicing into wedges to serve.

Caramel Apple Crumble

Servings: 6
Cooking Time: 50 Minutes
Ingredients:
- 4 apples, peeled and thinly sliced
- 2 tablespoons sugar
- 1 tablespoon flour
- 1 teaspoon ground cinnamon
- ¼ teaspoon ground allspice
- healthy pinch ground nutmeg
- 10 caramel squares, cut into small pieces
- Crumble Topping:
- ¾ cup rolled oats
- ¼ cup sugar
- ⅓ cup flour
- ¼ teaspoon ground cinnamon
- 6 tablespoons butter, melted

Directions:
1. Preheat the air fryer to 330°F (165°C).
2. Combine the apples, sugar, flour, and spices in a large bowl and toss to coat. Add the caramel pieces and mix well. Pour the apple mixture into a 1-quart round baking dish that will fit in your air fryer basket (6-inch diameter).
3. To make the crumble topping, combine the rolled oats, sugar, flour and cinnamon in a small bowl. Add the melted butter and mix well. Top the apples with the crumble mixture. Cover the entire dish with aluminum foil and transfer the dish to the air fryer basket, lowering the dish into the basket using a sling made of aluminum foil (fold a piece of aluminum foil into a strip about 2-inches wide by 24-inches long). Fold the ends of the aluminum foil over the top of the dish before returning the basket to the air fryer.
4. Air-fry at 330°F (165°C) for 25 minutes. Remove the aluminum foil and continue to air-fry for another 25 minutes. Serve the crumble warm with whipped cream or vanilla ice cream, if desired.

Sea-salted Caramel Cookie Cups

Servings: 12
Cooking Time: 12 Minutes
Ingredients:
- ⅓ cup butter
- ¼ cup brown sugar
- 1 teaspoon vanilla extract
- 1 large egg
- 1 cup all-purpose flour
- ½ cup old-fashioned oats
- ½ teaspoon baking soda
- ¼ teaspoon salt
- ⅓ cup sea-salted caramel chips

Directions:
1. Preheat the air fryer to 300°F (150°C).
2. In a large bowl, cream the butter with the brown sugar and vanilla. Whisk in the egg and set aside.
3. In a separate bowl, mix the flour, oats, baking soda, and salt. Then gently mix the dry ingredients into the wet. Fold in the caramel chips.
4. Divide the batter into 12 silicon muffin liners. Place the cookie cups into the air fryer basket and cook for 12 minutes or until a toothpick inserted in the center comes out clean.
5. Remove and let cool 5 minutes before serving.

Peanut Butter-banana Roll-ups

Servings: 4
Cooking Time: 20 Minutes
Ingredients:
- 2 ripe bananas, halved crosswise
- 4 spring roll wrappers
- ¼ cup molasses
- ¼ cup peanut butter
- 1 tsp ground cinnamon
- 1 tsp lemon zest

Directions:
1. Preheat air fryer to 375°F (190°C). Place the roll wrappers on a flat surface with one corner facing up. Spread 1 tbsp of molasses on each, then 1 tbsp of peanut butter, and finally top with lemon zest and 1 banana half. Sprinkle with cinnamon all over. For the wontons, fold the bottom over the banana, then fold the sides, and roll-up. Place them seam-side down and Roast for 10 minutes until golden brown and crispy. Serve warm.

One-bowl Chocolate Buttermilk Cake

Servings: 6
Cooking Time: 16-20 Minutes
Ingredients:
- ¾ cup All-purpose flour
- ½ cup Granulated white sugar
- 3 tablespoons Unsweetened cocoa powder
- ½ teaspoon Baking soda
- ¼ teaspoon Table salt
- ½ cup Buttermilk
- 2 tablespoons Vegetable oil
- ¾ teaspoon Vanilla extract
- Baking spray (see here)

Directions:
1. Preheat the air fryer to 325°F (160°C) (or 330°F (165°C), if that's the closest setting).
2. Stir the flour, sugar, cocoa powder, baking soda, and salt in a large bowl until well combined. Add the buttermilk, oil, and vanilla. Stir just until a thick, grainy batter forms.
3. Use the baking spray to generously coat the inside of a 6-inch round cake pan for a small batch, a 7-inch round cake pan for a medium batch, or an 8-inch round cake pan for a large batch. Scrape and spread the chocolate batter into this pan, smoothing the batter out to an even layer.
4. Set the pan in the basket and air-fry undisturbed for 16 minutes for a 6-inch layer, 18 minutes for a 7-inch layer, or 20 minutes for an 8-inch layer, or until a toothpick or cake tester inserted into the center of the cake comes out clean. Start checking it at the 14-minute mark to know where you are.
5. Use hot pads or silicone baking mitts to transfer the cake pan to a wire rack. Cool for 5 minutes. To unmold, set a cutting board over the baking pan and invert both the board and the pan. Lift the still-warm pan off the cake layer. Set the wire rack on top of the cake layer and invert all of it with the cutting board so that the cake layer is now right side up on the wire rack. Remove the cutting board and continue cooling the cake for at least 10 minutes or to room temperature, about 30 minutes, before slicing into wedges.

Strawberry Donuts

Servings: 4
Cooking Time: 55 Minutes
Ingredients:
- ¾ cup Greek yogurt
- 2 tbsp maple syrup
- 1 tbsp vanilla extract
- 2 tsp active dry yeast
- 1 ½ cups all-purpose flour
- 3 tbsp milk
- ½ cup strawberry jam

Directions:
1. Preheat air fryer to 350°F (175°C). Whisk the Greek yogurt, maple syrup, vanilla extract, and yeast until well combined. Then toss in flour until you get a sticky dough. Let rest covered for 10 minutes. Flour a parchment paper on a flat surface, lay the dough, sprinkle with some flour, and flatten to ½-inch thick with a rolling pin.
2. Using a 3-inch cookie cutter, cut the donuts. Repeat the process until no dough is left. Place the donuts in the basket and let rise for 15-20 minutes. Spread some milk on top of each donut and Air Fry for 4 minutes. Turn the donuts, spread more milk, and Air Fry for 4 more minutes until golden brown. Let cool for 15 minutes. Using a knife, cut the donuts 3/4 lengthwise, brush 1 tbsp of strawberry jam on each and close them. Serve.

Lemon Pound Cake Bites

Servings: 6
Cooking Time: 20 Minutes
Ingredients:
- 1 pound cake, cubed
- 1/3 cup cinnamon sugar
- ½ stick butter, melted
- 1 cup vanilla yogurt
- 3 tbsp brown sugar
- 1 tsp lemon zest

Directions:
1. Preheat the air fryer to 350°F (175°C). Drizzle the cake cubes with melted butter, then put them in the cinnamon sugar and toss until coated. Put them in a single layer in the frying basket and Air Fry for 4 minutes or until golden. Remove and place on a serving plate. Combine the yogurt, brown sugar, and lemon zest in a bowl. Serve with the cake bites.

Home-style Pumpkin Pie Pudding

Servings: 4
Cooking Time: 30 Minutes
Ingredients:
- 1 cup canned pumpkin purée
- ¼ cup sugar
- 3 tbsp all-purpose flour
- 1 tbsp butter, melted
- 1 egg
- 1 orange, zested
- 2 tbsp milk
- 1 tsp vanilla extract
- 4 vanilla wafers, crumbled

Directions:
1. Preheat air fryer to 350°F (175°C). Beat the pumpkin puree, sugar, flour, butter, egg, orange zest, milk, and vanilla until well-mixed. Spritz a baking pan with the cooking spray, then pour the pumpkin mix in. Place it in the air fryer and Bake for 11-17 minutes or until golden brown. Take the pudding out of the fryer and let it chill. Serve with vanilla wager crumbs.

Annie's Chocolate Chunk Hazelnut Cookies

Servings: 24
Cooking Time: 12 Minutes
Ingredients:
- 1 cup butter, softened
- 1 cup brown sugar
- ½ cup granulated sugar
- 2 eggs, lightly beaten
- 1½ teaspoons vanilla extract
- 1½ cups all-purpose flour
- ½ cup rolled oats
- 1 teaspoon baking soda
- ½ teaspoon salt
- 2 cups chocolate chunks
- ½ cup toasted chopped hazelnuts

Directions:
1. Cream the butter and sugars together until light and fluffy using a stand mixer or electric hand mixer. Add the eggs and vanilla, and beat until well combined.
2. Combine the flour, rolled oats, baking soda and salt in a second bowl. Gradually add the dry ingredients to the wet ingredients with a wooden spoon or spatula. Stir in the chocolate chunks and hazelnuts until distributed throughout the dough.
3. Shape the cookies into small balls about the size of golf balls and place them on a baking sheet. Freeze the cookie balls for at least 30 minutes, or package them in as airtight a package as you can and keep them in your freezer.
4. When you're ready for a delicious snack or dessert, Preheat the air fryer to 350°F (175°C). Cut a piece of

parchment paper to fit the number of cookies you are baking. Place the parchment down in the air fryer basket and place the frozen cookie ball or balls on top (remember to leave room for them to expand).
5. Air-fry the cookies at 350°F (175°C) for 12 minutes, or until they are done to your liking. Let them cool for a few minutes before enjoying your freshly baked cookie.

Holiday Peppermint Cake

Servings: 4
Cooking Time: 20 Minutes
Ingredients:
- 1 ½ cups flour
- 3 eggs
- 1/3 cup molasses
- ½ cup olive oil
- ½ cup almond milk
- ½ tsp vanilla extract
- ½ tsp peppermint extract
- 1 tsp baking powder
- ½ tsp salt

Directions:
1. Preheat air fryer to 380°F (195°C). Whisk the eggs and molasses in a bowl until smooth. Slowly mix in the olive oil, almond milk, and vanilla and peppermint extracts until combined. Sift the flour, baking powder, and salt in another bowl. Gradually incorporate the dry ingredients into the wet ingredients until combined. Pour the batter into a greased baking pan and place in the fryer. Bake for 12-15 minutes until a toothpick inserted in the center comes out clean. Serve and enjoy!

Peanut Butter Cup Doughnut Holes

Servings: 24
Cooking Time: 4 Minutes
Ingredients:
- 1½ cups bread flour
- 1 teaspoon active dry yeast
- 1 tablespoon sugar
- ¼ teaspoon salt
- ½ cup warm milk
- ½ teaspoon vanilla extract
- 2 egg yolks
- 2 tablespoons melted butter
- 24 miniature peanut butter cups, plus a few more for garnish
- vegetable oil, in a spray bottle
- Doughnut Topping
- 1 cup chocolate chips
- 2 tablespoons milk

Directions:
1. Combine the flour, yeast, sugar and salt in a bowl. Add the milk, vanilla, egg yolks and butter. Mix well until the

dough starts to come together. Transfer the dough to a floured surface and knead by hand for 2 minutes. Shape the dough into a ball and transfer it to a large oiled bowl. Cover the bowl with a towel and let the dough rise in a warm place for 1 to 1½ hours, until the dough has doubled in size.

2. When the dough has risen, punch it down and roll it into a 24-inch long log. Cut the dough into 24 pieces. Push a peanut butter cup into the center of each piece of dough, pinch the dough shut and roll it into a ball. Place the dough balls on a cookie sheet and let them rise in a warm place for 30 minutes.

3. Preheat the air fryer to 400°F（205°C）.

4. Spray or brush the dough balls lightly with vegetable oil. Air-fry eight at a time, at 400°F（205°C）for 4 minutes, turning them over halfway through the cooking process.

5. While the doughnuts are air frying, prepare the topping. Place the chocolate chips and milk in a microwave safe bowl. Microwave on high for 1 minute. Stir and microwave for an additional 30 seconds if necessary to get all the chips to melt. Stir until the chips are melted and smooth.

6. Dip the top half of the doughnut holes into the melted chocolate. Place them on a rack to set up for just a few minutes and watch them disappear.

Fall Pumpkin Cake

Servings: 6
Cooking Time: 50 Minutes
Ingredients:

- 1/3 cup pecan pieces
- 5 gingersnap cookies
- 1/3 cup light brown sugar
- 6 tbsp butter, melted
- 3 eggs
- ½ tsp vanilla extract
- 1 cup pumpkin purée
- 2 tbsp sour cream
- ½ cup flour
- ¼ cup tapioca flour
- ½ tsp cornstarch
- ½ cup granulated sugar
- ½ tsp baking soda
- 1 tsp baking powder
- 1 tsp pumpkin pie spice
- 6 oz mascarpone cheese
- 1 1/3 cups powdered sugar
- 1 tsp cinnamon
- 2 tbsp butter, softened
- 1 tbsp milk
- 1 tbsp flaked almonds

Directions:

1. Blitz the pecans, gingersnap cookies, brown sugar, and 3 tbsp of melted butter in a food processor until combined. Press mixture into the bottom of a lightly greased cake pan. Preheat air fryer at 350°F（175°C）. In a bowl, whisk the

eggs, remaining melted butter, ½ tsp of vanilla extract, pumpkin purée, and sour cream. In another bowl, combine the flour, tapioca flour, cornstarch, granulated sugar, baking soda, baking powder, and pumpkin pie spice. Add wet ingredients to dry ingredients and combine. Do not overmix. Pour the batter into a cake pan and cover it with aluminum foil. Place cake pan in the frying basket and Bake for 30 minutes. Remove the foil and cook for another 5 minutes. Let cool onto a cooling rack for 10 minutes. Then, turn cake onto a large serving platter. In a small bowl, whisk the mascarpone cheese, powdered sugar, remaining vanilla extract, cinnamon, softened butter, and milk. Spread over cooled cake and cut into slices. Serve sprinkled with almonds and enjoy!

Party S'mores

Servings: 6
Cooking Time: 15 Minutes
Ingredients:

- 2 dark chocolate bars, cut into 12 pieces
- 12 buttermilk biscuits
- 12 marshmallows

Directions:

1. Preheat air fryer to 350°F（175°C）. Place 6 biscuits in the air fryer. Top each square with a piece of dark chocolate. Bake for 2 minutes. Add a marshmallow to each piece of chocolate. Cook for another minute. Remove and top with another piece of biscuit. Serve warm.

Honey-roasted Mixed Nuts

Servings: 8
Cooking Time: 15 Minutes
Ingredients:

- ½ cup raw, shelled pistachios
- ½ cup raw almonds
- 1 cup raw walnuts
- 2 tablespoons filtered water
- 2 tablespoons honey
- 1 tablespoon vegetable oil
- 2 tablespoons sugar
- ½ teaspoon salt

Directions:

1. Preheat the air fryer to 300°F（150°C）.

2. Lightly spray an air-fryer-safe pan with olive oil; then place the pistachios, almonds, and walnuts inside the pan and place the pan inside the air fryer basket.

3. Cook for 15 minutes, shaking the basket every 5 minutes to rotate the nuts.

4. While the nuts are roasting, boil the water in a small pan and stir in the honey and oil. Continue to stir while cooking until the water begins to evaporate and a thick sauce is formed. Note: The sauce should stick to the back of a wooden spoon when mixed. Turn off the heat.

5. Remove the nuts from the air fryer (cooking should have just completed) and spoon the nuts into the stovetop pan. Use a spatula to coat the nuts with the honey syrup.
6. Line a baking sheet with parchment paper and spoon the nuts onto the sheet. Lightly sprinkle the sugar and salt over the nuts and let cool in the refrigerator for at least 2 hours.
7. When the honey and sugar have hardened, store the nuts in an airtight container in the refrigerator.

Tortilla Fried Pies

Servings: 12
Cooking Time: 5 Minutes
Ingredients:
- 12 small flour tortillas (4-inch diameter)
- ½ cup fig preserves
- ¼ cup sliced almonds
- 2 tablespoons shredded, unsweetened coconut
- oil for misting or cooking spray

Directions:
1. Wrap refrigerated tortillas in damp paper towels and heat in microwave 30 seconds to warm.
2. Working with one tortilla at a time, place 2 teaspoons fig preserves, 1 teaspoon sliced almonds, and ½ teaspoon coconut in the center of each.
3. Moisten outer edges of tortilla all around.
4. Fold one side of tortilla over filling to make a half-moon shape and press down lightly on center. Using the tines of a fork, press down firmly on edges of tortilla to seal in filling.
5. Mist both sides with oil or cooking spray.
6. Place hand pies in air fryer basket close but not overlapping. It's fine to lean some against the sides and corners of the basket. You may need to cook in 2 batches.
7. Cook at 390°F (200°C) for 5minutes or until lightly browned. Serve hot.
8. Refrigerate any leftover pies in a closed container. To serve later, toss them back in the air fryer basket and cook for 2 or 3minutes to reheat.

Famous Chocolate Lava Cake

Servings: 4
Cooking Time: 15 Minutes
Ingredients:
- ¼ cup flour
- 1 tbsp cocoa powder
- ⅛ tsp salt
- ½ tsp baking powder
- 1 tsp vanilla extract
- ¼ cup raw honey
- 1 egg, beaten
- 2 tbsp olive oil
- 2 tbsp icing sugar, to dust

Directions:
1. Preheat air fryer to 380°F (195°C). Sift the flour, cocoa powder, salt, vanilla, and baking powder in a bowl. Add in honey, egg, and olive oil and stir to combine. Divide

the batter evenly among greased ramekins. Put the filled ramekins inside the air fryer and Bake for 10 minutes. Remove the lava cakes from the fryer and slide a knife around the outside edge of each cake. Turn each ramekin upside down on a saucer and serve dusted with icing sugar.

Pecan-oat Filled Apples

Servings: 4
Cooking Time: 20 Minutes
Ingredients:
- 2 cored Granny Smith apples, halved
- ¼ cup rolled oats
- 2 tbsp honey
- ½ tsp ground cinnamon
- ½ tsp ground ginger
- 2 tbsp chopped pecans
- A pinch of salt
- 1 tbsp olive oil

Directions:
1. Preheat air fryer to 380°F (195°C). Combine together the oats, honey, cinnamon, ginger, pecans, salt, and olive oil in a bowl. Scoop a quarter of the oat mixture onto the top of each half apple. Put the apples in the frying basket and Roast for 12-15 minutes until the apples are fork-tender.

Mixed Berry Hand Pies

Servings: 4
Cooking Time: 15 Minutes
Ingredients:
- ¾ cup sugar
- ½ teaspoon ground cinnamon
- 1 tablespoon cornstarch
- 1 cup blueberries
- 1 cup blackberries
- 1 cup raspberries, divided
- 1 teaspoon water
- 1 package refrigerated pie dough (or your own homemade pie dough)
- 1 egg, beaten

Directions:
1. Combine the sugar, cinnamon, and cornstarch in a small saucepan. Add the blueberries, blackberries, and ½ cup of the raspberries. Toss the berries gently to coat them evenly. Add the teaspoon of water to the saucepan and turn the stovetop on to medium-high heat, stirring occasionally. Once the berries break down, release their juice and start to simmer (about 5 minutes), simmer for another couple of minutes and then transfer the mixture to a bowl, stir in the remaining ½ cup of raspberries and let it cool.
2. Preheat the air fryer to 370°F (185°C).
3. Cut the pie dough into four 5-inch circles and four 6-inch circles.
4. Spread the 6-inch circles on a flat surface. Divide the berry filling between all four circles. Brush the perimeter of

the dough circles with a little water. Place the 5-inch circles on top of the filling and press the perimeter of the dough circles together to seal. Roll the edges of the bottom circle up over the top circle to make a crust around the filling. Press a fork around the crust to make decorative indentations and to seal the crust shut. Brush the pies with egg wash and sprinkle a little sugar on top. Poke a small hole in the center of each pie with a paring knife to vent the dough.

5.   Air-fry two pies at a time. Brush or spray the air fryer basket with oil and place the pies into the basket. Air-fry for 9 minutes. Turn the pies over and air-fry for another 6 minutes. Serve warm or at room temperature.

Chocolate Bars

Servings: 4
Cooking Time: 30 Minutes
Ingredients:
- 2 tbsp chocolate toffee chips
- ¼ cup chopped pecans
- 2 tbsp raisins
- 1 tbsp dried blueberries
- 2 tbsp maple syrup
- ¼ cup light brown sugar
- 1/3 cup peanut butter
- 2 tbsp chocolate chips
- 2 tbsp butter, melted
- ½ tsp vanilla extract
- Salt to taste

Directions:
1.   Preheat air fryer at 350ºF (175°C). In a bowl, combine the pecans, maple syrup, sugar, peanut butter, toffee chips, raisins, dried blueberries, chocolate chips, butter, vanilla extract, and salt. Press mixture into a lightly greased cake pan and cover it with aluminum foil. Place cake pan in the frying basket and Bake for 15 minutes. Remove the foil and cook for 5 more minutes. Let cool completely for 15 minutes. Turn over on a place and cut into 6 bars. Enjoy!

Baked Caramelized Peaches

Servings: 6
Cooking Time: 25 Minutes
Ingredients:
- 3 pitted peaches, halved
- 2 tbsp brown sugar
- 1 cup heavy cream
- 1 tsp vanilla extract
- ¼ tsp ground cinnamon
- 1 cup fresh blueberries

Directions:

1.   Preheat air fryer to 380°F (195°C). Lay the peaches in the frying basket with the cut side up, then top them with brown sugar. Bake for 7-11 minutes, allowing the peaches to brown around the edges. In a mixing bowl, whisk heavy cream, vanilla, and cinnamon until stiff peaks form. Fold the peaches into a plate. Spoon the cream mixture into the peach cups, top with blueberries, and serve.

Custard

Servings: 4
Cooking Time: 45 Minutes
Ingredients:
- 2 cups whole milk
- 2 eggs
- ¼ cup sugar
- ⅛ teaspoon salt
- ¼ teaspoon vanilla
- cooking spray
- ⅛ teaspoon nutmeg

Directions:
1.   In a blender, process milk, egg, sugar, salt, and vanilla until smooth.
2.   Spray a 6 x 6-inch baking pan with nonstick spray and pour the custard into it.
3.   Cook at 300°F (150°C) for 45 minutes. Custard is done when the center sets.
4.   Sprinkle top with the nutmeg.
5.   Allow custard to cool slightly.
6.   Serve it warm, at room temperature, or chilled.

Brownies With White Chocolate

Servings: 6
Cooking Time: 30 Minutes
Ingredients:
- ¼ cup white chocolate chips
- ¼ cup muscovado sugar
- 1 egg
- 2 tbsp white sugar
- 2 tbsp canola oil
- 1 tsp vanilla
- ¼ cup cocoa powder
- 1/3 cup flour

Directions:
1.   Preheat air fryer to 340°F (170°C). Beat the egg with muscovado sugar and white sugar in a bowl. Mix in the canola oil and vanilla. Next, stir in cocoa powder and flour until just combined. Gently fold in white chocolate chips. Spoon the batter into a lightly pan. Bake until the brownies are set when lightly touched on top, about 20 minutes. Let to cool completely before slicing.

RECIPE INDEX

A

Albóndigas 43
All-in-one Breakfast Toast 34
Almond Cranberry Granola 30
Almond Topped Trout 69
Almond-crusted Fish 74
Almond-crusted Zucchini Fries 21
Almond-roasted Pears 105
Annie's Chocolate Chunk Hazelnut Cookies 112
Apple Cornbread Stuffed Pork Loin With Apple Gravy 48
Apple Fritters 31
Aromatic Pork Tenderloin 44
Asian Meatball Tacos 88
Asian Sweet Chili Chicken 91
Autenthic Greek Fish Pitas 76
Avocado Fries With Quick Salsa Fresca 15
Avocado Fries 20
Avocado Toast With Lemony Shrimp 12

B

Bacon, Blue Cheese And Pear Stuffed Pork Chops 53
Bacon, Broccoli And Swiss Cheese Bread Pudding 31
Bacon-wrapped Scallops 64
Baked Apple 106
Baked Caramelized Peaches 115
Baked Stuffed Pears 108
Balsamic London Broil 60
Balsamic Short Ribs 49
Baltimore Crab Cakes 65
Banana Bread Cake 106
Banana-blackberry Muffins 38
Bananas Foster Bread Pudding 107
Barbecue Country-style Pork Ribs 56
Barbecue-style London Broil 49
Basic Chicken Breasts(2) 86
Basil Cheese & Ham Stromboli 58
Basil Crab Cakes With Fresh Salad 66
Basil Feta Crostini 12
Basil Mushroom & Shrimp Spaghetti 73
Beef & Barley Stuffed Bell Peppers 46
Beef And Spinach Braciole 59
Beer-breaded Halibut Fish Tacos 72
Berbere Beef Steaks 57
Better-than-chinese-take-out Sesame Beef 47
Blueberry French Toast Sticks 33
Boneless Ribeyes 44
Bread Boat Eggs 36
Breaded Avocado Tacos 99
Breakfast Chimichangas 36
British Fish & Chips 65
Broccoli & Mushroom Beef 54

Brown Rice And Goat Cheese Croquettes 21
Brownies With White Chocolate 115
Buffalo Cauliflower 12
Buffalo Egg Rolls 85
Buttered Chicken Thighs 91
Buttery Radish Wedges 23
Buttery Stuffed Tomatoes 26

C

Cajun Breakfast Potatoes 30
Cajun Pork Loin Chops 61
Cal-mex Chimichangas 45
Calzones South Of The Border 58
Canadian Bacon & Cheese Sandwich 30
Canadian-style Rib Eye Steak 43
Caramel Apple Crumble 110
Caribbean Jerk Cod Fillets 75
Catalan Sardines With Romesco Sauce 75
Catalan-style Crab Samfaina 72
Catfish Nuggets 78
Charred Cauliflower Tacos 103
Cheesy Chicken-avocado Paninis 90
Cheesy Egg Bites 39
Cheesy Eggplant Rounds 102
Cheesy Green Pitas 12
Cheesy Tuna Tower 63
Cheesy Zucchini Chips 18
Cherry Cheesecake Rolls 109
Cherry Hand Pies 105
Chicago-style Turkey Meatballs 88
Chicken & Rice Sautée 86
Chicken Adobo 83
Chicken Breasts Wrapped In Bacon 92
Chicken Chimichangas 87
Chicken Cordon Bleu Patties 86
Chicken Fried Steak 54
Chicken Nuggets 82
Chicken Parmigiana 84
Chicken Pasta Pie 90
Chicken Pigs In Blankets 89
Chicken Scotch Eggs 42
Chipotle Pork Meatballs 55
Chocolate Bars 115
Chocolate Soufflés 108
Christmas Chicken & Roasted Grape Salad 83
Cinnamon Biscuit Rolls 33
Cinnamon Honeyed Pretzel Bites 16
Cinnamon Pear Oat Muffins 33
Cinnamon Roasted Pumpkin 28
Citrus Pork Lettuce Wraps 57
City "chicken" 55
Classic Chicken Cobb Salad 83

Coconut & Peanut Rice Cereal 39
Coconut Chicken With Apricot-ginger Sauce 83
Coconut Curry Chicken With Coconut Rice 93
Coconut Macaroons 108
Coconut-shrimp Po' Boys 71
Colorful Vegetable Medley 102
Corn And Pepper Jack Chile Rellenos With Roasted Tomato
Sauce 97
Corn Au Gratin 27
Country Chicken Hoagies 92
Country-style Pork Ribs(1) 51
Crab Cakes On A Budget 65
Crab Rangoon 15
Crab Stuffed Salmon Roast 76
Crabmeat-stuffed Flounder 69
Creamy Broccoli & Mushroom Casserole 102
Crispy Chicken Parmesan 82
Crispy Curried Sweet Potato Fries 18
Crispy Pork Medallions With Radicchio And Endive Salad 59
Crispy Pork Pork Escalopes 59
Crispy Tofu Bites 17
Crunchy And Buttery Cod With Ritz® Cracker Crust 78
Crunchy French Toast Sticks 35
Crunchy Spicy Chickpeas 13
Crunchy Tortellini Bites 19
Curried Cauliflower 100
Curried Fruit 27
Curried Sweet-and-spicy Scallops 74
Custard 115

D
Delicious Juicy Pork Meatballs 49
Dijon Shrimp Cakes 63

E
Easy Bread Pudding 105
Easy Scallops With Lemon Butter 70
Effortless Toffee Zucchini Bread 36
Eggless Mung Bean Tart 32
Enchilada Chicken Dip 11
Extra Crispy Country-style Pork Riblets 46

F
Fake Shepherd's Pie 103
Fall Pumpkin Cake 113
Famous Chocolate Lava Cake 114
Farmer's Fried Chicken 89
Favorite Blueberry Muffins 32
Fennel Tofu Bites 96
Fiesta Chicken Plate 80
Fingerling Potatoes 22
Firecracker Popcorn Shrimp 66
Fish Goujons With Tartar Sauce 78
Fish Tacos With Hot Coleslaw 72
Fish Tacos With Jalapeño-lime Sauce 67
Five-spice Roasted Sweet Potatoes 23

Flounder Fillets 71
French Grouper Nicoise 74
Fried Corn On The Cob 28
Fried Goat Cheese 17
Fried Gyoza 19
Fried Okra 21
Fried Oreos 108
Fried Oysters 64
Fried Peaches 16
Fried Potatoes With Bell Peppers 98
Fried Rice With Curried Tofu 104
Fried Snickers Bars 109
Fruit Turnovers 109

G
Garlic And Oregano Lamb Chops 52
Garlicky Bell Pepper Mix 22
Garlic-lemon Steamer Clams 74
Giant Buttery Chocolate Chip Cookie 106
Giant Oatmeal–peanut Butter Cookie 110
Goat Cheese Stuffed Turkey Roulade 89
Gorgeous Jalapeño Poppers 97
Granny Pesto Chicken Caprese 90
Greek Chicken Wings 92
Greek Gyros With Chicken & Rice 92
Greek Pork Chops 52
Greek Street Tacos 13
Green Egg Quiche 40
Green Peas With Mint 21
Grilled Cheese Sandwich Deluxe 18
Grilled Cheese Sandwich 104
Grilled Pork & Bell Pepper Salad 52
Grits Casserole 27

H
Halibut Quesadillas 76
Harissa Veggie Fries 96
Hashbrown Potatoes Lyonnaise 32
Hasselbacks 28
Hellenic Zucchini Bites 98
Herbed Baby Red Potato Hasselback 24
Herb-marinated Chicken 84
Herby Prawn & Zucchini Bake 69
Hole In One 41
Holiday Peppermint Cake 112
Holiday Shrimp Scampi 67
Holliday Lobster Salad 69
Home-style Buffalo Chicken Wings 17
Home-style Pumpkin Crumble 38
Home-style Pumpkin Pie Pudding 112
Honey Donuts 41
Honey Lemon Thyme Glazed Cornish Hen 85
Honey Mustard Pork Roast 45
Honey Pork Links 45
Honey-mustard Chicken Wings 11
Honey-roasted Mixed Nuts 113

Hot Calamari Rings 67
Hot Shrimp 15
Hungarian Spiralized Fries 17

I

Irresistible Cheesy Chicken Sticks 90
Italian Meatballs 58
Italian Sausage & Peppers 56
Italian Tuna Roast 75

J

Japanese-style Turkey Meatballs 84
Jerk Chicken Drumsticks 85
Jerk Rubbed Corn On The Cob 24

K

Kentucky-style Pork Tenderloin 45
King Prawns Al Ajillo 66

L

Lamb Chops In Currant Sauce 54
Leftover Roast Beef Risotto 43
Lemon Pound Cake Bites 111
Lemony Green Bean Sautée 29
Lime Flaming Halibut 78
Loaded Potato Skins 14

M

Magic Giant Chocolate Cookies 107
Malaysian Shrimp With Sambal Mayo 66
Mango-chocolate Custard 109
Maple Balsamic Glazed Salmon 68
Maple Loaded Sweet Potatoes 19
Masala Chicken With Charred Vegetables 91
Mascarpone Iced Cinnamon Rolls 35
Meat Loaves 60
Meatless Kimchi Bowls 100
Meatloaf With Tangy Tomato Glaze 61
Meaty Omelet 34
Mediterranean Potato Skins 18
Mediterranean Salmon Cakes 68
Mexican Twice Air-fried Sweet Potatoes 99
Mini Everything Bagels 34
Mini Meatloaves With Pancetta 44
Mixed Berry Hand Pies 114
Mixed Berry Pie 107
Mojo Sea Bass 68
Mongolian Beef 51
Moroccan Cauliflower 25
Mushroom & Quinoa-stuffed Pork Loins 50
Mushroom-rice Stuffed Bell Peppers 103
Mushrooms 25
Mustard-crusted Rib-eye 47

N

Natchitoches Meat Pies 55
Nutty Banana Bread 105

O

Oat Muffins With Blueberries 36
Oktoberfest Bratwursts 61
One-bowl Chocolate Buttermilk Cake 111
Orange Trail Oatmeal 37

P

Paprika Fried Beef 43
Parma Ham & Egg Toast Cups 35
Parmesan Crusted Chicken Cordon Bleu 80
Parmesan Eggplant Bites 13
Parmesan Pizza Nuggets 13
Party Buffalo Chicken Drumettes 81
Party Giant Nachos 96
Party S´mores 113
Peachy Chicken Chunks With Cherries 87
Peanut Butter Cup Doughnut Holes 112
Peanut Butter-banana Roll-ups 111
Pecan-oat Filled Apples 114
Pecorino Dill Muffins 23
Perfect French Fries 23
Pesto Chicken Cheeseburgers 82
Pesto Egg & Ham Sandwiches 37
Pickle Brined Fried Chicken 94
Pineapple & Veggie Souvlaki 95
Pinto Bean Casserole 95
Popcorn Crawfish 68
Pork & Beef Egg Rolls 54
Pork Cutlets With Almond-lemon Crust 48
Pork Cutlets With Aloha Salsa 46
Pork Loin 51
Potato Chips With Sour Cream And Onion Dip ... 20
Potato Chips 18
Potato-wrapped Salmon Fillets 64
Provençal Grilled Rib-eye 47
Provence French Fries 25
Pulled Turkey Quesadillas 91

Q

Quesadillas 31
Quick Chicken For Filling 82
Quinoa & Black Bean Stuffed Peppers 98

R

Rainbow Quinoa Patties 101
Red Curry Flank Steak 50
Rich Baked Sweet Potatoes 26
Rich Salmon Burgers With Broccoli Slaw 63
Roasted Bell Peppers With Garlic & Dill 28
Roasted Broccoli And Red Bean Salad 24
Roasted Fennel Salad 25

Roasted Red Pepper Dip 16
Roasted Vegetable Stromboli 101
Roasted Vegetable, Brown Rice And Black Bean Burrito 100

S

Sage & Paprika Turkey Cutlets 87
Sage & Thyme Potatoes 21
Sage Pork With Potatoes 50
Salmon Patties With Lemon-dill Sauce 74
Salmon 79
Salty German-style Shrimp Pancakes 77
Santorini Steak Bowls 45
Savory Brussels Sprouts 25
Scones 38
Seafood Egg Rolls 14
Sea-salted Caramel Cookie Cups 110
Sesame Orange Chicken 93
Shakshuka Cups 40
Shrimp "scampi" 72
Shrimp Po'boy With Remoulade Sauce 77
Shrimp, Chorizo And Fingerling Potatoes 76
Shrimp-jalapeño Poppers In Prosciutto 77
Skirt Steak Fajitas 53
Sloppy Joes 52
Smokehouse-style Beef Ribs 44
Southeast Asian-style Tuna Steaks 73
Southern Okra Chips 24
Southern Shrimp With Cocktail Sauce 63
Southern Sweet Cornbread 40
Southern-fried Chicken Livers 88
Southwest Gluten-free Turkey Meatloaf 81
Spiced Chicken Breasts 93
Spiced Shrimp Empanadas 70
Spicy Bean Stuffed Potatoes 22
Spicy Black Bean Turkey Burgers With Cumin-avocado
Spread 80
Spicy Hoisin Bbq Pork Chops 50
Spinach And Cheese Calzone 98
Spring Vegetable Omelet 40
Strawberry Donuts 111
Strawberry Streusel Muffins 39
Stress-free Beef Patties 47
Stuffed Pork Chops 60
Stuffed Portobellos 102

Stuffed Shrimp Wrapped In Bacon 71

Sugar-dusted Beignets 37
Summer Sea Scallops 73
Summer Watermelon And Cucumber Salad 26
Sweet Apple Fries 11
Sweet Corn Bread 95
Sweet Potato & Mushroom Hash 41
Sweet Potato Chips 14
Sweet Potato-cinnamon Toast 30

T

Taco Pie With Meatballs 57
Tacos 103
Tandoori Cauliflower 27
Tandoori Paneer Naan Pizza 104
Tasty Filet Mignon 55
Tasty Roasted Black Olives & Tomatoes 13
Teriyaki Chicken Bites 86
Thai Turkey Sausage Patties 33
The Best Oysters Rockefeller 64
The Ultimate Mac`n´cheese 27
Thyme Steak Finger Strips 62
Tilapia Teriyaki 75
Tomato & Squash Stuffed Mushrooms 100
Tortilla Fried Pies 114
Traditional Italian Beef Meatballs 57
Turkey Scotch Eggs 87

V

Vegan French Toast 99
Vegetable Hand Pies 95
Vegetable Roast 26
Vegetarian Paella 101
Veggie & Feta Scramble Bowls 41
Veggie Burgers 96

W

Wild Blueberry Lemon Chia Bread 32

Y

Yummy Maple-mustard Chicken Kabobs 84
Yummy Salmon Burgers With Salsa Rosa 70

Z

Zucchini Hash Browns 39
Zucchini Walnut Bread 37

Printed in Great Britain
by Amazon

16600620R10068